D0899579

The Social Dimension of Piety

Theological Inquiries

Studies in Contemporary
Biblical and Theological Problems

General Editor
Lawrence Boadt, C. S. P.

Editorial Advisory Board
Raymond Brown, S. S.   Scripture
Myles Bourke   Scripture
David Tracy   Systematic Theology
Michael Buckley, S. J.   Systematic Theology
Richard McCormick, S. J. Moral Theology

PAULIST PRESS

The Social Dimension of Piety

Andrew E. Barnes

PAULIST PRESS
New York ● Mahwah, N.J.

Copyright © 1994 by Andrew E. Barnes

All rights reserved. No part of this book may be reproduced or transmitted in any form or by any means, electronic or mechanical, including photocopying, recording or by any information storage and retrieval system without permission in writing from the Publisher.

Library of Congress Cataloging-in-Publication Data

Barnes, Andrew E., 1953–
The social dimension of piety : associative life and devotional change in the penitent confraternities of Marseille, 1499–1792 / Andrew E. Barnes.
p. cm.
Includes bibliographical references and index.
ISBN 0-8091-3395-4
1. Penitents—France—Marseille—History. 2. Confraternities—France—Marseille—History. 3. Catholic Church—France—Marseille—History. 4. Marseille (France)—Religious life and customs.
I. Title.
BX1533.M34B37   1994
267'.24244912'0903—dc20   93-41853
                                                                CIP

Published by Paulist Press
997 Macarthur Boulevard
Mahwah, New Jersey 07430

Printed and bound in the
United States of America

CONTENTS

Gift 11-16-94

DEC 7 1994

FIGURES

Chapter 1
INTRODUCTION

This is a study about the practice of religious devotions in the organizational context of lay-controlled brotherhoods, or confraternities. As will become clear, the devotions and the context in which they were performed were equally important. The story of penitent confraternities draws attention to those transformations in Catholic religious life during the early modern centuries that are routinely ignored because they do not fit neatly under the rubric *Counter-Reformation*. It is commonly accepted that what it meant to be a Catholic before the Reformation was different from what it meant to be a Catholic on the eve of the French Revolution. It is not so common to appreciate that many of the differences stemmed from changes in Catholic devotional life that were in process before the emergence of Protestantism.

These days, when one speaks of post-Tridentine Catholicism, one has in mind an episcopally controlled, parish-centered religious experience, supported by a Jesuit-inspired, if not Jesuit-maintained, school system.[1] Histories of the Counter-Reformation tend to look backward in detailing the evolution of this phenomenon coming into existence. This image obscures and submerges another one that also demands examination. In the cities and towns along the Mediterranean littoral, among the first expressions of the religious ferment that would change the nature of Christianity was the establishment of penitent confraternities.[2] These societies shaped and directed masculine religiosity for approximately a century and a half (1500 to 1650) before they gradually gave way to the Catholicism mandated by Trent.

In general, religious orders helped promote penitent confraternities, but between 1550 and 1650, the period of the confraternities' widest spread and influence, they did nothing more than try to isolate and control specific associations. In cities like Marseille penitent associations remained remarkably free of clerical control.

1

Understandably, post-Tridentine bishops sought to bring confraternities in line under their supervision. But to look at the story of penitent associations only from the perspective of this later development is to ignore why this type of association posed such an obstacle to episcopal plans for devotional reform, and why the devout Catholics in these associations displayed such resistance to episcopal intervention. It also obscures an extraordinary, and perhaps unparalleled, effort at lay evangelism.

Among the devotions performed by penitent confraternities, the rite of self-flagellation was initially *primus inter pares*. Beginning in the seventeenth century, however, the practice was replaced in most associations by other rituals of penance deemed by contemporaries as more efficacious. Confraternities of penitents began as confraternities of flagellants but evolved into something different. Historically, new devotions have given rise to new devotional societies. In this instance, however, the associations themselves were sufficiently vital that the devotions which provided their original raison d'être could be discarded, and new ones embraced.

From at least the time of the Black Death (1349), the lay practice of unsupervised self-flagellation was condemned by bishops and declared heretical, causing lay flagellants to attack clerics as culpable for the plague.[3] Far from leading the members of penitent confraternities away from the clergy, however, self-flagellation, and the rites that replaced it, confirmed a recurring acceptance of clerical guidance in ritual practice. From the perspective of the participants in penitent confraternities, the history of Catholicism between Luther and Voltaire, to use Delumeau's parameters, emerges as a remodeling of existing clerical ideals of sanctity into a lay-directed mission for the salvation of the male laity.[4]

It was the sociological dynamics behind this quest that came to fascinate me. Self-flagellation, and the devotional acts that replaced it, were voluntary acts. The associations that sponsored these devotions presented themselves as societies only for men truly serious about their salvation. That this seriousness could be manifested through commitment to the association, its governance, and its devotional activities, was both the primary reason penitent confraternities spread from Italy at the start of the sixteenth century, and why they flourished for centuries in cities like

Marseille. The lay prior of a confraternity possessed and exploited the kinds of authority and status normally reserved for the priesthood. The effort to obtain this office could become for members of Marseille's more affluent classes a life-long pursuit. Equally important were the ways in which confraternities, as organizations, evolved to permit each new generation of confreres to incorporate new rites and devotions and thus both spiritually renew themselves and revalidate their mission to promote collective salvation. Together these two factors help to explain why confraternities could serve as vehicles for the expression of successive waves of devotional change yet still retain their sense of themselves as organizations. These successive waves of devotional change have been well studied. Their significance to the organizational history of penitent confraternities has not. It is to this latter task that the following pages are primarily dedicated.

Other historians have written about penitent confraternities, but none have tried to understand how they functioned socially as a religious experience. There are a number of reasons for this, but a primary cause was an inability to recognize an essential difference between Protestant and Catholic religiosity. Arguably, since the appearance of Max Weber's *The Protestant Ethic and the Spirit of Capitalism,* historians have assumed that the essential way Christians express their faith is through verbal articulation. There is some validity to this assumption for Protestantism, for many Protestant creeds have retained the medieval practice of public confession in some form. For Catholicism this assumption is false. The verbalization stage, so essential for the Protestant religious experience, disappears in the Catholic expectation that private thought translates into public act. Contrition has to be demonstrated to be believed. The absence of verbal evidence of religious sentiment on the part of the Catholic laity did not reflect the absence of an internalized religiosity, as Weber implied, but the presence of a devotional ethic that placed the highest value on action.

Penitent confraternities equated fraternity with faith and participation in a confraternity with participation in the church itself. The devotional ethic of Catholicism translated this equation into a continuous effort on the part of confreres at keeping their associations vital as organizations. The following chapters present types of information not usually found in devotional studies. Taken from sets of statutes, registers of monthly council meetings, financial accounts, and enrollment registers, this information reflects the kind of institutional memory confreres themselves saw as necessary for the maintenance of their associations. These sources reveal an enormous amount of bickering, anguish, and frustration all centered around one concern—keeping the confraternities afloat as organizations. This concern made sense, for it was as corporations with the grace amassed from the devotions of past, present and future generations of confreres that confraternities presumed to play a role in their members' salvation. Once these corporations dissolved, so did their potential to aid their members' salvation. This explains why, among the confraternities reestablished in Marseille after the restoration of Catholicism in France, several had been suppressed by royal mandate decades before the Revolution. To learn how confreres sought to keep these treasuries of grace valid is to learn how they sought to be Christians.

Many scholars may take exception to the use of sociological and psychological theories to explain religious change. In defense I would point out that "religion as practiced," to mention a concept of the anthropologist William Christian to which I will later return, is not always accessible to the literate consciousness of the scholar. In any collective endeavor there are social and psychological dynamics that defy the search for patterns of behavior and of cognition discernable in individuals. Sociological and psychological theories try to understand how humans act and think unconsciously. They do not diminish but enhance other types of understanding. One of my purposes in this study is to illustrate how a focus on the material, the mundane aspects of a religious experience, can illuminate its spiritual dimensions. The theories of which I make use aid in this pursuit.

My initial ambition was to write a comparative study of the penitent societies of the major cities of southern France. I retreated from this ambition once I began to appreciate the differing external factors that influenced organizational evolution and made the religious experience occurring in the confraternities of the different locales sui generis.[5] Comparative study is still feasible, but to have any value, it must emerge through a survey of local studies of penitent associations and even of their analogues in other regions of France and Europe. My goal here is to utilize all of the available information to provide a sense of how penitent confraternities evolved as a reflection of the faith of one urban laity.

The most important reason for choosing Marseille for a detailed study is that there were twice as many brotherhoods there as anywhere else. From 1499, when the first confraternity was established, to 1792, when all were dissolved, the city witnessed the establishment of seventeen confraternities, of which twelve remained in existence for more than one hundred years. The long duration of their existence, most of it without close episcopal supervision, permitted the confraternities of Marseille, more so than those of any other city, to evolve according to their own impetus. External events, like the Wars of Religion, and ongoing change in the society around them, like Marseille's development as a major French port, influenced their development. But the responses to these outside stimuli were put forward by confreres, not clerical sponsors or diocesan officials. The confraternities of Marseille provide the best opportunity to study the development of penitent confraternities in France.

MARSEILLE IN THE EARLY MODERN AGE

Why penitent confraternities held so much attraction for the Marseillais is difficult to answer. It is tempting to account for their appeal by the proximity of the city to Italy. But the cultural connections between Marseille and urban Italy at the end of the fifteenth century were far less developed than those between Avignon or Lyon and urban Italy. Both of these cities had penitent confraternities decades before Marseille, but in neither city did they ever succeed to the same extent. A brief survey of the city's history during the centuries under consideration suggests some possible reasons.

Such a survey must begin by considering early modern Marseille as a French city, for the integration of the city into France is in fact the dominant theme of its history during this period. Through most of the late medieval centuries Marseille was part of the empire of the counts of Anjou, a cadet branch of the French royal line. Toward the end of the fifteenth century the cadet branch died out, and in 1481 Louis XI of France laid claim to Marseille along with the rest of Provence. The often violent struggle to make the city French can be considered in three stages.[6]

In the first stage (1481–1596) the citizens of Marseille were quite happy with their new French rulers. The Valois kings of France had ambitions to acquire more than just the Provençal part of the Angevin inheritance. The Angevins had once been rulers of Naples, so the Valois also had designs on the southern portion of the Italian peninsula. Marseille became a staging point of the French armies for the Italian campaigns. Royal monies poured into Marseille, and many of Marseille's ship captains and sailors gained glory and plunder serving in royal naval squadrons. The main opposition to the French came from the Hapsburgs of the Holy Roman Empire. In the early part of the sixteenth century the Hapsburgs reversed French gains on the Italian peninsula and actually invaded France. Marseille remained loyal when the tide turned against the Valois in their battle with the Hapsburgs. Both in 1524 and in 1536 imperial invasions foundered as a result of unsuccessful sieges of Marseille. Francis I rewarded the Marseillais for their fidelity. In 1533 the nuptials between the future Henry II and Catherine de Medici, niece of Pope Leo X, took place in Marseille. In the treaty he concluded with the Sultan of the Ottoman Turk Empire, Francis inserted a clause granting commercial concessions to the merchants of Marseille. In 1543 he also exempted the Marseillais from the obligation to quarter or supply royal troops.[7]

Yet, what Francis offered with one hand, he took away with the other. In 1501 his father, Louis XII, had established, over local opposition, a court of Parlement at Aix-en-Provence. Francis continued the effort to reduce Provençal autonomy. In 1535 in the edict of Joinville he stripped local officials of final authority in administrative matters and placed such authority in the hands of five *lieutenants de sénéchaussée* established in the major cities of the province. In 1539 in the ordinance of Villers-Cotterêts he prohibited the writing of official documents in any language other than French.[8]

The reaction by the Provençaux to royal efforts at centralization came during the Wars of Religion. In Provence, as in many parts of France, sectarian disputes became occasions of revolt against royal authority.[9] As for the Marseillais, from early on they had exhibited a marked animosity toward the ideas of Protestantism. Although there were Protestants in the city, primarily within the German merchant community, Protestant missions to the city were unsuccessful in expanding on this base. In 1560 several men suspected of Protestant leanings were lynched by a mob. In 1562 the city sent a delegation to the royal court to announce its desire "to live and die in the faith of its fathers" and to request royal sanction for an effort to expel all non-Catholics from within its walls.

During the Wars of Religion Catholic conservatism in Marseille became fused with the reaction against royal centralization. During the 1580s Marseille was a major center of the Holy League, producing money and troops for the Catholic struggle in Provence. In 1589, in the political vacuum created by the assassination of Henry III and the ascension of the Protestant Henry IV to the throne, the city decided to break free from France and the league and go its own way. In a solemn procession city leaders marched from the cathedral to the shrine of Notre Dame de la Garde on the hill overlooking the city. Once there they planted a cross to signify that the city recognized no master other than Jesus Christ. About this time Charles de Casaulx, a member of one of the local noble families and a leader of the league, began to gain control of the city. By 1591 Casaulx had established dictatorial control over the city. Though repeated attempts were made against his life, he maintained control for the next five years. During that time he succeeded in keeping the city independent of outside forces, beating back efforts by Charles Emmanuel, Duke of Savoy, to annex the city and stymying attempts by Henry IV to regain the city peacefully.

Casaulx dreamed of developing Marseille into a city republic. He established a mint, organized the first municipal archives, and arranged for the opening of the city's first printing press. He also rebuilt the fortifications of the city and opened negotiations with Philip II of Spain for the creation of a Spanish garrison. While these actions had the support of the popular classes, they alienated Marseille's mercantile elite. Through the latter group Henry IV arranged the assassination of Casaulx. On February 17, 1596, Pierre de Libertat, a Corsican mercenary Casaulx had taken into his service, committed the act. Simultaneously the gates to the city were opened and royal troops allowed in. On hearing of the assassination of Casaulx and the taking of Marseille, Henry IV remarked, "Only now am I truly king of France."[10]

During the second stage of the integration of Marseille into France (1596–1660), the Marseillais largely accepted royal rule. Primarily because the royal government was far away and absorbed with more important matters, it made little real effort to intervene in local affairs. Urban government was in the hands of royal officials appointed from among local notables. Political life during the first part of the seventeenth century was dominated by fighting between the two chief factions among these notables, headed respectively by the Valbelle and the Beausset families. For the most part the lower classes remained quiet during the period. Two issues, however, could and did bring them into the streets. During the Wars of Religion the city of Marseille went into debt for more than one and a half million livres. In the plan for the repayment of the debt a careful balance was struck between the portion expected of the general populace and the portion demanded of the city's merchants. Occasionally the merchants made an effort to restrike the balance in their favor, but protesting mobs of workers would quickly put a halt to this. The other issue which roused the lower classes was the ever-increasing burden of royal taxes. The battles over both these issues became confused with the fighting between the Valbelle and Beausset factions—the Valbelle faction defending the popular position and the Beausset defending the merchants'. In the background the republican issue still smouldered. In 1601 a plot to join Marseille to Savoy was put down. In 1605 a similar plot to deliver Marseille to the Spanish monarchy was foiled. In the 1620s and 1630s the republican issue also became embroiled in the factional fighting, the Valbelle faction taking the lead in the independence movement. The confusion created by the Fronde brought the republican element to the fore, and in 1650 the Marseillais once again broke free of France.

Antoine de Valbelle adroitly maintained control over the republican movement and the city for the last five years of his life.

When he died in 1655 his son Léon gained control. Léon was not as skilled at balancing the various interests against one another. In addition, he refused to respond to the entreaties of Louis XIV. By 1660 Louis felt strong enough to regain the city. In January 1660 he arrived before the city walls with an army of six thousand. The city capitulated. Louis tore down the city walls, stripped the municipal council of all powers, and established a royal garrison in the city. This broke the back of the republican movement.[11]

Yet the wounds created by Louis' destruction of Marseille's dreams of political autonomy were quickly healed by the prosperity brought about by his renovation of the city's port facilities. The final stage of Marseille's integration into France (1660–1789) was dominated by the city's development into the major French port on the Mediterranean. Prior to 1660 Marseille had competed with other Mediterranean ports for trade. While its natural harbor gave it a competitive edge, much of Marseille's economic prosperity in the first part of the early modern period can be traced to luck—luck in having been perfectly situated as a staging point for French campaigns in Italy, and in having been French and therefore neutral during the wars between Philip II and Suleiman the Magnificent. After 1660 most of Marseille's economic prosperity came as a result of the policies of Louis XIV and his minister Colbert. They saw Marseille as the perfect port for the products of an ever-expanding French empire in the Mediterranean and the southern seas. They rebuilt and expanded the port facilities. By the end of the seventeenth century the city was handling almost all of France's trade with the Middle East, as well as a significant part of its trade with Africa, the East, and the West Indies. Some industry also developed: Marseille became an important locale for soap manufacturing and sugar refining. It also became important in the manufacture of shoes, hats, and clothing for colonial markets. This industry was generated by the city's role as an international port; all aspects of Marseille's economy were tied to the sea.

After 1660 Marseille began to respond to the French initiatives. From that year can be dated its true integration into France. It is useful to sketch the major lines of its transformation. First, the city grew. Although Marseille suffered from constant recurrence of the plague (in 1720–21 the city lost an estimated 50,000 inhabitants), its population consistently increased. From an estimated 45,000 in 1600, the population of metropolitan Marseille rose to 65,000 in 1660, 100,000 in 1720, and 120,000 in 1790.[12]

Second, it became more cosmopolitan. Marseille's economic prosperity attracted skilled and unskilled workers from all over the Mediterranean world. A significant part of Marseille's population increase after 1660 came from immigration. Actual numbers for immigration do not exist, but the numbers for marriage partners from outside the city are revealing. Forty-one percent of the 757 marriages contracted in 1715 involved at least one partner born outside the city; by 1749 this had risen to 51 percent. Research led by Michel Vovelle has established that while immigrants came from all parts of the Mediterranean world, the bulk of this immigration came principally from other regions of Provence and secondarily from northwest Italy and Savoy. While there was some immigration by skilled craftsmen, most immigrants found employment as domestics and non-guild labor.[13]

The influx of new inhabitants caused few social problems. In the later years of the ancien régime, Marseille society was composed of a small patriciate of old noble and old mercantile families; a large maritime and commercial bourgeoisie headed by a few great *négociants,* but made up predominantly of shopkeepers and small master craftsmen; and a large working class of sailors, dockworkers, and artisans. Previously Marseille's patriciate had been politically dominant, but in 1660 Louis XIV outlawed noble participation in municipal affairs, and most political power fell to the economically dominant bourgeoisie. The bourgeoisie's control over urban government is perhaps one reason why there was little social and political conflict in Marseille in the century before the Revolution. Other possible reasons were the economic prosperity brought on by the development of the port facilities, which left few people with the time or cause to complain, and the outbreaks of the plague, which periodically wiped out Marseille's lower classes and thus gave them little opportunity to develop any sense of themselves as a group.

Third, Marseille expanded. In 1600 it covered sixty-seven hectares of land. In 1789 it covered 195 hectares. Most of the expansion was to the north where new docks were built as part of Louis XIV's redevelopment plan. Around them grew up new communities of fishermen, seamen, and dockworkers. The shift of port activities to the Rive Nord left the area around the old harbor, the Vieux Port, open for settlement. Gradually settlement filled in the area where the old docks had been and then spread outward into the hills immediately southeast of the harbor to give the city the sprawling appearance it has today.[14]

Finally, Marseille became culturally French. Before the coming of the French the Marseillais had been members of the Mediterranean world. Intellectually and spiritually they had faced southward toward Rome and Florence, rather than northward toward Paris. In their customs, values, and ideas of social relationships they had belonged to Occitania, the region along the Mediterranean coast from Genoa to Barcelona where the language of Oc (or Occitans) was once spoken. The French effort to transform them into Frenchmen took place only slowly and focused on making the transformation from the top of society downward. In this light the creation of the Parlement of Provence in 1501, its staffing with members of local families, and the publishing of the ordinance of Villers-Cotterêts can be perceived as aspects of the effort to gallicize elite society in Provence. During the Counter-Reformation, the church enhanced this process by the use of French in both clerical and lay instruction and through the dispersal of non-Provençal clerics throughout Provence. After 1660 gallicization was greatly aided by the presence of royal administrators and a royal garrison in Marseille.

By the eighteenth century royal policy bore fruit. Elite society in Marseille spoke and read French, looked toward Paris for intellectual and spiritual direction, and most importantly, identified itself as French. How deeply the process permeated the popular level of society is another question. As noted earlier, during the eighteenth century the popular milieu of Marseille was constantly renewed by people from the rural regions of Provence, Savoy, and northwestern Italy. The Occitanian tradition, therefore, was also continually replenished. Eighteenth-century Marseille, then, was an area where the normal split between elite and popular culture had as one of its dimensions a conflict between two cultural traditions: one, the French, literate and national in character, and the other, the Occitanian, customary and regional.[15]

In the eighteenth century Marseille brought back most of the political privileges Louis XIV had taken away. Yet there was no rebirth of the republican movement; the economic prosperity brought on by Louis' development of the port facilities made French nationality too lucrative for that. Thus, three hundred years after Louis XI claimed the city as a prize of territorial expansion, the integration of Marseille into France was complete. Both the city and its people had changed. Economic development and the influx of new inhabitants had forced the city outside its medieval walls into the surrounding hills. The royal carrot of economic prosperity reinforced by the royal stick of military coercion had changed its citizens into contented provincial Frenchmen. Three hundred years of conscientious courting by the French had led the city to wed its fate, for better or for worse, to that of France.

Historically, the presence of a comparatively affluent nobility and an exceptionally prosperous bourgeoisie promoted the success of penitent devotions. From their beginnings in Marseille penitent confraternities were an expression of the elite religious sensibilities, though over the course of their history the nature of this expression changed. Still, the presence of a wealthy elite willing to subsidize the cost of maintaining the confraternities helps explain both the large number of confraternities in Marseille and their organizational longevity. At the other end of the social scale, the constant replenishment of the city's lower classes by men from lower Provence, Savoy, Italy (i.e., places where penitent confraternities were already recognized and approved as vehicles for the expression of faith) insured a constant supply of new recruits for the religious experience occurring in confraternal chapels. In sum, Marseille's economic prosperity and demographic growth during the final centuries of the ancien régime were key factors in the success of penitent societies there.

THE CONFRATERNITIES OF PENITENTS OF MARSEILLE[16]

The first confraternity, the *pénitents blancs de Saint Catherine d'Alexandre,* appeared in 1499. Over the next twenty-five years it was followed by four others: the *pénitents bleus de Notre Dame de Pitté* (1506); the *pénitents blancs du Saint Esprit* (1511); the *péni-*

tents blancs de la Sainte Trinité (1515); and the *pénitents noirs of Saint Jean Baptiste* (1521). A few years later in 1531, the penitents of Notre Dame de Pitié split in two, one group of brothers remaining in the chapel at Saint Martin's parish, the other moving to a nearby chapel rented from the Carmelite monastery. As of 1531 Marseille had six companies of flagellants. Why did the confraternities appear when they did, and why did they experience such success?

An answer to the first question has already been suggested: penitent associations began to appear outside of Italy toward the end of the fifteenth century, because by then they had evolved an organizational form that emphasized lay devotional autonomy at the expense of clerical supervision. The second question is more complicated. Before 1560 penitent confraternities are known to have been established only in Marseille, Avignon, Aix-en-Provence, and Montpellier—that is, only in the southern portion of the Rhone valley and the northwestern littoral of the Mediterranean. Here the Dominican Vincent Ferrer made the value of self-flagellation as an act of penance a main theme of his revivalistic preaching toward the start of the fifteenth century. Ferrer's association of the act of self-flagellation with the status of "penitent" in fact may be the explanation of why Italian confraternities of *disciplinati* appeared in France as confraternities of *pénitents*. It would seem that the connections Ferrer made in the popular mind between self-flagellation, penance, and salvation remained after his evangelical efforts had waned. When a new type of confraternity appeared that featured flagellant devotions, the laity in the area where Ferrer had proselytized proved receptive to it.[17]

The problem with this explanation is that while it provides cultural background for the diffusion of penitent devotions north of the Alps, it does not explain why penitent confraternities generated so much interest in so short a time. In *La Comptabilité de l'Au-Dela*, his magnificent study of burial practices in late medieval Avignon, Jacques Chiffoleau furnishes a possible clue. Chiffoleau argues that the demographic effects of the bubonic plague, coupled with the fear and anxiety caused by the plague's constant recurrence, combined to alter burial practices. The need of Avignon and the other cities of Provence for new inhabitants to replace those killed by the plague uprooted the rural population. The material success to be gained in the city appealed to these displaced peasants, but they were alienated from the anonymity of the urban environment. They also lived in terror that their new-found prosperity would be cut short by death from the plague. As Chiffoleau shows, newly arrived city-dwellers gradually abandoned attitudes about death and the afterlife formed in their native countryside and small towns and replaced them with attitudes more reflective of the psychic and emotional climate of the plague-ridden cities. Behind these new attitudes was what might be labeled an obsession with assuring salvation. Under pressure from endemic plague, lay testators became fixated with preparing their souls for a sudden departure from this earth.

At first laymen sought to assure salvation by seeking access to clerical sanctity. Across the fourteenth century this desire resulted in a growth in requests by testators to be buried in the habits of mendicants and to have mendicants present at their burials and sing masses for the good of their souls after death. This quest for sanctity can also be detected in a declining concern on the part of testators for burial among "kith and kin" and a growing preference for burial within urban churches, especially those of the mendicants. Through the fifteenth century though, particularly after 1450, lay eagerness for access to mendicant sanctity declines. To a certain degree it is replaced by a desire for access to the sanctity of secular priests. But most distinctive is the increasing reliance of testators on confraternities as vehicles to salvation. Chiffoleau uncovered steady increases in the number of confraternities being established, in the average number of confraternities to which testators claimed membership, and in the number and amount of bequests being left to confraternities. He read this growing popularity as reflective of the role confraternities played in the burial process. In effect, confraternities provided urbanites with new, albeit artificial, families who guaranteed members proper burial and proper prayer after death. Chiffoleau's study reveals a two-stage evolution in lay attitudes about death and the pursuit of salvation. In the first stage, deracinated peasants abandoned the ideal of dying among their families and original communal associates to embrace the psychic security of mendicant spirituality. In the second stage, disillusionment with the mendicants led urbanites to re-create, through confraternities, a new familial structure from which to contemplate death and salvation.[18]

Confraternities of disciplinati were not initially organized as burial societies. All the more striking, then, is the fact that available statutes for the earliest French associations display a concern with regulating obligations to deceased confreres out of proportion to other organizational concerns. Penitent confraternities appeared in Avignon in the decades just after the period of Chiffoleau's study, and thus are not considered by him. Based on his discussion, however, I would speculate that part of what made them so attractive to the Avignonnais, as well as other southerners, was their potential as burial societies. The relatively quick spread of penitent confraternities can thus be explained as a result of an impulse on the part of the laity to direct its devotional energies toward the establishment of burial societies. Along the northwestern Mediterranean coastline in the fifteenth and early sixteenth centuries, no one doubted the efficacy of self-flagellation in lessening the time to be spent in purgatory. Laymen exploited this potential to assure their salvation.

The first three confraternities in Marseille were established through lay initiative. Yet while the laity may have taken the initiative in introducing penitent devotions to Marseille, it was not long before the clergy began to challenge with confraternities of their own. In fact, with the exception of the *pénitents Bourras,* and excluding the aborted brotherhoods of the civil war era, it appears that every other confraternity established was the result of clerical initiative. What is striking about Marseille is the initial rapport between penitent confraternities and the secular clergy. The association of flagellant devotions with the religious orders in Italy (and later in France and Spain), the fifteenth-century confrontation between Jean Gerson and Vincent Ferrer over the orthodoxy of flagellation rites, and the struggles between penitent confraternities and reforming bishops that occurred throughout the Counter-Reformation, all confirm the existence of antipathy between the secular clergy and the performers of flagellant devotions. Yet sixteenth-century Marseille had four parishes, and by 1550 each had its own confraternity.[19]

The attractiveness of parish churches to the founders of the earliest confraternities may have been a function of the former's ability to offer confreres secluded locales in which to practice their devotions. The peregrinations of the original confraternity of Notre Dame de Pitié—from an abandoned chapel outside the city walls, to an unused *crypte* under one of the local hospitals, to a chapel in the cemetery attached to Saint Martin parish—indicate the degree to which seclusion was prized. Of the four confraternities situated at parish churches, three built their chapels in cemeteries, the other in the parish garden.

In 1515 the Trinitarians founded the first company under the supervision of a religious order. The *pénitents blancs de Notre Dame de Bonne Aide,* or as they were popularly known, "the penitents of the *Trinité vieille*" were auxiliaries to the centuries-old Trinitarian confraternity of lay questors (alms gatherers) of the same name. The establishment of this confraternity is an indication that penitent associations were beginning to become attractive to the regular clergy. The penitents of Notre Dame de Bonne Aide were followed six years later by the pénitents noirs of Saint John the Baptist. Nominally this confraternity was an extension of the surviving remnants of the military order of Saint John of Jerusalem, but their location in and dependence upon the monastery of the Observant Franciscans suggests a Franciscan project from the start.

The split in two of the confraternity of Notre Dame de Pitié in 1531 provided the Carmelites with the opportunity to provide shelter and chaplain services for a penitent confraternity. Although they expelled the confraternity ten years later, financial necessity led them to resell the chapel to the confraternity in 1551. The Fathers of Saint Anthony also had an empty chapel and in 1550 formed a confraternity of penitents there. The monastery had in its possession some of the relics of Saint Anthony, father of monasticism. They decided to pass on these relics to the confraternity for safekeeping. In exchange the confraternity was expected to carry the relics in the procession held annually by the order on the feast of Saint Anthony. Three years later, however, the penitents of Saint Anthony moved to the Dominican monastery and placed themselves under the spiritual direction of the members of that order, taking the relics with them.

As the story of the Carmelites and the penitents of Notre Dame de Pitié suggests, part of the appeal of penitent confraternities for clerical groups may have been their potential as sources of revenue—from rent for chapel space, fees for chaplain service, and bequests from deceased confraternity members. Both the Fathers of Saint Anthony and the chapter of canons at the cathedral created confraternities to carry relics in processions. Part of the appeal to churchmen of penitent confraternities must have been the prestige and flourish they brought to processions and other religious events.

How the competition among clerical groups to possess their own confraternities affected the goals of the laymen who joined these associations is impossible to determine. There was no necessary conflict between the confraternities' service as both burial societies and ceremonial auxiliaries to a clerical group. Clearly the indulgences and other spiritual inducements offered by the clergy were well received; otherwise the confraternities would not have attracted members. Still, it seems that the lay initiative that led to the introduction of penitent confraternities in Marseille was swallowed up by the eagerness of clerical groups to promote such associations.

Evidence indicates that the original memberships of most of Marseille's confraternities were small groups of committed men with a history of some prior social interaction. (Problems in determining the social composition of the earliest associations will be discussed in the next chapter.) This was obviously the case with the successive groups who left the penitents of Saint Catherine to found the penitents of Notre Dame de Pitié and the penitents of the Holy Spirit, and with the later split of the penitents of Notre Dame de Pitié. The penitents of Notre Dame de Bonne Aide were essentially an extension of an existing confraternity. And if Fontanier is right about the aristocratic origins of the pénitents noirs, then the confraternity of Saint John the Baptist can be seen as an effort on the part of the nobility of Marseille to found their own association.

There is no way to ascertain how quickly confraternities outgrew these original groups. But there is no evidence that any of the original brotherhoods were very active in the recruitment of members. It stands to reason that if any had been, the ability of successive clerical groups to attract others to their new associations would have been much weaker. The socio-economic status of the founders and other members of penitent confraternities cannot be established with any degree of certainty. It is doubtful that all these men were the local social and cultural elites insisted upon by generations of local historians. Still, the costs associated with membership in a penitent confraternity, the rigor and uniqueness of penitent devotions, and the presumption of literacy were all factors that limited to the middle and upper classes the pool of possible participants.

By 1561, the eve of the Wars of Religion, Marseille had eight functioning confraternities, already more than any other French city would ever have. An indication of neither mass appeal nor mass acceptance, this probably reflected the intensity of clerical competitiveness. The confraternities at that time were composed of small, closely-knit groups of financially comfortable men, undoubtedly the protégés of some clerical group, who maintained a moderate but still relatively demanding devotional life, and an active part in the ceremonial life of their clerical sponsors. This situation probably changed somewhat in the 1550s as tensions mounted between Catholics and Marseille's small Protestant community. But it is doubtful that this change was sufficient to make a qualitative difference in the experience occurring within confraternal chapels.

The 1560s brought a new concern to the confraternities. In 1561 the Protestant community of Marseille sent a small painted figure of a flagellant in robe and hood to the Admiral de Coligny, "pour lui faire connaître l'habit de leur persécuteur."[20] What triggered the emergence of the confraternities as centers of anti-Protestantism is difficult to determine. Part of the answer would involve the *politicization* of their devotional life in response to Protestant attacks on Catholic ideas of penance. By the same envoy who carried the statuette to the Admiral de Coligny, the Protestants of Marseille sent a letter to Catherine de Medici requesting that she enforce a royal ordinance issued by Francis I in 1539 suppressing the confraternities of penitents. Guibert reports an incident in Aix-en-Provence in 1560 when Protestants interrupted a procession by the pénitents noirs of that city by sprinkling pepper-corns along the route of the procession that burned the bare feet of the participants. Penitent confraternities and their activities were being singled out by Protestants for scorn.

The ideas of the social psychologist Charles Kiesler help to interpret the effects of such attacks on the Catholic psyche. Kiesler has defined commitment as cognitive resistance to behavioral change in the face of cognitive dissonance concerning that behavior. Kiesler suggests, then, that commitment represents the reaffirmation of an attitude in response to an attack.[21] He further theorizes what he calls a "boomerang effect," the idea that the cognitive dissonance created by an attack on a behavior, once resisted, leads to a greater commitment to the behavior in response to the attack.[22] As Protestants began to proselytize in southern cities and towns, they subjected all Catholic devotional acts to derision. These attacks forced those who remained Catholics to reaffirm their faith in Catholicism and its rites and pushed their commitment to new extremes. And while it would be misleading to suggest that the increase in Catholic militancy on the eve of the Wars of Religion was purely a response to Protestantism, it may explain why certain Catholic rites, like self-flagellation, became rallying points for Catholic reaction.[23]

The specific connotations that the rite of self-flagellation took on merit consideration. The perception of the confraternities of Marseille by the Protestant community has already been mentioned. A study by Linsolas indicates that during the 1540s and 1550s penitent confraternities were established in a number of small towns and villages around Avignon. Linsolas relates the appearance of these associations to the presence of Protestants (though he does this without much supporting evidence). Pecquet reports that it was among the loyal Catholics massed before Toulouse in anticipation of a Protestant assault that the movement began which culminated in the establishment of the first penitent confraternity of that city (the penitents of the Holy Circumcision of Our Redeemer Jesus Christ).[24] For militant Catholics, performance of the rite of self-flagellation was an act of defiance, a repudiation of Protestant attacks upon the sacrality of Catholic ritual. Its prestige in this regard was sufficient to make self-flagellation the cornerstone of the collective Catholic response to Protestantism.

Exactly what Henry III saw in the rite has been the subject of speculation and controversy for more than four centuries. What is certain is that Henry, too, wanted to exploit the rite for galvanizing Catholics into collective action.[25] His congregation of the Annunciation of Our Lady, inaugurated with much fanfare in the spring of 1583, failed to stimulate the development of the anticipated realm-wide network of affiliates. Henry's promotion of it, though, as well as his patronage of penitent confraternities in general was probably a major factor in the appeal of penitent confraternities to moderate Catholic elites in such places as Toulouse and Lyon, and as such, an important factor in the survival of such confraternities in those cities after the wars.

For Henry, the rite of self-flagellation was essentially an act of penance whose collective performance could only help assuage heavenly ire—the source of France's present misery. The rite for him was a symbol whose sanctity and integrity could not be questioned, and was thus a starting point for a policy of reconciliation within Catholic ranks. His instincts were right. Historians have been blinded by the disdain of northern commentators such as Pierre de l'Étoile for "southern" devotions, thinking that flagellation received a negative reception in Paris. Actually, evidence suggests that Parisian crowds did not question the act as much as the king's sincerity in performing it.[26]

No one questioned the sincerity of the leaders of the Holy League when they performed the rite. As Frances Yates observed, the Holy League, "stole Henri's thunder," meaning that they succeeded where Henry had failed in making political capital out of the performance of penitent devotions. How they stole Henry's thunder is important.[27] Yates describes how, after they had taken control of the confraternity of Our Lady of the Annunciation, the leaders of the league altered its processions:

> Henri's processions had used lights and beautiful music, and allegorical figures expressive of charity and the works of mercy. In the League processions, the priests and monks, as well as the soldiers, carried guns which they

fired at intervals. . . . The symbolism of the League processions was specifically aimed against the King. Lighted
tapers were carried which the bearers every now and then
stopped to extinguish, with imprecations against the
House of Valois. This process seems to have "magical"
intentions of injuring the King, just as the wax images of
the King which League fanatics placed on altars and
pricked in the region of the heart during Mass were in-
tended to cause his death.[28]

For the leaders of the league, performance of the rite of self-
flagellation became an act of defiance against not only Protestantism, but also against a king who permitted Protestants to live.
Thus, a few years after Henry had tried to develop a realm-wide
network of confraternities to support his religious policies, the
Holy League attempted the same. By the end of the 1580s, especially in the north of France, penitent confraternities had been
established to serve as, or had evolved into, radical egalitarian
Catholic cells like those the league had fostered in Paris. As such,
penitent confraternities became targets of local authorities once
political order had been reestablished.[29]

During the period 1560–1600 the rite of self-flagellation became a political act, and the brotherhoods who performed the rite,
political organizations. The *politicization* of penitent confraternities
also led to their *popularization,* an ambiguous term used here to
signify the related phenomena of an increase in the number of existing brotherhoods, an increase in total memberships within chapels,
and last but perhaps most controversial, a transformation of the
social mix within chapels to include men from the lower classes.

Between 1560 and 1600 penitent confraternities spread across
France. The total number is unknown, but at least one confraternity was established in cities as far-flung as Cahors, Grenoble
and Rouen, while Paris, Lyon and Toulouse all witnessed multiple
foundations. The increase in total memberships within given chapels likewise is fairly easy to document. Boucher, for example,
notes that in their initial procession of 1578, the penitents of Notre
Dame de Gonfalon of Lyon had one hundred members. Five years
later the papal nuncio reported the confraternity as containing five

hundred members. That a membership of that magnitude was not unusual by this time is indicated by the fact that in 1574, five hundred pénitents blancs of the Holy Cross marched in procession with Henry III through the streets of Avignon.[30]

The assumption that penitent confraternities experienced only in the seventeenth century what Maurice Agulhon has labeled a *gonflement democratique,* or "democratic explosion," has been around for several generations. Thus, the question of the transformation of the social mix within chapels deserves some discussion. When the Protestants of Aix-en-Provence attempted to repeat their humiliation of the pénitents noirs of a few weeks earlier, they met with a violent Catholic counterattack. Guibert describes this counterattack as a cooperative effort between several "capitaines catholiques," and an "assez grand nombre de manouvriers."[31] Figures presented by Venard for confraternities in Avignon and Carpentras and by Boucher for confraternities in Avignon and Lyon also strongly support the conclusion that the transition within confraternal chapels from small homogeneous groups to large heterogeneous ones actually took place during the latter decades of the sixteenth century.[32]

The politicization of penitent confraternities probably advanced more in Marseille than in most cities, a reflection in part of the fact that politicization began there earlier than in most cities. A more significant factor, however, was the later emergence of the confraternities as the recruitment grounds and meeting places for the radical egalitarian fringe of the Catholic Holy League. While this development occurred elsewhere in France also, nowhere did it reach the extent it did in Marseille, where it was behind Casaulx's successful establishment of a popular dictatorship in the 1590s. It is actually difficult, in fact, to differentiate during the reign of Casaulx between the confraternities and his government. During the five years he was dictator of Marseille, Casaulx was simultaneously prior of the penitents of Saint John the Baptist. Most of the men who made up his government were also members of the confraternity. Another indication of the intimate relationship between the Casaulx government and penitent confraternities is the fact that two, possibly three, confraternities were founded during his short reign. One of them was begun by Casaulx's son Fabio; another was a sort of boys' club that sought to train teen-age males in penitential skills. Neither of these associations lasted beyond Casaulx's assassination. A third confraternity, however, the *pénitents gris du Très-Saint-Nom-et-Très-Auguste-Nom-de-Jésus,* popularly known as the "pénitents Bourras" (1591), went on to become possibly the most successful of Marseille's penitent associations. It was founded by Antoine Mascaron, another member of Casaulx's entourage.

The popularization of the confraternities of Marseille followed a different dynamic than elsewhere owing to the fact that by the start of the Wars of Religion penitent confraternities there were already so well-established. To be sure, the war years did see the establishment of five new confraternities, of which only two, the above-mentioned pénitents Bourras and a second Trinitarian confraternity under the patronage of Notre Dame de Miséricorde (1558), survived. But the chief effect of the wars on the confraternities of Marseille was to transform them from small, somewhat intimate associations to large, fairly impersonal organizations.

This point can be comfortably asserted even though very little direct evidence exists to support it. First, that such a transformation occurred is beyond debate; the only real question is when. Just as it happened in Avignon (the only comparable city) during the war era, logic supports its occurrence in Marseille at approximately the same time. In 1558 an accord was reached between the pénitents gris de Notre Dame de Miséricorde (also known as the *"pénitents of the Trinité nouvelle"*) and the Trinitarians, establishing the monastery's obligations toward the fledgling association. It is worth noting that Jean Roquier, "marchand," and Gabriel Maté, "cordier," are listed as representing the confraternity.[33] In this instance members of the popular classes were not only joining confraternities but founding them.

Second, circumstantial evidence points toward a significant increase in chapel populations during this period. Data is scanty, but it can be said that as of 1626 the penitents of Saint Lazarus had at least one hundred members whose enrollment dated back to the civil war era. Obviously, at the end of the sixteenth century the population of the chapel must have been larger. And the confraternity of Saint Catherine experienced such growth during the second half of the sixteenth century that by 1604 it had to build a new chapel.

Third, the creation of the penitents of Our Lady of the Annunciation—the boys' confraternity mentioned above—may be taken as an indication that the diversity of the men who were entering confraternal chapels was a source of concern. The symbology and meaning of the rather stylized devotions performed by penitent confraternities probably were very difficult for ordinary illiterate laymen to grasp. The innovative solution to this problem offered by the confraternity of Our Lady of Annunciation was to take boys between the ages of ten and twenty and train them in the rudiments of penitential devotion, after which they would seek acceptance into one of the adult confraternities.

Last, perhaps the best evidence for the transformation of chapel populations from homogeneous to heterogeneous groups is the concern (expressed in the statutes of all new confraternities from the pénitents Bourras onward) to avoid what the Bourras described as, "confusions et desordres que le plus souvent survienent [sic] aux grandes multitudes." Controls were placed on both the number and type of men permitted to enroll. Such procedures were aimed at reestablishing a type of homogeneity among the brethren, one that would not offend the egalitarian sensibilities of the radical Catholic fringe, but would still allow the organization to establish some type of control over the type of men they admittted.

The Bourras were an example of what became known as *reformed* confraternities, a type of association that began to appear around the end of the wars. These confraternities were characterized organizationally by innovative responses to the structural problems that politicization and popularization caused earlier associations.[34]

Earlier confraternities evolved through an initial stage when the laity used them primarily as burial societies to an antebellum stage when they served as ceremonial auxiliaries to clerical groups. Reformed confraternities sought first and foremost to be vehicles of religious instruction and edification. To a certain extent earlier goals were suppressed, but to an even greater extent they were transcended by a new focus on the cultivation of an interior spirituality. Thus the organizational evolution of penitent confraternities toward becoming more purely prayer societies fitted with their evolution toward the devotional sensibilities of the Counter-Reformation that placed less emphasis on the performance of physical acts of faith and more on an internal, intellectualized piety. While it is true that reformed confraternities intensified their performance of certain rites, these rites were always performed with the intention that the performance bring about some interior change of mind. Earlier confraternities had promoted the exchange of temporal mortification for eternal suffering. Reformed confraternities placed less faith in the act of mortification itself than in the state of contrition that the act helped to induce.

Reformed confraternities, like their predecessors, were introduced to Marseille as a result of lay initiative. Very quickly, however, their promotion was appropriated by clerical groups. The *pénitents rouges de la Sainte Croix* was the outcome of a mission preached in Marseille in 1607 by a member of the Minims order. Originally they met in a chapel at the monastery of the Fathers of Saint Anthony vacated only a short time before by the Bourras. In 1612 they moved to a chapel they had constructed next to the Carmelite monastery. In 1641 the confraternity established itself as a third order of Saint Francis of Paoli, the founder of the Minims order. The *pénitents gris de Notre Dame de Mont Carmel* (1621), also know as the "pénitents Carmélins," were an extension of a centuries-old Carmelite scapular confraternity of the same name. Lazare de Cordier wrote that soon after their establishment the Carmélins alienated themselves from the Carmelites. This is not so surprising, given that it must have been difficult for members of the scapular confraternity to adjust to the more rigorous devotional demands of a reformed penitent association. Lazare de Cordier reports that eventually the confraternity returned to the monastery's good graces.[35]

The fact that the *pénitents de la Charité,* founded in 1663, limited their membership to thirty-three in honor of the years of the life of Christ suggests that they also were a reformed confraternity. The probability that the confraternity was founded by a clique of dissenting members from the pénitents Bourras also supports this conclusion. But several factors argue against it being considered among reformed confraternities. Fontanier asserts that most of its members were clerics, an assertion that fits in with the other story of the confraternity's origins as a project of the reformed Benedictines dedicated to Saint Maur (hence the confraternity's popular name, the "penitents of Saint Maur"). Whatever the case, the confraternity does not appear to have had much organizational vitality, disappearing several decades after it came into existence. It came to life again in 1714 when Monseigneur Belsunce, the bishop of Marseille, reestablished it to serve as a model for the other confraternities. Rather than including it with the three reformed confraternities created between 1590 and 1620, it seems fairer to place it in a special category as a later, essentially clerical effort to fine-tune the ideals behind reformed confraternities.

This decision places it in the same category as the *pénitents gris de Saint Henri* (1717), the confraternity Belsunce created three years after reactivating the penitents of Saint Maur. That the penitents of Saint Henry did not practice self-flagellation reflects the fact that the practice had declined over the course of the seventeenth century. In fact, it had so declined by the early eighteenth century that it was possible to define as "penitential" a confraternity that did not even include it among its devotional exercises. The penitents of Saint Henry were another effort by Bishop Belsunce to provide a model for the confraternities of Marseille of what a confraternity of penitents should be. Here, as with the pénitents de la Charité, he was only partially successful. Twelve years after their foundation, the penitents of Saint Henry threw off his tutelage and reorganized more in conformity with the other confraternities.

From the start of the Wars of Religion onward, only three religious orders expressed interest in housing confraternities of penitents: the Fathers of Saint Anthony who failed to keep the confraternity they created, the Bourras, and the penitents of the Holy Cross. The more successful Trinitarians eventually maintained three confraternities on the grounds of their monastery, as did the Carmelites. Perhaps only these monasteries were large enough to incorporate the chapels of new associations. More probable is a decline in interest by religious orders in having confraternities of penitents on the premises once these confraternities became large popular organizations. The confraternities accepted as tenants by the Trinitarians and the Carmelites after 1560 were either extensions of devotions already promoted by those religious orders, reformed confraternities, or both. Neither the Trinitarians nor the Carmelites were especially gracious landlords, taking their various tenants to court for a multitude of reasons over the course of the seventeenth and eighteenth centuries. Their willingness to take in the confraternities could not have had much to do with pastoral concern.

If their appeal as an aspect of clerical piety had a great deal to do with the initial spread and growth of penitent confraternities, it can be concluded that once they began to emerge as popular lay organizations, their appeal in this regard began to decline. Their very success as lay organizations may be the reason why, while new confraternities were appearing all over the rest of the south of France during the seventeenth century, comparatively few came into existence in Marseille. None of the confraternities founded during the seventeenth or eighteenth century (except for the confraternity of Saint Maur, which had its own unique problems) had difficulties finding members, which suggests that there was a market for new associations. New confraternities did not appear in Marseille because few clerical groups were willing to take on the challenge, and those that did seem to have been more interested in the monetary reward.

Still, Marseille, more so than any other city, had several different types of penitent confraternities. Contemporaries recognized a distinction between *unreformed* and *reformed* confraternities, seeing the latter as both more rigorous and more pious. To these two types can be added later variations such as the penitents of Saint Maur and the penitents of Saint Henry. While bishops certainly attempted to make all confraternities conform to one ideal, the laity apparently perceived no contradiction in having a multitude of types of associations all defined by the same name. They appear to have seen the various confraternities as providing a hierarchy of possible confraternal experiences, going from more civic-minded associations such as the penitents of the Trinité vieille to spiritually motivated associations such as the penitents of Saint Maur. For the laity the diversity of confraternities provided a devotional world catering to individual devotional taste and needs.

An Outline of the Chapters

The rest of the study will be divided into six chapters. Because debate about social composition has bogged down past research, and since the transformation of social composition played such an essential part in the later development of the companies of Marseille, chapter 2 will focus on this topic. The discussion will center on answers to two sets of questions. Maurice Agulhon, in his path-breaking study of the penitent confraternities of southern Provence, concluded that the introduction of the lower classes into confraternal chapels eventually alienated the upper classes, which in turn was a major factor in the confraternities' eighteenth-century decline. Can the alienation of the elite be discerned in Marseille's confraternities, and if so, can it be related to confraternal decline? More importantly, what were the general connections between social composition and organizational vitality in penitent confraternities and in what ways did they evolve or change over the course of the centuries?

It was suggested above that the original confraternities were composed of small homogeneous groups of participants. It was further suggested that reformed confraternities sought to reestablish a type of homogeneity after the social transformation which occurred during the war era. Implicit here are several assumptions about groups, their natures and roles in the organizational life of associations. The second set of questions tests these assumptions. The homogeneity of the memberships of the earliest confraternities cannot be established. Neither can the effect on these memberships of the influx of new members of diverse origins be studied except by model building. But the role of preexisting groups in the functioning of later socially heterogeneous chapels can be studied, and from there some conclusions about social composition and group dynamics put forward.

Chapter 3 will provide information on government and operations. Officially confraternal organization and structure changed very little over the course of the ancien régime. Eighteenth-century confreres reverently swore to maintain statutes first written in the sixteenth century. But it is possible to detect in the amendments and addenda major changes in the structure and operation of the confraternities. As I shall argue, most of these changes can be traced back to forces set in motion by the popularization of the confraternities during the sixteenth century. Furthermore, it is to these forces that one must look to explain the decline and demise of several confraternities toward the end of the eighteenth century.

Distinct from questions of organization and structure are questions about the maintenance of internal order. Conflict between groups competing for control of confraternities could become violent. The threat posed by this competition was perceived by contemporaries as the major source of organization instability. Statutes aimed at maintaining internal discipline thus provide a useful perspective on the weekly operation of confraternities as associations. Statutes display a concern to regulate three processes in particular: the election and installation of new officers, the enrollment of new members, and the expulsion of offending members. In an effort to explain changes in the way internal order was maintained, chapter 4 regards the evolution in the procedures for regulating these processes, as well as supporting evidence taken from extant minutes of council meetings.

The next chapter will reprise several of the key themes presented in chapters 2 and 3. One of the real treasures in the archive of material on the confraternities of Marseille is a register compiled in the nineteenth century of all of the members of the pénitents Bourras, and of the confraternal offices they occupied over the course of their participation in the company. Information is scarce for the seventeenth century, but for the eighteenth century the register appears fairly complete. Using this register, it is possible to examine the nature of participation in a confraternity and to come to some conclusions about the rewards for such participation. Chapter 5 will offer an extended analysis of official life in one confraternity, with a desire to ascertain the nature of participation and the internal and external factors that influenced it.

The listing of topics to this point may appear odd to many, considering that the role of confraternities first and foremost as religious organizations has not even been broached. My justification for tackling the religious aspects of confraternal life last will emerge by the end of Chapter 5. Chapter 6, on devotional life, will consider two distinct but related topics. The cult of the confraternities, that is, the material aspects of their devotional life, attracted (and continues to attract) attention far beyond its importance. The robes, the hoods, the whips, and the secluded chapels made penitent confraternities the object of much conversation. But if confraternal statutes and records are any indication, for most confreres these things were primarily sources of nagging concern. The discussion will center around a description of chapels and their furnishings, robes, hoods and other devotional paraphernalia. The second part of the chapter will consider evolution and change in confraternal devotional life. To a certain extent that has been done already for the sixteenth century, but full contact between penitent confraternities and the religious sensibilities of the Counter-Reformation did not occur until the seventeenth century. The results of this contact will form the substance of most of the discussion.

Over the course of the ancien régime the nature of the interaction between the confraternities as lay organizations and the clergy changed. As chapter 7 seeks to demonstrate, the withdrawal of the regular clergy from any pastoral mission relative to the confraternities of penitents occurred by the beginning of the seventeenth century, leaving the confraternities virtually free of any clerical directive for most of that century. When clerical authority was reasserted, it came in the eighteenth century from a reformed episcopacy determined to force the confraternities to acknowledge its control. The nature of this battle and its result will be spotlighted.

NOTES

1. On the Counter-Reformation in France see John Bossy, "The Counter-Reformation and the Catholic People of Europe," *Past and Present,* 46 (1970), and his *Christianity in the West 1400–1700* (Oxford, 1985); Philip Hoffman, *Church and Community in the Diocese of Lyon, 1500–1789* (New Haven, 1984); René Taveneaux, *La Catholicisme dans la France Classique, 1610–1715,* 2 vols. (Paris, 1980); Alain Lottin, *Lille, Citadelle de la Contre-Réforme (1598–1668)* (Dunkerque, France, 1980). On the Jesuits see A. Lynn Martin, *The Jesuit Mind: The Mentality of an Elite in Early Modern France* (Ithaca, N.Y., 1988); Louis Châtellier, *The Europe*

of the Devout: The Catholic Reformation and the Formation of a New Society (Cambridge, 1989), chaps. 2–4.

2. On the appearance of penitent confraternities in France see Louis Guibert, *Les Confréries de Pénitents en France et notamment dans la diocèse de Limoges* (Limoges, 1879; reprint, Marseille, 1978); Marc Venard, *L'Église d'Avignon au XVI siècle* (Lille, 1980); A. E. Barnes, "Religious Anxiety and Devotional Change in Sixteenth Century French Penitential Confraternities," *Sixteenth Century Journal* 11, no. 3 (Fall 1988). On penitent confraternities in Spain see William A. Christian, Jr., *Local Religion in Sixteenth Century Spain* (Princeton, 1989).

3. Gordon Leff, *Heresy in the Later Middle Ages*, 2 vols. (New York, 1967), 2: 485–93.

4. Cf. Jean Delumeau, *Catholicism between Luther and Voltaire* (London, 1977).

5. These factors include the date when penitent confraternities were introduced into a locale, the type of confraternity that was introduced, the composition of local clerical culture, and the appearance of the first reforming bishop.

6. The following narration is drawn primarily from Raoul Busquet, *Histoire de Marseille* (Paris, 1978); Edouard Baratier, ed., *Histoire de Marseille* (Toulouse, 1973); Mireille Zarb, *Les Privilèges de la ville de Marseille; Du Xe siècle à la Révolution* (Paris, 1962). See also E. Baratier, ed., *Histoire de Provence* (Toulouse, 1969); Jean-Jacques Antier, *Marins de Provence et du Languedoc; Vingt-cinq siècles d'histoire du littoral français méditerranéen* (Avignon, 1977).

7. Zarb, 159–60.

8. Baratier, *Histoire de Provence,* chap. 8.

9. Robert R. Harding, *Anatomy of a Power Elite: The Provincial Governors of Early Modern France* (New Haven, 1978), 55–67.

10. Busquet, 212.

11. A. Cremieux, *Marseille et la royauté pendant la minorité de Louis XIV,* 2 vols. (Paris, 1917); Beatrice Henin, "L'agrandissement de Marseille (1660–1690): Un compromis entre les aspirations monarchiques et les habitudes locales," *Annales du Midi* 98 (1986).

12. Figures by Charles Carrière in Baratier, *Histoire de Marseille,* 163–68. For a lower estimate of the city's population see

Michel Terrisé, "La population de Marseille vers 1750: Évidences et problèmes de la démographie des métropoles de type ancien," *Annales du Midi* 98 (1986).

13. For example, based on the census of 1793, twenty-five percent of the shoemakers in Marseille at the end of the ancien régime, twenty-four percent of the masons and thirty-nine percent of the bakers came from outside the city. See studies by Carrière and Terrisé (previous note) and Michel Vovelle, *De la Cave au Grenier: Un itineraire en Provence au XVIIIe siècle: De l'histoire sociale à l'histoire des mentalités* (Quebec, 1980), 74–129.

14. On the transformation of Marseille see Felix Tavernier, *La vie quotidienne à Marseille de Louis XIV à Louis-Phillipe* (Paris, 1973), especially pp. 81–88, and the classic work by Augustin Fabre, *Les Rues de Marseille,* 6 vols. (Marseille, 1867–69; Reprint, Marseille, 1977).

15. On this point see Michel Vovelle, "Y a-t-il eu une 'Révolution culturelle' au XVIIIe siècle?" in his *De la cave au Grenier,* 313–67. Also see the discussion in Baratier, *Histoire de Marseille,* 227–60, and the classic work on Provençal culture, Fernand Benoit, *La Provence et le Comtat Venaissin; Arts et traditions populaires* (Avignon, 1978).

16. In order to save space, the details of the histories of the individual confraternities have been placed in the Appendix. References for the following discussion have also been placed there.

17. *Dictionnaire de spiritualité ascetique et mystique doctrine et histoire* (Paris, 1962), 399; M.-M. Gorce, *Saint Vincent Ferrer* (Paris, 1924), 185–86.

18. Jacques Chiffoleau, *La Comptabilité de l'au-del'à: Les hommes, la mort et la religion dans la région d'Avignon à la fin du Moyen Age (vers 1320–1420)* (Rome, 1980), especially part 2.

19. Note that excluding Saint Laurent parish, all of Marseille's parishes had chapters of canons associated with them. In all three cases, chaplain services for the resident confraternity of penitents were provided by members of the chapter, so that only with the first confraternity was spiritual supervision actually performed by a parish priest.

20. Antoine De Ruffi, *Histoire de la Ville de Marseille,* 2 vols. (Marseille, 1696), 2: 89.

21. Charles Kiesler, *The Psychology of Commitment: Experiments Linking Behavior to Belief* (New York and London, 1971), chaps. 3 and 4 in general and page 48 in particular.

22. See chapter 4 below.

23. Harding, "The Mobilization of Confraternities against the Reformation in France," *Sixteenth Century Journal* 11 (1980): passim. Also see Natalie Zemon Davis, "The Rites of Violence," in her *Culture and Society in Early Modern France* (Stanford, 1975).

24. Marguerite Pecquet, "La Compagnie des pénitents blancs de Toulouse," *Annales du Midi* 82 (1972): 213–24.

25. Jacqueline Boucher, "Henri III, mondain ou dévot? Ses retraites dans les monastères de la région parisienne," *Cahiers d'histoire* (1970); and in general her *Societé et Mentalités autour de Henri III,* 4 vols. (Lille/Paris, 1981), especially vol. 4. See also A. Lynn Martin, *Henri III and the Jesuit Politicians* (Geneva, 1973).

26. Pierre L'Etoile, *Mémoires-Journaux,* 4 vols. (Paris, 1875), 2: 112–17.

27. Yates, *French Academies of the Sixteenth Century* (London, 1947), 220.

28. Ibid., 221.

29. Guibert, 28–32.

30. Boucher, 1, 374.

31. Guibert, 64–65.

32. Venard, 1581–83; Boucher, 1377.

33. Transactions of the Order of the Holy Trinity, Archives départmentales des Bouches-du-Rhône, 50H-48 (hereafter cited as Transactions of the Holy Trinity).

34. For a more detailed discussion of the differences between unreformed and reformed penitent confraternities, see A. E. Barnes, "The Wars of Religion and the Origins of Reformed Confraternities of Penitents: A Theoretical Approach," *Archives de Sciences Sociales de Religion* 64/1 (juilliet-septembre 1987): 117–36.

35. "Analyse autographe de la travail de Lazare de Cordier, 'De poenitentibus civitatis Massiliae' par Francois de Marin de Carrannais," Collection Fontanier 24F-3, bk. 2 chap. 13 in the Archives départementales des Bouches-du-Rhône, (hereafter cited as *Lazare de Cordier*)

Chapter 2
SOCIAL COMPOSITION

INTRODUCTION: THE AGULHON THESIS

Other than an occasional notation that an individual was a member of a religious body, a master of some craft, or a *noble,* during their period of growth and expansion confraternities rarely bothered to register the social status of new recruits. Such information was not deemed worthy of record until the middle of the eighteenth century. An absence of systematic data did not pose a problem for the local historians who conducted the first studies of penitent societies, content as they were to certify popular belief about the "elite" composition of the earliest associations and the "democratic" composition of later ones. Agulhon's *Pénitents et Francs-Maçons,* the first modern study of French confraternities, retains the prevailing notion that confraternities began as elite societies and gradually evolved into popular organizations. Agulhon directed his energies toward developing a three-stage schema for this transformation.

In the first stage, which began near the end of the sixteenth century, confraternities were composed of men from the social and cultural elites. Agulhon draws on previous local studies, all of which are unanimous in arguing that the early confraternities were composed of local magistrates, prelates, professionals, and patricians. In the second stage, which occurred during the seventeenth century, the confraternities experienced a *gonflement democratique.* Across Provence new confraternities were being established, and old confraternities were opening their doors to men from all social classes. During this stage the confraternities became a type of classless society, to Agulhon's mind uniquely Mediterranean. In the final stage, which began early in the eighteenth century but accelerated during later decades, the upper classes, disgusted and embarrassed by a perceived moral decline within confraternal chapels, deserted these chapels to establish freemason lodges. This left the confraternities in the hands of the lower classes, who transformed them from religious societies into popular, fraternal associations and thus set the stage for their eventual organizational decline.[1]

In eastern Provence where Agulhon did his work, it is perhaps true that confraternities were initially established during, and as a result of, the Wars of Religion. But in Marseille and other Provençal cities penitent confraternities were already established decades before the outbreak of the religious wars. What Agulhon identifies as the first stage of confraternal growth more accurately can be conceived as secondary expansion stimulated by sectarian conflict.

Agulhon's chronology leaves unanswered the question of when the transition from elite to popular associations occurred. If urban confraternities had an elitist stage, it would have been during the earliest decades of the century. Confraternities established during the war years either quickly made the transition into multiclass associations or were that way from the beginning.

The very assumption of an elitist stage needs to be examined. There are very little data on the original membership of the earliest confraternities. Into this void generations of local historians have projected their era's notions about the pedigrees of original confreres. A classic example is provided by Jean Baptiste Thouron, a member of the *pénitents bleus* of Saint Jerome of Toulouse, who in his history of the confraternity published in 1688 lists a long line of distinguished individuals among the founders of the confraternity. Yet, as P.E. Ousset pointed out in 1928, in a much overlooked article, the rediscovered original membership register of the confraternity reveals that its first initiates were actually a class of schoolboys recruited by the confraternity's founder, the Jesuit Emond Auger.[2] Available data simply does not justify the generalization that the initial memberships of penitent confraternities were drawn primarily from local elites.

In researching the social composition of the penitent confraternities of Toulouse in the late eighteenth century, Boursiquot discovered that each of the city's four confraternities had a different social clientele: the *bleus* and the *noirs* drew their memberships from among the local elites; the *blancs* and *gris* attracted the *menu peuple*. In Toulouse, at least, the elite classes were never distributed evenly throughout the confraternities but congregated in only a few. Given the large number of confraternities established in

Marseille, Avignon, Lyon, and the other main centers of the devotion, it is worth speculating that the same situation applied in these cities also.[3]

Now consider the last stage in Agulhon's transformation of the confraternities, the "decline" during which the confraternities were deserted by the elite. Two types of problems suggest that this notion should be accepted with caution. The first concerns the ability of the "model" to incorporate all the facts. As Boursiquot's research suggests, many confraternities did not have many notables to begin with. So desertion by this group was not a general problem. Also the question may be raised whether all confraternities suffered from desertion by the elite. This is especially pertinent for reformed confraternities. Smaller and stricter in their enrollment requirements and more rigorous in their devotions, these confraternities escaped much of the censure heaped on larger confraternities. And both their admission procedures and higher dues would have limited their memberships to the middle and upper classes. Third, here also the urban/rural dichotomy demands attention. Agulhon's model appears to work for the villages and towns of eastern Provence, but it is not clear that it works for the cities in the western part of the region.

The second type of problem with Agulhon's notion of "decline" emerges from consideration of the sources he used. Agulhon based his schema on the work of nineteenth-century local historians. For his last stage he apparently drew heavily on the ideas of Louis Guibert, the best of these historians, which focused on the impetus behind the transformation within confraternal chapels. It was Guibert who first described the seventeenth century as the period of the confraternities' greatest flowering but also of the beginning of their decline into spiritual decadence. He wanted to counter the impression that something intrinsic to the confraternities themselves led to their decline. He claimed instead that it was the confraternities' popularity which attracted large numbers of the wrong sort of individuals. These in turn distracted the confraternities from their spiritual mission, which eventually led to their decline. Who were these individuals? They were the sort who joined the confraternities only to participate in the processions and ceremonies, and to take part in festive celebrations—in short, those who joined the confraternities for social, as opposed to religious, reasons.[4]

The impression that confraternities were experiencing spiritual decline was fostered by episcopal pastoral letters and ordinances. These sources cannot be taken as unbiased. One of the primary goals of Counter-Reformation bishops was the suppression of whatever competition confraternities posed to the devotional activities occurring in the parish. Their letters and ordinances reflect this concern. They were also unsympathetic, if not outright antagonistic, to all lay devotional activities that retained vestiges of the ritualistic piety of the late Middle Ages. Guibert was defending the confraternities against an invalid charge.[5]

Still, Agulhon took Guibert's argument and sought to explicate it as a social process:

> Pensons enfin à tout ce que nous avons dit, louguement, dans les chapitres qui précédent, sur les attaques menées contre les pénitents. Qui pouvait être sensible à l'argumentation des évêques, qui pouvait prêter l'oreille aux inclinations de l'ère de lumières, ou aux raisons des magistrats municipaux, ou à tout cela à la fois? Les classes populaires? ou les classes aisées et cultivées? Évidemment ces dernières. Les deux processus—déviation profane des confréries et défection des notables—ont pu d'ailleurs aussi s'enchaîner et réagir l'un sur l'autre (les critiques contre les pénitents provoquent le départ des notables, qui fuient le blâme ou le ridicule; à l'inverse le départ de ceux-ci laisse les humbles, livrés à eux-mêmes, aggraver les déviations folkloriques, et par la même la rigueur des réprobations), sans que l'on puisse savior dans cette hypothèse le quel de ces deux processus fut le premier.[6]

As just suggested, the "déviation profane" of the confraternities was to a great extent an episcopal ploy. As in the case of the "défection des notables," it was probably a factor in some cases, but not a generalized phenomenon. The social process Agulhon sketches may have occurred in eastern Provençal villages, but I question whether it can be perceived as determining the fate of penitential associations elsewhere.[7]

So was there a decline? Without a doubt there were fewer men associated with a confraternity of penitents in the second half of the eighteenth century than there were in the second half of the seventeenth. I hesitate, however, to characterize this as a decline. In seventeenth-century Marseille confraternities overextended themselves, enrolling anyone who appeared at the chapel doors. For a great many of these recruits, participation was, as Guibert correctly surmised, more a social than a religious act. In the eighteenth century fewer men may have come knocking, but on the whole they were more specifically religious. Instead of "decline," "retrenchment" better describes the organizational situation of confraternities in the eighteenth century.

A CASE STUDY OF SOCIAL COMPOSITION.
THE PENITENTS OF NOTRE DAME DE PITIÉ (SAINT MARTIN PARISH)

There is an excellent source on the social composition of one of Marseille's confraternities toward the end of the ancien régime. In 1785 the penitents of Notre Dame de Pitié (Saint Martin parish) prepared a register of all their members and their members' financial obligations to the confraternity. Included in this register for most of the members was notation of their occupation, their year of enrollment, and the amount of dues they owed as of 1785.[8]

Eleven of the 763 names listed in the register lack all the pertinent data; nineteen are noted as religious. There remain 733 dues-paying members as of the end of 1784. The penitents of Notre Dame de Pitié would appear to be quite a large confraternity, but this appearance is deceptive. Only 192, or twenty-six percent of the members, actually were current in their dues. Further, 137 of the men listed in the register, or nineteen percent, had never paid dues. Assuming the payment of dues to be an indication of commitment, and commitment in turn a sign of participation, the evidence indicates that the *active* membership of the confraternity, that is, the membership actually involved in the affairs of the confraternity, was significantly smaller than the listed membership.

But dues payment may be an inaccurate measurement of

participation. Confraternities often admitted men who had no capacity to pay dues and often allowed other members under financial duress to go several years without paying. So the active membership was probably larger than the twenty-six percent current in their dues. Inclusion in the register of such individuals as the Lamottes, Jean and Paul, "bourgeois," who joined the confraternity in 1699, argue against overstating the size, however. Neither man had paid dues since 1731, yet they were still being listed as members fifty-four years later. Perhaps they were still alive (though both would have to have been at least octogenarians), and perhaps they were still in Marseille, but it seems unlikely. Many modern voluntary organizations keep on their rolls lapsed members in the hope that they may one day choose to participate again. Such inclusive practices evidently were common also during the ancien régime. Some of the 137 men listed as having never paid dues were probably active participants; most probably had had second thoughts soon after joining and never returned.

In light of this, it seems pertinent to ask if the confraternity of Notre Dame de Pitié declined during the second half of the eighteenth century. The enrollment data included in the register do not provide a complete picture of enrollments during the eighteenth century. Members who died and were buried by the confraternity would not be included among confreres owing dues, and this lacunae would be particularly significant for the first decades of the century. The names of members who officially left the confraternity or who were officially expelled also would not be included. There is, nonetheless, sufficient information to establish some trends in enrollment and to determine whether the confraternity experienced a decline over the course of the century.

Figure 2A presents a graph of enrollment by year starting with the Lamottes and going to 1784. The continuous black line indicates the number of individuals listed as having enrolled in a given year. It dispels any notions that the confraternity declined in the latter decades of the century. Rates fluctuated, but throughout the sixties, seventies and early eighties, the confraternity averaged between ten and fifteen enrollments per year. If anything, it was going through something of a renaissance toward the end of the century.

Figure 2A: Enrollment Contrasted with Active Participation in the
Confraternity of Pénitents Bleus de Notre Dame de Pitié, 1700–1784

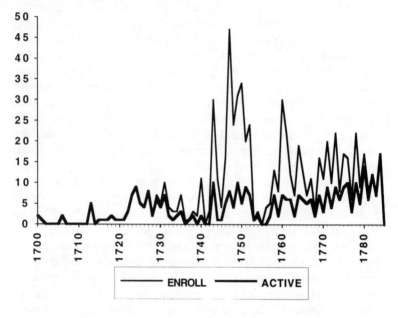

The most remarkable thing that the graph demonstrates, however, is the intense effort to recruit new members which began in the early 1740s and continued into the early 1750s. During the period 1742–52, 245 or approximately one-third of all the men listed as members in 1784 enrolled. The magnitude and consistency of this surge, especially in contrast with what went before and after, suggests a conscious change in admission policy on the part of the leaders of the confraternity. Is it possible that the confraternity actually did go through a decline, only earlier in the century? If so, then the massive recruitments of the forties and fifties may have been an effort to turn around the fortunes of the confraternity.

Whatever its motivation, how successful was this effort? We have seen that enrollment was not an accurate barometer of participation. Some other criterion is needed. The data on dues paying come to mind, but they pose special problems. Because the register took no account of men who after years of participation either left Marseille or died without the confraternity's knowledge, measuring participation simply by assessing who was current, versus who was not, with dues payment as of 1785 would be misleading. Take again the example of the Lamottes. Both men paid dues for thirty-two years before the confraternity lost sight of them. According to the register, both were fifty-four years behind in their dues, yet it is clear that in their time both had been committed members. In order to establish past participation, the simplest and most effective method is to count the actual number of years dues were paid.

But how many years of dues paying are needed to indicate committed membership? Did payment of dues for one year indicate commitment? Did five or ten? A graph of the 733 members of the confraternity plotted against the number of years they actually paid dues reveals that starting with the 141 who paid no dues and moving to the 181 who paid one year's dues, there is thereafter a steady drop in numbers until a plateau is reached between seven and eleven years when the number of paying members fluctuates between sixteen and twenty. In other words, the bulk of those who had no real commitment to the confraternity left in the first two years, with the rest leaving by the end of six years. Seven years of dues paying, then, appears as the minimum amount which might be taken as an indication of commitment. Yet accepting seven years of dues paying as the criterion of participation generates another problem. How do you evaluate men who joined after 1778, too late to have paid seven years' dues? Suppose, as one possible approach, that one recognizes these men as active participants if they had paid at least fifty percent of the dues owed for their period in the confraternity. A man who entered in 1779 would have to have paid three years' dues to be considered active; a man who entered in 1780 likewise would have to have paid for three years.

The results of such an analysis are represented by the broken black line in figure 2A. It indicates that from the point of view of the actual yield of committed members, the recruitment drive of the forties and early fifties was a failure. Of the 245 men who entered during this period, only sixty-one, or twenty-five percent went on to become active members. This can be contrasted with the numbers for the first four decades of the century. From the period 1699–1741, 113 names remained on the books. Of these 113 individuals, eighty-six, or seventy-six percent, had been active participants in the confraternity. The yield during the later period was somewhat better. Of the 305 men who enrolled from 1753 to 1778, 130, or forty-three percent, stayed with the confraternity for at least seven years. Actually 103 of these 130 men were current with their dues payment in 1785. So the evidence suggests that those who stayed seven years tended to stay a much longer period of time. This tendency is discernible in the men who entered the confraternity in the six years before the register was edited, when the criterion for active participation changes to payment of fifty percent or more of dues for the period in the confraternity. Seventy men joined the confraternity in the period 1779–84. Of these, sixty-one, or eighty-seven percent, had paid dues for at least half the years they had been in the confraternity. Fifty were actually paid up to 1785. These individuals had been in the confraternity too short a time to evaluate their commitment. Still, the impression remains that in the final years of the ancien régime the penitents of Notre Dame de Pitié succeeded in attracting the kind of men who would be committed members.

Who were these men? Using registers much like that of the penitents of Notre Dame de Pitié, Agulhon categorized memberships according to their social class, then created tables displaying the percentage of chapel populations represented by each group. As demonstrated above, however, confraternal membership registers often contained the names of men who enrolled but never participated, and the names of men who had died or who had long since moved on without the knowledge of confraternal record keepers. The inclusive membership policies of many confraternities means that their registers of members cannot be taken at face value.

Agulhon's main concern was to establish the presence or absence within confraternal chapels of members of the social elite. In light of this it made sense that he lumped all artisans together into one group. But by now it should be clear that the assumption that the presence or absence in confraternal chapels of members of the social elite was the key indicator of organizational vitality is mistaken. Further, to base an analysis of confraternal social composition on the listed membership for a given year is to proceed on the unproven assumption that social composition was static and unchanging. Leaving aside the question of the disappearing elite, did the composition of the rest of the chapel population remain constant? Or did it change, and if so, in what ways?

Did the composition of the confraternity change over the course of the eighteenth century and if so in what directions? Was there any relationship between occupation or profession and committed membership, that is, did occupational group have any influence on dues payment and were some groups more committed to the confraternity than others? To answer these questions totals were tallied for the occupations and professions listed in the register of the penitents of Notre Dame de Pitié. This data was then correlated with that on active participation used earlier.

Figure 2B displays information on enrollment patterns for the fourteen occupations and professions mentioned more than ten times in the register. These fourteen groups account for forty-seven percent of the members. Three of these groups, the négociants, the bourgeoisie and the seamen are composites, that is, they are composed of individuals who presumably did not interact with each other in some formal, organizational context. All eleven of the others were guilds. It can be noted in passing that for eight

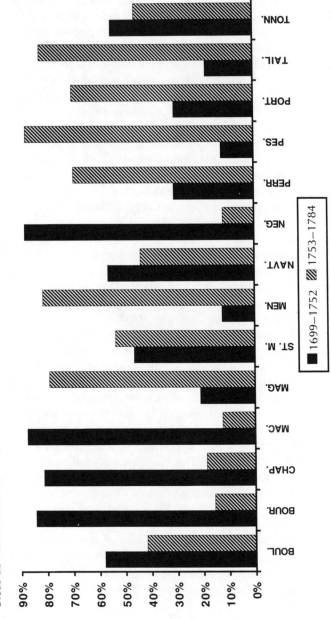

Figure 2B: Enrollment before and after 1753 of Selected Occupational Groups in the Confraternity of Pénitents Bleus de Notre Dame de Pitié, 1699–1784

of the eleven it is possible to establish the location of their devotional chapel and/or meeting hall. In seven out of eight cases, these locales were either at the church of Saint Martin itself or at monasteries located in the parish.[9] The evidence suggests, then, that locale had an influence on the decision of specific groups to frequent specific confraternities. The penitents of Notre Dame de Pitié served as a sort of neighborhood confraternity for guilds that met in the immediate area.

Figure 2B indicates that enrollment patterns during the great recruitment drive tended to follow preexisting enrollment patterns. This is most discernable in the cases of the négociants, the hatmakers, the restaurant and hotel workers, seamen and those labeled, "bourgeois," that is, those who lived on their investments. These five groups, who accounted for approximately one-third of the pre-1742 enrollment, accounted for roughly one-fifth of the men enrolled during the period 1742–52. Groups already in the confraternity apparently took on the onus of recruiting new members.

Figure 2B also indicates, however, that during the period 1742–52 patterns began to change, as the wide net cast in search of new members brought in the initial enrollees of groups that would later become more significant in terms of their representation in the chapel population. It is interesting to compare two sets of groups whose presence in the confraternity across the eighteenth century went in opposite directions. Négociants and those labeled "bourgeois" are well represented in the confraternity in the early decades of the eighteenth century, but after 1753 few men from either category joined the confraternity. Their places were taken by men from groups such as the *magasiniers* and *peseurs*. In this instance at least, the drift of the upper classes away from a confraternal chapel and their replacement by members of the lower classes seems clear. But this was only one level of the transformation that took place. Within the artisanal population of the chapel there was change also, as enrollments from groups such as the seamen, the *maçons,* and the *chapeliers* decreased to a trickle, while those from groups such as the magasiniers, peseurs and portefaix increased to a steady stream.

The answer to the question of whether confraternal social

composition changed during the eighteenth century must be yes. On the one hand there was a decline in upper class enrollments and an increase in lower class enrollments. On another there was a change in artisanal makeup as enrollments by members of groups prominent in the early part of the century gave way to newer groups.

Figure 2C presents the data on enrollments analyzed according to the criterion of active participation. It provides affirmative answers to the questions on the relationship between occupational group and active participation. Not every guild exerted an influence on its members' behavior in the confraternity. But in at least four cases, those of the magasiniers, the menuisiers, the peseurs, and the portefaix there is a marked tendency toward dues paying that in the context of the available information, can only be explained as the result of prior, external group affiliation. (Discounting the data for the period 1742–52, the *boulangers* and *tonneliers* would also fit in this category.) As for the other groups, their patterns of participation are best interpreted as the results of individual decisions. In other words, in at least four cases, guild affiliation appears to have been a prod toward greater participation in the confraternity of Notre Dame de Pitié. With the other groups this impetus was lacking, with the result that only those individual members of these groups genuinely interested in the confraternity stayed.

Is it coincidence that the groups most committed to the confraternity as of 1785 made their presence felt in the chapel only after 1742, or that the groups that figured most prominently in confraternal social composition before 1742 are insignificant both in terms of actual enrollments and yield of committed participants after that date? The great recruitment drive was a disaster for the confraternity in yielding active participants. But from the perspective of the composition of the confraternity in 1785, this turns out to have been a transitional period during which the occupational old guard within the confraternity gave way to the new.

Enrollment and participation for the penitents of Notre Dame de Pitié can best be assessed by their occupational group, which for many was their primary group affiliation. This affiliation exercised some influence over both the decision to enroll and continued

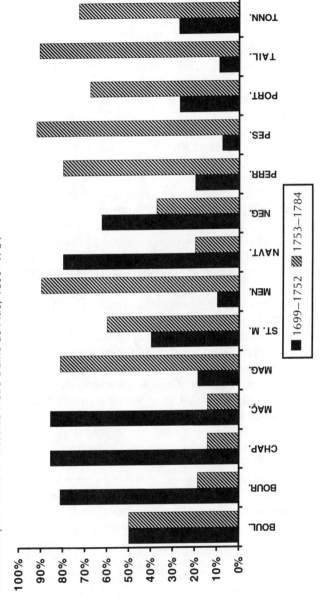

Figure 2C: Yield of Active Participants before and after 1753 for Selected Occupational Groups in the Confraternity of Pénitents Bleus de Notre Dame de Pitié, 1699–1784

participation. In sum, men joined and participated in the confraternity as part of cliques.

There is one solid piece of independent information that serves
to confirm this conclusion as the general case. Ironically it has to do
with the portefaix who seem to have been so conscientious as members of the penitents of Notre Dame de Pitié. In 1629 an assembly
general was called of the members of the penitents of Saint Anthony
in order to "c[h]asser et rayer," that is, to expel with no possibility of
readmission all of the "portefaix" in the chapel. The longshore-
men's crimes were ones we will hear about again: not attending
services, not paying their dues, not participating in the burial services of deceased confreres, and refusing to buy robes and hoods.
Already by 1629 cliques were being identified as a source of disrup-
tion in the chapel. These cliques were perceived to have formed
outside the confraternity, and their external formation was recognized to have resulted from some prior organizational affiliation.[10]

The social composition of penitent confraternities was not
static. The composition of the chapels was constantly changing, and
to a certain extent the vitality of the confraternities as organizations
was tied to this change. The continued existence of the confraternity
of Notre Dame de Pitié at the end of the ancien régime was clearly
tied to the committed participation of groups who enrolled in abun-
dance only after 1742. One-third of the men current with their dues
as of 1785 came from either the magasiniers, the menuisiers, the
peseurs, or the portefaix. There is some evidence to suggest that,
although it was explicitly condemned in confraternal by-laws,
confraternities often accepted men with prior affiliation to other
confraternities.[11] So the arrival in the chapel of the penitents of
Notre Dame de Pitié of portefaix, magasiniers, etc., is perhaps best
taken as an indication of the alienation of these groups from, or as
we have just seen, the expulsion of these groups by, other chapels.
By the same token, the disappearance of the chapeliers, bourgeois,
and négociants may have been to other chapels.

SOME COMPARISONS AND CONTRASTS

There are no other data on social composition of comparative
value to those on the penitents of Saint Martin parish. Data on

enrollments do exist for three other confraternities for the eighteenth century: the pénitents Carmélins, the pénitents Bourras, and the pénitents blancs of the Trinité vieille. These data support the characterization of the eighteenth century as a period of retrenchment, not decline, for the confraternities.

The data on the two reformed confraternities have been tabulated by decade and displayed in figure 2D. As the graph shows, the low point in terms of new recruits for both confraternities occurred during the decade of the 1730s. This was the decade during which the early eighteenth-century bishop of Marseille, Monseigneur Belsunce, made his greatest effort at scrutinizing the activities of the confraternities, an effort which culminated in 1739 with his personal inspection of every chapel and every set of statutes. I would speculate that this was the cause for the reluctance of men to join confraternities over this span. In the decades after the 1730s, enrollments fluctuated, one decade bringing in large numbers, the following bringing in fewer, probably because the organization needed time to assimilate the recruits it already had. On the whole, though, it appears that the confraternities were in much better shape toward the end of the eighteenth century than toward the beginning.

Figure 2E indicates the massive numbers of yearly enrollments experienced by the confraternity of the Trinité vieille across the middle of the eighteenth century. In this instance also a trough can be discerned during the period of Belsunce's most intense efforts at reform, followed by a sharp increase during the following period: over the decade 1726–35, the confraternity admitted 266 new members; from 1736–45 it admitted 190; in the following decade, 1746–55, it more than doubled the last figure, recruiting 406 new confreres. The register unfortunately terminates in 1775, but there is no evidence to suggest that the confraternity's popularity declined in the last few years of the ancien régime.

For the pénitents Bourras data on expulsions permit some comparisons on active participation. Using again the same criterion of seven years of active membership as the sign of true participation, of the 284 men who joined the confraternity over the course of the eighteenth century, twenty-five, or nine percent, either resigned or were expelled within seven years of joining.

Figure 2D: Enrollment in the Confraternity of Pénitents Gris de Notre Dame de Mont Carmel (Carmélins), 1699–1791

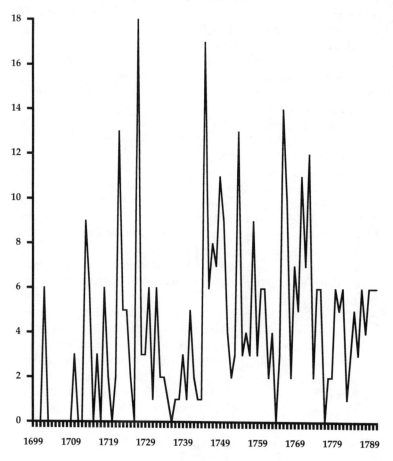

Figure 2E: Enrollment by Year in the Confraternity of Pénitents Blancs de Notre Dame de Bonne Aide (la Trinité Vieille), 1716–1775

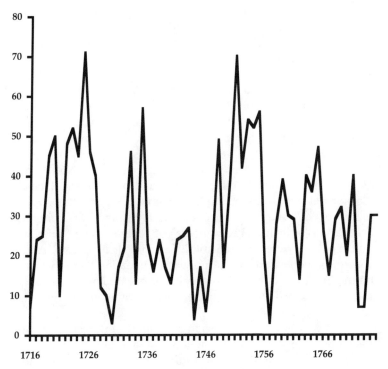

Reformed confraternities appear to have followed the practice of Italian confraternities of disciplinati in expelling those who failed to participate.[12] Essentially one out of every two men who enrolled in the penitents of Notre Dame de Pitié went on to become an active member. The ratio for the pénitents Bourras was nine out of ten. As will be discussed next, there is reason to see the yield of active members obtained by the penitents of Notre Dame de Pitié as exceptionally low. And it is unlikely that even the other reformed confraternities were as successful in attracting committed members as the Bourras. So it is probable that these two ratios represent the extremes in terms of the recruitment of active members.

It is curious that in the register of the penitents of Notre Dame de Pitié, most of its enrollees noted adult occupations. That the register was not always updated is clear from the fact that some of the enrollees going as far back as the fifties and sixties list their occupations as living "chez son père" or "chez sa mère," an indication that they were children still living with their parents. And of course the confraternity had no way of updating the information on the hundreds of men who simply disappeared after attending a few services. Most of its enrollees were adults at the time they sought admission.

A second interesting aspect is that most of the enrollees were the only members of their families listed. The aforementioned Lamottes were one of the few instances where individuals sharing the same last name joined the confraternity. Research led by Michel Vovelle has shown that at the end of the eighteenth century Saint Martin parish was the locale for most of the hotels and hostels frequented by migrant artisans and laborers in search of work. Many of these men were single, and it appears that a large portion of them joined the penitents of Notre Dame de Pitié.

These impressions can be contrasted with those created by the data available for the penitents of the Trinité vieille. Toward the end of its register, the confraternity began to record the age of its enrollees. For sixty-one of the sixty-seven individuals who entered between 1773 and 1775, this information is included. The oldest enrollee noted was sixty, the youngest was five months. Overall, three of the enrollees were age ten or younger; twenty-three were between eleven and twenty; twenty-four were between twenty-one and forty; and eleven were over forty. Forty-three percent of the individuals enrolled in the three years were twenty years of age or younger. Most of these boys were signed for by their fathers. The only exceptions were two young men, ages sixteen and twenty, who already claimed occupations. Sometimes fathers came along with their sons, as was the case with Jean Honneré Caillot, "portefaix," who enrolled with his son Jean André in 1774. Altogether the brief glimpse provided by the register of the social composition of the confraternity suggests a very different situation from that which existed in the penitents of Notre Dame de Pitié. The Trinitarian confraternity under the patronage of Notre Dame de Bonne Aide, for whom the penitents of the Trinité vieille were auxiliaries, collected funds for the purchase and manumission of slaves. This commendable activity evidently appealed to many men as something in which their offspring, and sometimes even they themselves, might participate.

The pénitents Bourras provided a different sort of family context. Over its two hundred years, the confraternity enrolled seven members of the Roubaud family and nine members of the Martin family.[13] There were many other families just as committed to the confraternity. Whether the other reformed confraternities were family associations to the same degree is not known. Among the larger confraternities the penitents of Saint Anthony are noteworthy for their decision to permit the sons of members to enroll at a lower rate than other new entrants.[14] It was argued above that occupational affiliations were a motivating force in both enrollments and continued participation. The evidence from the other confraternities suggests that family ties could exert the same type of influence. Further, given the correlation between family bonds and active participation suggested by the information on the pénitents Bourras, it is worth speculating that the relatively low net yield of active participants of the penitents of Notre Dame de Pitié reflected the transient character of much of their membership.

Churchmen, a group ignored to this point comprised approximately two percent of the entries (or nineteen of the 763) in the register of the penitents of Notre Dame de Pitié. This is actually a low percentage, though perhaps representative of the situation in unreformed confraternities.[15] In reformed confraternities the percentage of the membership drawn from the clergy was much higher. One out of every five men who joined the pénitents Bourras and the pénitents Carmélins over the second half of the eighteenth century was an ecclesiastic.[16] Much has been written about the spiritual decline of confraternities in the eighteenth century. But would churchmen have continued to join them so willingly if they had been truly decadent? Here is some of the best evidence in support of the argument that the episcopal condemnation of confraternities was motivated by something other than spiritual lassitude. Churchmen were honored men among their confreres, who saw their prayers as making the confraternity's efforts for collective salvation just that much more efficacious. A statute from the penitents of Saint Anthony from 1672 politely invited all clerical confreres to say a mass for the confraternity every January 17, the feast of Saint Anthony. According to Lazare de Cordier, a distinction was made between regular and secular churchmen. Members of religious orders, like paupers, were free of any obligation to pay dues. But like paupers also, they could not hold office, whereas secular priests could.[17]

One last group is left to consider. During the seventeenth century the confraternities opened their chapel doors to impoverished men. What percentage of the membership of a given chapel was made up of paupers is impossible to establish. Occasionally in their financial accounts for the early seventeenth century the penitents of Saint Lazarus would note "franc" next to an individual's name, an indication that he was not expected to pay dues. But whether these men were paupers or simply confreres who for some reason were not expected to pay dues that year cannot be established. Although paupers were not expected to pay dues, they do not appear to have been placed in a separate category as were churchmen. Presumably the leaders within the confraternities knew who the indigent members were.

This rather liberal attitude, not to treat separately the "scholarship students," was not shared by reformed confraternities. In 1658 the pénitents Carmélins reached the decision that poor members, who paid no dues, should dutifully perform for free the unwanted tasks of standard bearers and pallbearers.[18] In the financial accounts of the pénitents Bourras for the second half of the eighteenth century, there existed a "table particulière" composed of all those confreres not expected to pay dues. Most of the men noted here were religious, though occasionally there would be a member with an unexplained "gratis" next to his name. In this instance, however, there was no expectation of labor service.

Some Answers to Questions of Size

The number of men associated with penitent confraternities at any given time is impossible to determine. Still, an idea of the magnitude of participation can provide insight into both the dynamics of social life within the confraternities and the role the confraternities played in the religious life of Marseille.

The last five confraternities all limited their official size. The pénitents Bourras kept their number to seventy-two in honor of the seventy-two disciples of Christ. The pénitents rouges of the Holy Cross limited their number to ninety-six in honor of the years in the life of Christ and the Virgin Mary. The pénitents Carmélins set their size at 120 in honor of the number of disciples who elected Saint Mathias to replace Judas. The penitents of Saint Maur limited their number to thirty-three in honor of the years in the life of Christ. The pénitents gris of Saint Henry originally set no limits on their membership but later established a maximum of 130 members (why they chose that number is not known). All told, the five confraternities had a maximum total of 451 members.

For three of the larger confraternities, it is possible to develop some idea of their official sizes at some point in their existence. The penitents of Notre Dame de Pitié had 763 official enrollees as of 1784. Data on the penitents of Saint Lazarus for the years 1611–51 indicate that the confraternity grew from 451 members in 1611 to 593 in 1646, and then fell back to 575 in 1651. They enrolled new members at a rate of fifteen a year, and the average number of members in a given year was 496.[19]

This information is useful in interpreting the data for the pénitents blancs of the Trinité vieille. For them there are no figures for total yearly membership; but over the period 1716–75 they averaged thirty new enrollments a year. Assuming the same relation-

ship between total number of members and number of new receptions per year as in the case of the penitents of Saint Lazarus, their
average number of members in any given year can be estimated as
being between 950 to 1000.[20]

These numbers can help to determine a working idea of the
number of Marseillais officially involved in penitent confraternities. Suppose we assume that all nine of the earlier confraternities
reached the size of the confraternities of the Trinité vieille and
Notre Dame de Pitié (Saint Martin parish) we would reach a figure
of between seven and nine thousand men involved in the confraternities of seventeenth and eighteenth-century Marseille.[21] On the
other hand, if we assume that these confraternities were exceptions, and that the other confraternities only reached the size of
the confraternity of Saint Lazarus, a figure of between five and six
thousand penitents would result.[22]

Actual active participants were another matter entirely. As we
have seen, only about a quarter of the men on the register of the
confraternity of Notre Dame de Pitié participated in organization
life. On the other hand, in the later eighteenth century the Bourras
were circumventing the statute that limited their membership to
seventy-two by placing non-dues paying members on the "table
particulière." In 1788 the confraternity had eighty-eight members
on its rolls.

Other data support the conclusion that active enrollments of
between 100 and 200 were typical for unreformed confraternities.
A budget that also lists the number of members paying dues that
year is available for the pénitents noirs of Saint John the Baptist for
the year 1696. Fontanier assumed that the 110 names listed represented the total number of members in the confraternity at that
time.[23] This seems doubtful since the list is composed only of those
members who actually paid. Unless the penitents of Saint John the
Baptist were extraordinarily effective in pressuring members to
pay their dues, it is highly unlikely that this is the total membership
and is probably a partial list of only the more conscientious members. Incorporated into the register of deliberations of the penitents of Saint Lazarus is a narration of the events of the burial of
Bishop Bernard Poudeaux in 1709. Included is a list of the

confraternities of penitents and the number of their members who marched in the funeral procession. The narration notes, for example, that twenty-two members of the pénitents Bourras, forty-two members of the pénitents Carmélins, 114 members of the penitents of the Trinité vieille, and 108 members of the penitents of Saint Martin parish marched. These figures suggest some correlation between the size of a confraternity and the number of penitents who participated in public processions. The fact that 101 members of the penitents of Saint John the Baptist also marched in the procession adds to the suspicion that the confraternity was much larger than Fontanier assumed.[24]

The size of the contingents marching in the funeral of Monseigneur Poudeaux suggests one of the problems with trying to determine active memberships. Confraternal memberships, to borrow a phrase from Natalie Zemon Davis to describe Catholic devotional patterns in general, "breathed in and out," that is, expanded and contracted in accordance with the liturgical and social calendar year. Processions brought out many occasional participants who, as Guibert complained, appeared only to be part of the show. There is one good example of this. The secretary of the penitents of Saint Anthony for the year 1641–1642 was exceptionally diligent about noting the number of brothers who left the chapel to participate in processions. In the thirteen burials in which the confraternity played a role over the course of the year, the number of confreres who marched with the body from the house of the deceased to the burial site could be as few as fifty or as many as 108, presumably a reflection of the popularity of the deceased. The procession which took place every Easter Sunday to the shrine of Notre Dame de la Garde just above the city brought out 168 confreres. The annual procession on January 17, the feast of their patron saint, brought out 178. The Christmas Eve procession made jointly with the Dominicans, however, attracted only ninety-three participants. On the Wednesday before the feast of the Assumption (August 15) eighty-eight confreres started off on a four-day pilgrimage to Sainte Baume. In his summation of the event, the secretary noted with both pride and pleasure that each pilgrim had comported himself well and that each had brought his own robe and hood. The one devotion performed by the confraternity that year in its chapel, a candle-lighting ceremony and mass in honor of the Virgin (February 2), interested only fifty-two confreres.[25]

With the danger of using numbers from processions to determine active memberships in mind, it is useful to consider three contemporary "guesstaments." In his brief visit to Marseille in 1597, Thomas Platter reported that the confraternities of penitents, as punishment for their role in Casaulx's rebellion, were required by royal authorities to make a procession in honor of the city's "deliverance." Platter was a spectator at this procession and estimated that more than four thousand penitents marched. Marseille had only nine companies of penitents at this time, but considering the closeness of this date to the end of the Wars of Religion and the period of the confraternities' greatest popularity, this seems a reasonable figure.[26] The second estimate is from 1626. A Marseillais writing to his brother claimed that there were eighteen thousand penitents present for the reception of the new bishop, François de Lomenie.[27] Even if one includes the confraternities of penitents from the villages of the territory outside the city walls, this seems a fantastic number.

The final estimate is by François Marchetti, a local servant who, when writing about the funeral in 1643 of the Blessed Jean Baptiste Gault, noted that "plus de trois mille" penitents marched in the procession. With eleven companies of penitents marching, this appears to be a conservative but probably reasonable estimate.[28]

The above estimates give some sense of the difficulty in establishing the approximate number of participants in penitential associations in Marseille. For any hope of accuracy, the time and number of confraternities then in existence must be included. Were there, for example, more penitents in Marseille at the opening of the seventeenth century when there were only ten confraternities at the height of their popularity? Or were there more penitents in the middle of the eighteenth century when there were fourteen confraternities with their popularity on the decline? And while on one level it makes sense to disregard official enrollments as inflated, they cannot be totally dismissed. As suggested above, confraternities probably had a large number of occasional members who appeared only for major ceremonial and religious events.

These men saw themselves, and were seen by more assiduous members, as part of their confraternities.

To develop a working sense of the number of *active* participants, let us first assume that the memberships of the reformed confraternities were on the whole conscientious. Let us further assume that the number of active members in the larger confraternities fluctuated between 100 and 200. This would generate a figure between 1500 and 3000, remarkably close to Marchetti's estimate of the total number of penitents at Gault's funeral.

The local historian Henry Villard once boasted that, "Bien rares sont les familles marseillaises qui n'ont pas eu un des leurs enrolé sous la bannière d'une de ces associations."[29] The population of Marseille went from 45,000 in 1600 to 120,000 in 1790. Villard was correct in the sense that a large part of the male population did at least join a penitent confraternity. Most of these men, however, made no effort at serious participation. The confraternities were a valid part of the social and religious lives of only a small portion of the men enrolled in their membership registers. We must conclude that their importance as a social and religious option was much greater than their actual social and religious impact.

THE SOCIAL TRANSFORMATION WITHIN PENITENT CONFRATERNITIES AND ITS CONSEQUENCES

The question of the social transformation occurring within confraternities remains to be settled. Agulhon's schema in which middle and working-class men remained, at best, exceptions to the rule until the seventeenth century is not supported by the evidence. In Marseille artisans were forming confraternities even before the religious wars.

The earliest confraternities in Marseille can be characterized as extensions of previously formed social sub-groups, or cliques, into a new devotional realm. Initially confraternal chapels were not places where diverse groups of men met or mixed. Agulhon and the local historians who preceded him were right to emphasize the homogeneity within the earliest associations. But they erred in the assumption that this homogeneity was one of social status, when it actually reflected the common group allegiances of all members.[30]

This homogeneity was destroyed during the religious wars by the influx into confraternal chapels of diverse groups of men with no commitment to the group norms that had evolved therein. An ability and willingness to fit into the existing group had been the attribute sought in new recruits before the wars. Penitent associations, willing to fight and die for the faith, emerged as a sort of advance guard of Catholic reaction during the wars. Such zeal became the new criterion in recruitment. The most important social transformation that occurred within confraternal chapels was not a transition from single-class associations to multi-class associations, but a transition from single-group associations to multi-group associations. Antebellum confraternities may not have been elitist, but they were exclusive. Sectarian conflict broke down this exclusivity and forced the confraternities to admit any and all who displayed sufficient sectarian combativeness. The result of the process was the transcendence of exclusivist notions of fraternalism by an inclusivist glorification of Catholic fidelity.

The Wars of Religion permanently altered the social dynamics occurring within penitent confraternities. The popularity and prestige the associations garnered during the war years made them even more attractive in the decades that followed. Request for admission did not decline but increased. And in the spiritually charged climate of the early seventeenth century, confraternities found it difficult to go back to the exclusionary policies of the antebellum years. The idea of a confraternity being the extension or the expression of the values and norms of a single self-generated group could no longer be maintained in its original form.

In Marseille two responses to the transformation of memberships can be identified. Confraternities established after the wars attempted to make spiritual commitment the basis for a return to an exclusivist ideal. The three-week waiting period for admission and the rigorous scrutiny of a candidate's past life instituted by reformed confraternities had as their objective the exclusion of men lacking in spiritual commitment. The statutes of the pénitents Bourras best reflect the concerns of confraternal organizers at the end of the sixteenth century. They went so far as to stipulate that when a vacancy in the confraternity arose, the candidate chosen to fill the spot from among those on the waiting list would be regarded as the most "spiritually" capable. Spiritual commitment, however, was not an end in itself; rather it was expected to motivate the candidate to endure the socialization process during which he would be instilled with the desired group values. Only after the candidate had spent three months on probation, during which his success at fitting in was carefully monitored by the master of novices, was he truly received into the confraternity. Clearly group norms, not religious convictions (though people at the time would not have recognized a distinction between the two), were being monitored here. The earliest statutes of both the pénitents Bourras and the pénitents Carmélins established a group of officers whose primary duty was to monitor the maintenance by later generations of the original values of the confraternity. At least with the Bourras, the group of officers, known collectively as the Founders, had the right to expel men who did not conform to the expected fraternal values.

The response of older, unreformed confraternities is not so clear, there being a tendency in the reedition of statutes to emphasize continuity with the past, rather than present innovation. The above findings on the confraternity of Notre Dame de Pitié, however, do provide one clue. Participation in this confraternity was tied to previous group affiliation, while the groups actively participating in the confraternity's affairs at any given time changed. I would speculate that in a very real sense the confraternity of Notre Dame de Pitié functioned as an extension of the guilds located in Saint Martin's parish. The confraternity permitted the guilds, or more accurately, cliques from the guilds, to appropriate it as a religious institution for the expression of their own private religious sensibilities. Competition among various groups kept this appropriation a temporary thing, the threat of desertion by groups out of power (theoretically) serving to restrain any tendency toward monopolization. More important from the standpoint of organizational vitality, appropriation of the confraternity as an organization allowed subgroups to re-create the initial experiences of fraternal closeness and fraternal exclusiveness that were part of the confraternities' appeal.

Older, unreformed confraternities continued to maintain the inclusivist policies first adopted during the war years. However, the groups that these policies brought in were given free rein to function as heterogeneous subgroups within the context of the confraternity. Local guilds produced most of these groups in the case of the penitents of Notre Dame de Pitié. But one can imagine that in other confraternities such groups were produced from family/clan ties, neighborhood networks, or even other religious associations. If the example of the penitents of Notre Dame de Pitié is any guide, then group loyalty to specific confraternities was slight. One or perhaps two generations of a given group might join and participate in the activities of one confraternity. But if the group's situation changed in that confraternity, that is, if the position of influence of that group in confraternal affairs was claimed by a competing group, then the group would move on to another confraternity in search of favorable terms for its participation.

Theorists of organizational behavior would argue that the emergence within confraternal chapels of groups of individuals with no commitment to the values and norms of the original members was an expected sign of the *formalization* of the confraternities as organizations. They would also expect this process to sap organizational vitality. Two centuries after the transformation of their memberships, however, penitent confraternities maintained their vital signs. Their success in staying alive reflected their success in restructuring themselves as organizations to incorporate diversity among their constituent elements. What is fascinating is that both the older confraternities and those that came into existence after the transformation sought, in different ways, to re-create the group dynamics that occurred in the earliest associations. The earliest ideals of fraternalism could not be maintained, but they could be re-created.

NOTES

1. Maurice Agulhon, *Pénitents et Franc-Macons de l'ancienne Provence* (Paris, 1968), 139–45.

2. P.E. Ousset, "La confrérie des pénitents bleus de Toulouse," *Revue historique de Toulouse* 11 (1924): 23.

3. Jean-Luc Boursiquot, "Pénitents et Societé Toulousaine au siècle des Lumières," *Annales du Midi* 88 (1976): 159–75.

4. Guibert, passim, especially page 33.

5. On the episcopacy and penitent confraternities, see chapter 7 below.

6. Agulhon, 144.

7. Further, it begs the question of why associations in such disrepute emerged as centers of right-wing Catholicism during the Revolution. See Robert Sauzet, "Sociabilité et Militantisme: Les Pénitents Blancs de Nîmes au XVIIIe siècle," *Actes du Colloque de Rouen 24/26* (November 1983). See also Yves Marie Bercé, *Fête et Révolte: Des Mentalités populaires du XVIe au XVIIIe siècle* (Paris, 1976); Hoffman, *Church and Community.*

8. "Nomenclature des Frères et Cotes versés par des Pénitents de Notre Dame de Pitié de Saint Martin," Collection Fontanier, Archives départementales de Bouches-du-Rhône, 24F-111 (hereafter cited as Nomenclature des Frères et Cotes).

9. The boulangers, the portefaix, the menuisiers, and the chapeliers all met at the monastery of the Augustinians. The perruquiers met in the monastery church of the Recollects. The tailleurs had their chapel in the parish church of Notre Dame des Accoules, but their meeting hall was located near the Dominican monastery. Finally the confrèrie de Sainte Marthe which contained various crafts involved in hotel and restaurant work, met at Saint Martin itself.

10. *Déliberations* of the Penitents of St. Anthony, Collection Fontanier, Archives départementales des Bouches-du-Rhône, 24F-132 (hereafter cited as DSA).

11. Lucien Fontanier, *Histoire de la Confrèrie des pénitents noirs de la Decollation de Saint Jean Baptiste* (Marseille, 1922). See also chapter 5 below.

12. See the régiment of the penitents of the Holy Cross on December 26, 1704 when a general housecleaning was made of all brethren with poor records of participation, *Livre des Pénitents de la Sainte Croix* (1672–1782), Bibliothèque Municipale de Marseille, manuscript 1191 (hereafter cited as *Livre de la Sainte Croix*). Also see the discussion of the Bourras practice of expelling members, chapter 4 below.

13. "Registre Matricule de la Confrairie des Penitents du Bon Jesus dit Bourras de Marseille," composed by frère Michael Marie Bresson, with revisions by L. de Gonzague in 1858, and L. Fontanier in 1895, Collection Fontanier 24F-51.

14. *Statutes of the Penitents of Saint Anthony,* Collection Fontanier 24F-111, art. 21 (hereafter cited as SPSA).

15. In the other example we have, that of the penitents of Saint Lazarus for the period 1611–1651, the percentage of the membership composed of ecclesiatics consistently remained three to four percent. See *Livre des cotes pour la compagnie de Saint Lazare, 1612–1652,* Bibliothèque Municipale de Marseille, manuscript 1190 (hereafter cited as *Livre des cotes Saint Lazare*).

16. On the Bourras see Collection Fontanier, 24F-66; on the Carmélins see Collection Fontanier, 24F-95bis.

17. On the penitents of Saint Anthony see SPSA, art. 18; on Lazare de Cordier see *Lazare de Cordier,* bk. 1, chap. 8.

18. *Déliberations of the Pénitents Carmélins, 1634–1672,* Collection Fontanier, 24F-90, ff. 76–77 (hereafter cited as DC-B).

19. *Livre des cotes Saint Lazare.* Note that these numbers are based on five year samplings starting in 1611.

20. *Livre des réceptions des Pénitents de Notre Dame de Bonne Ayde, 1716–1775,* Collection Fontanier, 24F-121 bis (hereafter cited as *Livre de Notre Dame de Bonne Ayde*).

21. Assuming the penitents of Our Lady of Compassion = 800, and the penitents of Trinité vieille = 1000, then the total for nine confraternities is 7,200-9,000 + 451 for the final five confraternities.

22. Assuming the penitents of Saint Lazarus = 500, then the total for the seven other Renaissance confraternities is 3,500 + 800 for the confraternity of Our Lady of Compassion + 1,000 for the confraternity of the Trinité vieille + 451 for the final five confraternities.

23. Fontanier, *Pénitents noirs,* 37. On the budget see Collection Fontanier, 24F-35.

24. *Livre des pénitents de Saint Lazare de Marseille, 1611–1719,* Bibliothèque Municipale de Marseille, manuscript 1189, ff. 342–44 (hereafter cited as *Livre de Saint Lazare*).

25. DSA, ff. 65–66.

26. *Félix et Thomas Platter à Montpellier, 1552–1559 et 1593–1599* (Paris, 1892; reprint, Marseille, 1979), 311.

27. H. Villard, "La Chapelle des Pénitents Bourras de Marseille et le Musée des Pénitents," *Bulletin official de Musée du Vieux Marseille* 10 (1934): 22.

28. François Marchetti, *La Vie de Jean Baptiste Gault, évêque de Marseille* (Marseille, 1645); Fontanier, in his *Pénitents noirs,* page 35, notes that only eleven companies of penitents marched in this procession.

29. Villard, 23.

30. For a more in-depth discussion of this point, see Barnes, "Wars of Religion."

Chapter 3
FINANCE AND GOVERNMENT

INTRODUCTION

French associations inherited from their Italian predecessors an organizational structure modeled on that of a monastery. Monasteries, in comparison with other types of organizations, are relatively closed, with complete control over membership, little interference from outside, and clear hierarchies of command. None of these conditions applied to penitent confraternities. Thus it is not surprising to find evolution away from a monastic ideal a major theme of the latter's organizational history. The next three chapters will demonstrate that two interrelated forces influenced the directions of this evolution. Robert Nisbet has argued that modern organizations are the sum total of "whole networks of small, informal, social groups within the larger structure."[1] The same can be said of penitent confraternities. Most of the positive experiences associated with confraternal participation resulted from the existence of cliques. These positive experiences had to be balanced against the negative effects the presence of cliques had on organizational stability. Mitigating the negative effects of the entry and exit of cliques became a primary concern.

Over the centuries the elected heads of confraternities came to centralize most decision-making power in their hands. Pushing the growth of political centralization was a parallel growth in the financial dependency of confraternities on the wealth of their more affluent members. Neutralizing the negative effects of *encephalization* became the other major concern of organizers. On several levels these concerns came together: elected heads depended upon their cliques to elect them and to help them rule; but in other ways the two remained distinct. Cliques had more to do with the nature and rewards of participation, while centralization of political power affected to a greater degree the promotion and realization of organizational goals. The main focus of this chapter will be the centralization of authority in the offices of prior and rector. The focus of chapter 4 will be on efforts to regulate the effects of cliques on organizational stability. Chapter 5 presents a case study in the dynamics of associative life in one confraternity, the pénitents Bourras, during the eighteenth century. It will provide some indications of how political centralization and the emergence of cliques converged to influence the experience of confraternal participation.

FINANCE

In order to understand developments in confraternal government, it is first necessary to understand the financial forces at work behind these developments. The financial records available for the confraternities of Marseille do not permit systematic study. Sufficient information does exist, however, to develop a picture of financial operations.[2]

Expenses

It was required in the statutes of the confraternities of pénitents that the treasurer on his final day in office present an account of the receipts and expenses for his year. Examples of such accounts exist for three confraternities: the pénitents blancs of Saint Lazarus for 1640, the pénitents noirs of Saint John the Baptist for 1689, the pénitents Bourras for 1743. Together these three accounts provide an idea of the various costs entailed in maintaining a confraternity. They have been summarized in the form of pie graphs in figures 3A, 3B, and 3C.

First and most important were the costs associated with the purchase of clerical services. The greatest of these costs was the annual fee for the services of a chaplain, usually performed by one or more members of one of the religious orders. The basic duties of the chaplain were to say mass in the chapel of the confraternity on Sundays and on the feast day of the confraternity, to confess the brothers before the feasts on which they made communion, to march in all processions, and to perform the funeral rites at the grave site of the deceased member.[3]

Some confraternities, such as the pénitents blancs of Saint Lazarus and the pénitents bleus of the Trinité Nouvelle, paid to

Figure 3A: Graph of Expenditure of the Pénitents Gris of Saint Lazarus for 1640

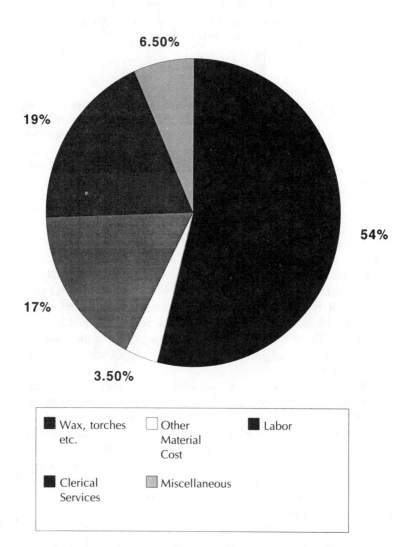

Total = £496.8.3

Legend:
- Wax, torches etc.
- Other Material Cost
- Labor
- Clerical Services
- Miscellaneous

Figure 3B: Graph of Expenditure of the Pénitents Noirs of Saint John the Baptist for 1689

Total = £125.14

Wax, torches, etc | Clerical services | ⦀ Labor | Miscellaneous

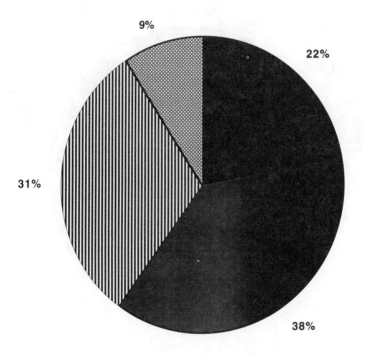

Figure 3C: Graph of Expenditure of the Pénitents Bourras for 1743

Total = £167.9

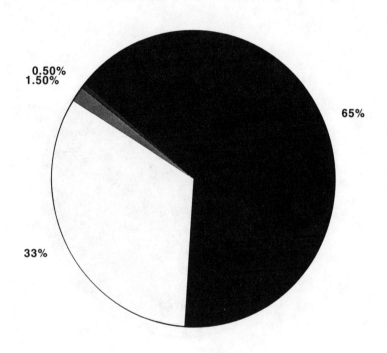

have four requiem canticles sung on the major feasts of Christmas, Easter, Pentecost, and the Assumption. Other confraternities offered prayers for the souls of their deceased on a more regular basis. The pénitents blancs of Saint Catherine in their glory years arranged for a requiem mass, celebrated with deacon and subdeacon, to be said daily for the souls of their departed. The pénitents blancs of the Holy Spirit arranged for the same type of mass to be sung, but only on Mondays and Fridays.[4]

The graph for the pénitents Bourras indicates that an extraordinary percentage of their expenses covered clerical services. Such a percentage is probably representative of the other reformed confraternities as well. Because these confraternities outlawed many of the activities that contributed to the expenses of earlier confraternities, a greater percentage of their expenses went for clerical services.

As revealed in the accounts of the penitents of Saint Lazarus and the pénitents Bourras, confraternities paid not only for the wax consumed in their chapels, but for wax consumed by clergymen in performance of services for them. Several stratagems for removing expenses from the general account had developed by the latter part of the seventeenth century. To deal with the cost of wax, the penitents of Saint John the Baptist followed such strategems, which explains the absence of this item in their account.

The last major type of expense indicated in these accounts was labor. The accounts of the confraternities of Saint Lazarus and of Saint John the Baptist make explicit the degree to which penitent confraternities remained burial societies. Labor costs from burials came from the performance of three separate tasks. The first two of these tasks, those of washing and preparing the body of the deceased and then summoning the other members for the funeral procession, were performed by an individual called the "subsacristan." The final task, that of carrying the body to the grave site, was performed by pallbearers.[5]

Other than the cost involved in the burial of members, the two unreformed confraternities also paid for the carrying of their statutes in processions, and for other, lesser acts of labor, usually also involving the carrying of objects. Because they saw processions as an occasion for prideful display, reformed companies limited to twice a year the number of times confreres could leave the chapel on procession—on Maundy Thursday and the feast of their patronal devotion. They also elected members to perform these duties on an unpaid basis. As the accounts of the penitents of Saint Lazarus and the penitents of Saint John the Baptist demonstrate, a significant portion of the expenditure of the larger confraternities stemmed from the expenses involved in making processions. Thus, in limiting the number of processions they made and enlisting members to perform the labor services involved for free, reformed confraternities curtailed a major expense.[6]

The salary for the sub-sacristan was one major labor cost all confraternities found a way of hiding; thus it did not appear in the accounts.[7] Along with the tasks involved in preparing the bodies of deceased members for burial, the sub-sacristan was the caretaker and janitor for the chapel of a confraternity and performed odd jobs. It seems to have been a general practice that the salary of the sub-sacristan be paid partly or totally out of the pockets of the sacristans.[8]

Two other major, but occasional, expenses round out expenditure. The lesser of the two was legal fees. Confraternities were forever in the courts, contesting their contracts with the ecclesiastics who served as their landlords and/or chaplains, settling disagreements with dissenting confreres, and prosecuting the heirs of deceased members for back dues. Legal expenses came to be a fairly regular confraternal expenditure.[9]

A far more significant type of occasional expense was that of building repair. In the earlier years, during the time of their expansion, confraternities built large chapels. Over time, keeping these buildings in good repair became a drain on funds. For example, in 1642 rain falling from the roof of the Dominican monastery next door broke through the roof of the chapel of the penitents of Saint Anthony, causing major damage. The confraternity had to take out a loan of six hundred livres to pay for the repairs. In the account of the pénitents Bourras for 1763, it was noted that the confraternity received a loan of 742 livres from frère Pierre Martin Grimaud to help pay a repair bill of £1002.12. They also paid £33.19 in interest on a past loan of 920 livres from frère Elzear Lion, taken also for repair on the chapel.[10]

Revenue

First and foremost, confraternities were supposed to pay ordinary expenses out of the monies collected as dues and initiation fees. Dues were six sous a year for unreformed associations and twelve a year for reformed associations at the start of the seventeenth century. By the middle of the century dues had jumped to sixteen and twenty sous, respectively. By the end of the eighteenth century the penitents of Notre Dame de Pitié (Saint Martin parish) were paying thirty sous in dues yearly, while the pénitents Bourras were paying six livres. Rates of inflation for ancien régime Marseille are not known, but over the course of the seventeenth and eighteenth centuries dues in unreformed confraternities increased 400 percent, while those in reformed confraternities shot up 900 percent.[11] Initiation fees for unreformed confraternities were three livres, though in the middle of the seventeenth century the penitents of Saint Lazarus were accepting many fees much lower than that. Initiation fees for reformed confraternities were six livres. These fees were relatively constant for most of the period, though the pénitents Bourras raised theirs to twelve livres at some point in the eighteenth century. Occasionally the monies received in dues and fees were sufficient to cover yearly expenses. For example, the receipts for the penitents of Saint John the Baptist for 1689 totaled £234.12, while expenses equaled £125.14. The confraternity was left with a surplus of £108.18. However, more often than not, revenue from dues and fees was not sufficient to cover expenses, primarily because members were not paying their dues.[12]

Data on the penitents of Saint Lazarus illustrate the problem. In the register of their accounts for 1616 the confraternity had 463 members of whom 184 paid dues. The total revenue from dues that year was £78.12. The total expenditure for the confraternity equaled £499.18.6. In 1636 the confraternity had 493 members of whom eighty-seven paid dues totaling £131.10. The account of expenditure for that year is missing. In 1646 the confraternity had 593 members of whom ninety-two paid dues totaling £161.6. Expenditure for that year totaled £338.15. Finally, in 1651, the last entry in the register, the confraternity had 575 members of whom only 48 members paid dues. Dues that

year brought in £76.16.9 in revenue. Expenditures, however, totaled £263.18.6.[13]

Several factors help to ameliorate the bleakness of this picture. As in the case of the penitents of Notre Dame de Pitié, a
large number of the men listed as members of the penitents of
Saint Lazarus had probably long since ceased to participate. The
confraternity also maintained a large number of clerics and paupers on their membership rolls whose presence was not always
identified. Of the 593 members listed in 1646, forty-seven were
noted as not expected to pay dues. Of these, only twenty-three are
listed as religious. The penitents of Saint Lazarus appear to have
increasingly permitted the practice of members paying dues when
they could. Twenty-nine of the 184 men who paid dues in 1616 paid
dues for more than one year. By 1651 this had jumped to thirty-
eight out of forty-eight. Over the period 1616–51, dues increased
from six sous a year to sixteen. Perhaps it was the inability of many
confreres to pay the large amount on a consistent basis that
prompted the lenient policy on dues payment. An indication that
this was a general trend comes from the statutes of the penitents of
Saint Anthony from 1671 where it is stated (art. 35) that no member will be permitted to fall further than three years in arrears in
his dues. Twelve of the forty-eight members of the penitents of
Saint Lazarus paying dues in 1651 are noted as paying for both
themselves and their sons. This suggests that the confraternity had
a large underage population which was not expected to pay for
itself.

All confraternities suffered from the refusal of members to
pay their dues, but there was a distinction in its magnitude in
unreformed versus reformed confraternities. The latter appear to
have been able to demand a higher degree of conscientiousness in
dues payment. Compare the following data on dues payment for
the pénitents Bourras with that for the penitents of Saint Lazarus.
In 1743 the Bourras had seventy-seven members of which fifty-six
were expected to pay dues, and of these, fifty-five paid. In 1753
they had seventy-seven members; of the sixty-three members expected to pay dues, fifty-six did so. In 1763 the confraternity had
decreased to only sixty-six members; of the fifty-three members
expected to pay dues, thirty-one did so. By 1773 the confraternity

had returned to health. It had eighty-one members, sixty of whom were expected to pay dues, forty-nine of whom actually did. In 1783 the confraternity had eighty-one members, and fifty-two of the fifty-eight members expected to pay dues, paid. Finally, in 1791, forty-eight of the seventy-one members paid dues. (There is no notation of the number of members expected to do so).[14]

Here, as in so many other instances, the Bourras probably represented an extreme. Complaints about members not paying their dues are a regular topic in the monthly deliberations of the pénitents Carmélins in the seventeenth century. Still, the smaller memberships, selective admissions procedures, and willingness to expel lukewarm participants of the reformed confraternities appear to have translated into a comparatively smaller problem with non-payment of dues.

Confraternities adopted various schemes to force members to pay their dues. The pénitents Carmélins went so far as to require members to sign a pledge promising to pay their dues so that if they failed to do so, they could be legally prosecuted. The penitents of Saint Anthony created a treasurer and secretary to look after the collection of dues. Other confraternities, such as the penitents of Saint Lazarus, followed the practical expedient of refusing to bury a deceased member until his heirs paid his back dues. In 1651 this stratagem brought in seventy-nine livres, ten sous, or roughly one-third of all revenue received. This was an effective way to generate revenue, but it also led to some ugly court cases, as in 1664 when the penitents of Saint Martin parish took the heirs of André Masse to court for having secretly buried his body in order to avoid paying his back dues.[15] Overall, the various measures taken by the confraternities do not appear to have been very effective.[16]

Reception fees could represent a significant windfall. Sometimes they brought in more than dues payment, as in 1616 when the reception of seventeen new confreres brought into the treasury of the penitents of Saint Lazarus more than 102 livres, while dues brought in only seventy-eight. This was a banner year, however, both in that so many men joined and that all paid the full fee. Confraternities also often received gifts from the wills of deceased frères that went toward the payment of ordinary expenses. In the revenue of the penitents of Saint John the Baptist for 1689, for example, was a gift of twenty livres from "feu frère Jean Chenue." How important this factor was is not known, although Jullien does mention the arrival in Marseille in 1692 of a royal commission charged with investigating the various gifts of land, houses, and pensions that confraternities held in *mortmain*.[17]

A third source of occasional revenue was the fees charged for burial of outsiders. Both Agulhon and Vovelle allude to the "status" confraternities of penitents added to the funeral processions of the elite. Such trappings were expensive. In 1635 an assembly general of the penitents of Saint Anthony decided that although Honneré (?), "maître cordonier," and Blaise Michel, "marchant mercier," "soict devenu mallade," they should be admitted among the brethren since both had "offrant et bailler une somme raisonable."[18] In 1651 the pénitents Carmélins established the fee for the burial of outsiders as eight ecus (twenty-four livres). How regular or how important a source of revenue this was is impossible to establish. But it was sufficiently important that in 1698 Bishop Vintimille sought to put a stop to the practice.[19]

The actual solution to the problem of meeting expenses, however, was the practice of having priors and rectors pay the difference between the revenue and expenses for their year in office. To return to the data on the penitents of Saint Lazarus, in 1646 Prior Louis Bayard paid the £141.9 difference between revenue and expenditure. Five years later, Prior Jean Baptiste Rambaud was more fortunate. Although the confraternity took in only seventy-six livres from dues, and only sixty-eight from receptions, its success in getting heirs of deceased members to pay their back dues meant that he paid only £39.9 from his pocket.[20]

Exactly when the practice of having the prior pay the difference between revenue and expenses began is not certain. By the early seventeenth century it was clearly widespread; by the latter part of the century it was written into statutes. By this later date also, several of the confraternities had begun to divide the obligation between the prior and the sub-prior, the prior paying two-thirds of the difference between revenue and expenses, the sub-prior paying one-third.[21]

This last innovation was only one of many aimed at spreading throughout the officer list the expenses involved with maintaining the chapel. Already in their 1558 statutes the penitents of the Holy Spirit expected the two men chosen as sacristans each year to pay the cost associated with lighting the chapel. By the seventeenth century other expenses had become the responsibility of specific officers. Along with paying part of the salary of the sub-sacristan and the cost of the candles used in illuminating the benches of the prior and sub-prior and the grand chandelier before the altar, the sacristans of the penitents of Saint Anthony were responsible for the "bouquets de fleurs qu'ils ont acoustumé de donner aux frères pendant le mois de Mai," the oil burned in the lamp of the chapel, and half the cost of washing the tapisserie of the chapel. The two chorists of the confraternity were held accountable for the candles necessary to illuminate the choir during their year in office. As for the oil burned at the altar to Saint Anthony, that and all other expenses associated with that shrine were paid by the four annually elected priors. Because they paid such expenses, these officers were not expected to pay dues.[22]

Agulhon noted the tendency of confraternities to elect members of the social elite as officers and attributed this to the status and prestige the elite could bring to the confraternities. This was undoubtedly a factor, but an even greater influence was the ability of these men to pay the cost associated with holding office. Personal affluence was an attribute not simply sought-after, but necessary in confraternal leaders. Penitent associations, even the more affluent ones such as the pénitents Bourras, depended upon the pockets of their elected officers to make ends meet. This meant that the pool of candidates for the most important and more costly posts was limited to those with the ability to pay.

Seen from an organizational perspective, the seeds for the financial crisis that the confraternities experienced during the eighteenth century were sown very early, most likely in the late sixteenth century during the Wars of Religion. It was during this time that the confraternities opened their doors to any and all militant Catholics. Apparently, it was also during this period that more affluent members accepted the obligation to pay the annual short-fall in revenue generated by the inability of many of these new members to pay. This practice did not cease after the wars, but actually increased, permitting the confraternities to open their doors to an even wider spectrum of individuals.

Penitent confraternities undertook as part of their mission the economic upkeep of their impoverished members. Subsidization of the confraternity itself was only the most obvious level of this effort. The porters and other laborers paid by the two unreformed confraternities noted above were members of their confraternities, as was the sub-sacristan. In 1673 the confraternity of Saint Lazarus decided that because there were few lepers anymore in the leper hospital outside of Marseille, the alms in the box traditionally maintained to help the lepers should go instead "pour des frères et des malades de la chapelle." In 1687 it went further and decreed that of the various chests the confraternity kept to receive alms, the chest dedicated to the relief of indigent members would hence-forth be first in importance.[23]

Much has been written about the emergence of social activism as a dominant value of Counter-Reformation piety,[24] but the degree to which penitent confraternities realized this value, not so much in their external acts of charity, but in their internal mainte-nance, has gone unrecognized. For more than two hundred years one group of Catholic laymen subsidized the religious devotions of another. What officers got in return for their benevolence will be the subject of later discussion. Here it is necessary to mention that not only were they willing to pay for the honor of being elected, but were actually willing to compete for it.

The price the confraternities paid for the "popularity" the financial resources of affluent members permitted was a progres-sively greater dependency upon these resources. And even though officers were committed to giving, they were hard pressed to cover all the costs associated with keeping the confraternities afloat. As was recorded in the deliberations of the penitents of Saint An-thony in 1662:

> Lequel jour frère Jacques Foucou, prieur de ladicte Com-pagnie avoit assemblée la banque et autres frères. . . Et leur avoir remonstre que ladicte Compagnie se va des-truict par moyen de ce que aucun des frères de ladicte

Compagnie negligé payent de leur Cottes et Arrérages. En Sort que comme les prieurs et sous prieurs susport touts les charges et frais à leur propre il luy estant impossible de fere aucune reparation dans ladicte Chapelle laquelle en a grandement de besoin.[25]

The Eighteenth-Century Financial Crisis

Was there any time when the confraternities were financially solvent? The absence of relevant data from the sixteenth century makes this a difficult question to answer. Prewar associations were still small enough, and prewar memberships still committed enough, that the confraternities of that era probably were financially healthy. The popularity confraternities gained during the war era translated during the following period into general prosperity. Supporting evidence for this conclusion is the ability of the penitents of Saint Catherine, who met at the parish church of Saint Laurent, the poorest parish in town, to erect in 1604 a large new chapel, of "très belle construction, ornée de mosaïques, de marbres, et enricheé de vitraux de couleurs variées." The comparative wealth of the confraternity at that time can be discerned also in its founding in the same year the requiem mass alluded to earlier.[26]

Available evidence on enrollment patterns confirms the impression of early seventeenth century prosperity. Over the period 1591–1630 the pénitents Bourras took in 206 new members, or one-third of the men they would admit over their two hundred year existence during the ancien régime. Seventy-eight percent of the members of the confraternity of Saint Lazarus in 1626 had enrolled since 1596—the year after the end of the wars in Marseille. It appears that all confraternities, from the most exclusive to the most inclusive, were expanding during the first decades of the seventeenth century.

By that time the confraternities were already in financial trouble. The largess of the officer corps remained sufficient to compensate for unpaid dues. But as the complaint of the prior of the penitents of Saint Anthony suggests, this compensation came at the expense of officers directing their donations toward building repair. The penitents of Saint Catherine were not atypical in their decision to construct a new chapel during the early years of the seventeenth century. The sanguine expectations of these decades that penitent devotions would permeate all of masculine society, however, were never realized. Joining a confraternity of penitents may have been a popular thing to do, but committed participation was beyond most men. The large chapels built to shelter these multitudes, undoubtably half to three-quarters empty on most Sundays, were like stones around the necks of later generations of confreres, dragging them deeper and deeper into debt.

By the eighteenth century most of the confraternities had accumulated enormous debts they had no hope of repaying. In a report to the diocesan office in 1727, the penitents of Saint Catherine listed debts totaling more than 1200 ecus. In the same report the penitents of Saint John the Baptist listed debts of 1500 livres, and the penitents of Saint Anthony more than 5300 livres. In 1762 in a report to the Parlement of Provence, the penitents of the Holy Spirit listed debts of 3500 livres. From the record of the municipal commission appointed in 1792 to handle the disestablishment of confraternities comes the lists of debts for both confraternities of Notre Dame de Pitié. The debts of the confraternity of Saint Martin parish totaled 4700 livres, while those of the confraternity attached to the Carmelite's monastery totaled more than 5000 livres.[27]

The bulk of these debts was in the form of long-term loans for which the confraternities annually paid five percent interest. Since this interest had to come out of ordinary expenses, by the end of the eighteenth century, most confraternities faced interest payments greater in magnitude than their ordinary expenditure. In 1783, for example, of their £353.16 in expenses, the pénitents Bourras paid £234.13.6 in interest on their loans. The Bourras was a fortunate confraternity, however. All of their loans in 1783 were from frère Pierre Martin Grimaud. Thus, besides dues-paying members enabling it to pay the interest on its loans, the confraternity had members rich enough that all its loans came from within the organization. None of the other confraternities seems to have been so lucky.[28]

Compounding financial troubles were complaints of corruption and mismanagement of funds. In 1761 the Parlement of Provence, officially concerned that confraternities of penitents were borrowing money without reporting it to authorities, making loans they could not repay, and/or using funds earmarked for the support of the poor for "despenses superflués," required all confraternities to send an account of their financial condition to the office of the seneschal.[29]

In Marseille, the financial crises in several confraternities became so acute in the late 1760s that the royal authorities stepped in. In 1768 by royal decree the chapels and goods of the confraternities of the Holy Spirit and of Saint Catherine were auctioned off to pay their debts, and their remaining members forced to combine with the confraternity of Saint Lazarus.[30]

In research on eighteenth-century Marseille, Michel Vovelle found that penitent confraternities were being mentioned comparatively more as beneficiaries in the wills of the petite bourgeoisie and participants in "le petit monde de l'échoppe," than in the wills of the bourgeoisie and nobility.[31] This piece of information may be interpreted in two ways. Shopkeepers and artisans had comparatively fewer occasions to display commitment to their confraternities during their lives than more affluent members, who could demonstrate their commitment by assuming the cost of serving as prior or rector or by making a donation toward upkeep. Modest bequests were one way less affluent members could show that they cared.

Then again, Vovelle probably assumed a relationship between bequests and commitment in which the absence of bequests from the upper classes signaled an absence of commitment on their part to the confraternities. If so, this would support the conclusion that by the end of the eighteenth century the economic, as well as social, backbone of the confraternities had become the artisanal and petit bourgeois classes. It would also support Agulhon's argument that desertion by the elite precipitated the decline of confraternities.

Such an argument would hold, however, only by proceeding on the incorrect assumption that the elite initially had had a presence in all chapels. A more interesting question is whether the huge debts of the confraternities frightened away more affluent members. This certainly was not the case with the Bourras who could depend on the deep pockets of more than one member to keep the cost of building repair from destroying them financially. It does not seem to have been the case elsewhere either. One of the unappreciated points about the results of the royal investigation of 1768 is that they certify the ongoing financial solvency, if not health, of the associations that survived the investigation. While buildings were only marginally maintained, these confraternities were still capable of electing men willing to pay the cost of governing.

OFFICERS AND THEIR DUTIES

The Prior, Sub-Prior, and Syndics

The significance of developments in the areas of finance and government will be discussed in the next section. For that discussion to make sense, some idea of the governmental structure of confraternities is needed.

At the head of every confraternity was an officer called in the earlier confraternities, *prior;* in the reformed confraternities, *rector;* and in the penitents of Saint Henry, *prior* once more. Whether the change in title indicated any substantive difference in the nature of the office in the different types of confraternities will be considered later, but for the sake of convenience, the term *prior* will be employed throughout the discussion here. The chief duties of the prior were to direct the spiritual lives of the confrere during his year in office, to oversee the maintenance of the statutes of the confraternity, to act as final arbiter of all ordinary problems which developed, and to police the behavior of members.[32]

Each confraternity also invested its prior with other, secondary duties to conform with its needs. The penitents of Saint Anthony specifically granted their prior and sub-prior the right to negotiate new contracts with the monastery of the Dominicans of Marseille, their landlords and chaplains. The penitents of Saint Henry left it to their prior to choose, each week, four members of the confraternity to visit nightly the dying patients at the Hôpital Saint Esprit.[33]

Last, in some of the confraternities it was the prerogative of the prior to select individuals to fill many of the lesser offices during his term. With the pénitents blancs of Saint Anthony the new prior and sub-prior had the right to name individuals to all offices lower than the Banque, subject to the approval of the assembled members. In the confraternity of Saint Lazarus, the prior had the right to nominate a portion of the Banque also. In the 1717 edition of their statutes, the penitents of Saint Henry granted their prior the right to select his own sub-prior, sacristan and porter. In the later edition of their statutes the prior of the penitents of Saint Henry lost the power to select his own sub-prior, but retained the right to name individuals to the offices of sacristan and porter.[34]

The duty of the sub-prior was to substitute as leader of services for the prior when he was absent. Both the information in the statutes and research into the organizational dynamics of the confraternities indicate that the office was not especially important in confraternal government. As mentioned, the penitents of Saint Henry in their original statutes granted their prior the right to appoint someone to fill this office. Perhaps this can be taken as a statement of the status of the office by the early eighteenth century. Only one of the sets of statutes mentions specific duties. In the 1731 reedition of their statutes, the penitents of Saint Henry granted the sub-prior, now elected along with the other officers, the right to oversee the sacristan and porters in the performance of their duties.[35] In only one set of statutes, those of the penitents of Saint Anthony, did the sub-prior appear to have any power or authority distinct from that of the prior. And in this case it was only a right to help select the members of the nominating committee, which chose candidates for prior.[36]

Upon completion of their term in office, the retiring prior and sub-prior served for a term as heads of the Banque. In most of the confraternities this term lasted a year. In larger confraternities, such as the penitents of the Trinité vieille and the penitents of Saint Lazarus (both of whom had Banques numbering twenty-four members,) in the first year after his priorship a man served as head of the twelve upper *banquiers,* in the second year, as head of the lower twelve banquiers. Originally in this capacity the prior and sub-prior were known as *régidours,* but midway through the seventeenth century this gave way to the title of *syndic.*[37] Why the change, and why the change to syndic, is difficult to establish.[38]

The Banque

After the prior and the sub-prior, all sets of statutes mention groups of counselors who helped govern the confraternity. This practice was evident also in the Italian confraternities where groups of *consigliere*—from four to twenty-four in number—helped govern. The chapels of the confraternities of penitents were built on the plan of a monastic choir, with benches perpendicular to the altar coming down from the wall. The confraternities reserved the lowest benches on either side of the altar for the use of the counselors. From this practice derived the use of the term the *Banque*, "Bench," to denote the body of counselors sitting in session.

There was no universal procedure by which men became banquiers.[39] In some cases they were elected; in other cases they were appointed; in some cases membership on the Banque was the automatic result of service in another office. As of 1671 the penitents of Saint Anthony elected twelve of their sixteen banquiers, the other four spots being filled automatically by the retiring prior and sub-prior and two sacristans. With the penitents of Saint Lazarus a curious procedure existed. Each year eight of the twenty-four "rectors" on the Banque were replaced. The prior leaving office and the prior entering office each had the right to name four of the replacements. Terms of office for banquiers also varied. For the penitents of Saint Anthony it was one year. For the penitents of Saint Lazarus it was two years, one-half of the men being chosen annually. For the pénitents Bourras it was three years. The size of the Banque also varied from confraternity to confraternity. The penitents of the Holy Spirit and the pénitents Bourras had twelve banquiers. The penitents of Saint Henry had four conseillers. The penitents of Saint Lazarus and the penitents of Trinité vieille had twenty-four banquiers.

Statutes required that the Banque meet once a month, usually the first Sunday, to discuss the affairs of the confraternity. These meetings were called *régiments*. Banquiers who missed régiments without legitimate excuses paid a fine up to the third time at which point they were dismissed from office. Once in session the Banque discussed the problems of the confraternity as presented to them by the prior and sub-prior. Major decisions made by the régiment had to be ratified by a general assembly of the members. The record of these decisions was then noted in the register of the confraternity with the signature of the prior, sub-prior, and members of the Banque.

The Treasurer and the Secretary

In the confraternities of disciplinati the treasurer was often the second most important lay officer, which reflected the central importance of the gathering and managing of money. The importance of this office declined somewhat in French confraternities but not totally. The treasurer had two primary responsibilities: First, he had to collect dues from the members; second, he had to pay out all usual expenses for the confraternity. With the pénitents Bourras this included the fee charged by the Trinitarians for mass to be sung upon the death of a member. Presumably this was an ordinary expense with other confraternities also. Extraordinary expenses could be paid only under written direction of the prior.[40]

The secretary also had two primary duties. He was expected to be in the chapel early Sunday morning to take attendance, noting in his register who was absent and who was tardy. He then would turn over this information to the prior who would reprimand the erring members, and/or to the treasurer who would collect the fines for these infractions. The second major duty of the secretary was to write down in the register of the confraternity the minutes of the régiments as well as any letters received or contracts completed.[41]

The Chorist and Master of Ceremonies

Every confraternity had two chorists and/or two masters of ceremonies. It is difficult to discern the difference in their functions. The title "chorist" suggests that this officer had control over all singing done by the confraternity. Since the regular Sunday services of the confraternities were structured around chants, this would suggest that the chorist had an active role in the regular observances. The problem here is that the chant was led by the prior during these services. The duties of the chorists at this point, as defined by the statutes of the Carmélins, were to determine the appropriate offices for the day; to lay out whatever ornaments were required; to signal the beginning of the services with their bâton de cérémonie; to announce the prior when he stood; to lead the singing; and to orchestrate the members for any ritual to be performed during the services. One of the statutes of the penitents of Saint Anthony requires the chorist to pay for all printing of chants done for processions. In sum, the duties of the office appear to have been to serve in the role of deacon during the regular chapel services and to lead in the chants performed by confraternities while in procession.[42]

In contrast, the masters of ceremonies seem to have been expected to supervise the ceremonial rather than the sacramental aspects of the confraternities' activities. The office appears to have been of later origin than that of chorist. Mention of the latter first appears in the early seventeenth century. Mention of the former only began to appear around mid-century. It would seem that, as the ceremonial life of the confraternities became more sophisticated, a new officer was created to supervise it.[43]

The Master of Novices

Every confraternity had a procedure for accepting new members. Usually the aspirant, called either a "novice" or a "prétendant," had to attend services for a certain time period, ranging from the three weeks required in the 1621 statutes of the pénitents Carmélins, to the four months required in the 1731 statutes of the penitents of Saint Henry. During this novitiate it was the duty of the master of novices to initiate the aspirants into the rules and rituals of the confraternity. In an area of the chapel set aside for that purpose, he observed the novices, answered their questions, and later, after the services, lectured them on the statutes of the confraternity. As his final act, the master of novices led them in their ceremonial reception into the confraternity.[44]

Other Officers

All the confraternities had lesser, more service-oriented offices. The sacristans were essentially the managers of the chapel. The statutes of the pénitents blancs of the Holy Spirit called them either *sacristains* or *custodes*. Two was the usual number mentioned for them. They held the keys to the chapel and were expected to arrive at least a half hour before the service. Sacristans were responsible for making sure the altar ornaments and other chapel furnishings were in good order. They were also responsible for cleaning the altar linen and for maintaining chapel lighting, the money for these expenses coming from their pockets.[45]

The chapel proper, as opposed to the vestibule and meeting rooms, was a sacred place, to be entered only by those prepared to worship God. The porter's main duty was to regulate entry to and exit from it. Non-members were not allowed to enter without the prior's permission. Members improperly dressed (i.e., without their robes and hoods in place) were also prohibited entry. More of a guard than a doorkeeper, the porter in the pénitents Bourras was expected to police the behavior of the members while in chapel and to maintain decorum. Perhaps he functioned similarly in other confraternities.[46]

As with all other Christians, the culmination of the religious year for the confraternities of penitents was Easter week. As part of their observance of this week, they reenacted the last supper, complete with foot-washing ceremony. This event in French is called the "Cène," and the men appointed by the confraternities to oversee the preparation of the chapel for it were called "cènaires." While it is fairly certain that the last supper was celebrated by all the confraternities, not all, apparently, created officers to oversee the preparation for it. For certain the pénitents Bourras elected a cenaire whose duties were to furnish bread and flowers and fruit to be blessed and displayed on the altar and to spread aromatic plants along the floor of the chapel. The penitents of Saint Anthony did not elect cenaires until the late 1630s, at which point they began appointing four men on the first Sunday of Easter week to prepare the chapel for the following Thursday. Later it appears they began electing four men to the office at the time of their regular elections on the Monday after Easter.[47]

As the ceremonial life of the confraternities developed, the need for men to carry statues and other artifacts increased. Three kinds of *porteurs* are mentioned in the various lists of officers. The earliest mentioned were cross-bearers. The Bourras had one, while the penitents of Saint Anthony and the penitents of Saint Lazarus each had two. Penitent confraternities, like all other ancien régime corporations, had their own banners. In the seventeenth century many of them began to elect standard-bearers. Finally, several of the confraternities elected pall-bearers. Their number was always four and they were expected to be young and strong enough to lift heavy weights. These *porteurs des morts* carried the coffins of deceased members in funeral processions. In festive processions they carried the various statues, usually of the Virgin Mary, possessed by the confraternities.[48]

In reformed confraternities there existed one other office, that of mandataire or éveille-matin. Very simply, the duty of the mandataire was to knock on the door of each member of the confraternity on Saturday night and waken him for Sunday services. The mandataire was equipped for his task with a lantern, a clock, and a wooden mallet. If a confrere, once awakened, wanted to know the hour, the mandataire would strike the door with one blow for each hour, using a blow with the handle of the mallet to indicate the half hour. The task of the mandataires was perceived as strenuous enough that the pénitents Bourras allowed theirs to return to sleep after the fulfillment of their duties. The small size of reformed confraternities appears to have been key to the utility of the mandataire. In 1645 the penitents of Saint Anthony elected four mandataires. The large size of the confraternity must have made this an unsuccessful experiment, however, because the next year they disappear from the office list.[49]

Evolution and Change in the Office of Prior

Religious Duties and Sacerdotal Pretensions

Service as the prior of a confraternity of penitents could be an expensive proposition. Among the factors that would lead individuals to willingly seek to pay such costs no doubt were peer recognition and the satisfaction of a desire to lead others. Of greater importance in explaining the attraction of the office were its religious and devotional prerogatives. For the year he was in office the prior was the spiritual director of his confraternity, guiding his brethren in their prayers, rituals, processions, feasts and fasts. Many confraternities required that the members address the prior and sub-prior as "père," and that immediately after entering the chapel for services the members perform some ritual of obeisance to the prior and sub-prior, seated on or near the altar, before continuing on to their seats. In all of the confraternities the prior was expected to exhort, cajole, correct and chastise the members to maintain the level of piety advanced in the statutes.

Every confraternity had a chaplain, hired to perform mass and other rites. But as regards their week-to-week spiritual life and the needs of individual confreres for spiritual and pastoral guidance, confraternities remained fairly autonomous from clerical directive. Most of the initiative in these areas fell to the prior, with the result that many of the services provided for ordinary laymen by the priest were provided for members of penitent confraternities by the prior.

In the earliest confraternities of disciplinati, the office of prior was overshadowed by that of the clerical director. As it states, for example, in the statutes of the disciplinati of Saint Dominic of Siena:

> In percio che l'anima e piu nobile che 'l corpo, diesi in prima avere a richiedere el consiglatore dell'anima e della vita spirituale, e in percio ordieniamo che la nostra compagnia sempre abbia uno frate, prete dell'ordine del beato santo Domenico, el quale sia nostro correttore e ghovernatore. El quale di ciascheuno de' frategli volemo che sia ubidito e riverito si como padre spirituale. Et allui concediamo che possa corregiere e dirizzare el priore nostro e penitentiare e farne quello che allui piace, qundo esso priore non facesse quello che avesse a fare. Et generalmente, gli concediamo licentia li corregiare tutti e'fatti de la compagnia nostra secondo la forma de' nostri capitogli. Et esso correctore volemo che sia dat e creduto per lo priore de'fratri.[50]

The key term here is *corregiere,* the Italian verb meaning "to correct." In the statutes of the confraternities of disciplinati, it signified the power to denounce and punish spiritual as well as moral faults and transgressions. Initially the power was exercised either by a friar, as in the above case, or by a committee headed by a friar. These officers were to oversee and correct the behavior of all members and were granted powers, both pastoral and legislative, to do this. While the confraternities had lay governments, they were actually under the control of clerical spiritual directors, who ruled through the art of "correction." The chief function of the priors was to implement the decisions of the spiritual directors.[51]

Over the fourteenth and fifteenth centuries the power of the mendicants over the confraternities under their supervision waned, and the office of prior expanded to fill the vacuum. By the fifteenth century mention of such an office as *correttorre* began to disappear, the office of prior incorporating the correction of morals. In the statutes of the disciplinati of Saint Dominic of Bologna, edited in 1443, for example, the prior of the confraternity had three duties. The first was to set a good example for all others to follow, the second was to be zealous and solicitous in maintaining watch over the morals of the members, and the third was to correct the faults of the members. In this the prior was to "sempre observando modo e prudentia com ogni carita e benignita a auctorita de padre e non de signore." To facilitate this the prior was expected to converse monthly with each of the members of the confraternity in order to correct any of his defects.[52]

There are several clear indications that the priors of Marseille's confraternities of penitents maintained the priestly pretensions of their Italian forerunners. One of the clearest is the printed books of offices or liturgy that the confraternities followed. In these the prior assumes the role reserved for the priest in other liturgies.[53] In his treatise on the confraternities of Marseille, Lazare de Cordier centered a chapter around the question: "Can the prior of a confraternity preach?" He answered the question in the affirmative, using as evidence the examples of two priors: Balthazar de Catin, as prior of the penitents of Saint John the Baptist, preached every Friday during Lent in 1564; Louis de Felix, as prior of the penitents of the Holy Spirit in 1640, did the same, in his case with Alfonse du Plessis de Richelieu, Cardinal Archbishop of Aix, in the audience. Lazare de Cordier later used these precedents as

the justification of his own efforts at preaching during his term as
the prior of the penitents of the Holy Spirit in 1661. Times had
changed, however, because for his efforts he was soundly chastised
by the bishop.[54]

Several examples exist of priors attempting to make "corrections" in the spiritual lives of individual confreres. In 1594 François
de Paul and Jean Baptiste Imperial, members of the penitents of the
Holy Spirit, chose to march in a procession with their hoods pulled
back far enough to expose their beards. As punishment for this act
of pride, Jean Jacques de Cordier, prior of the confraternity that
year, required each man to recite the psalm *Miserere,* and to pay half
the cost for the repair of the windows of the confraternity's chapel.
In 1591 when Charles de Casaulx was prior of the pénitents noirs of
Saint John the Baptist, his son Fabio came rushing into the chapel
wearing his sword and scabbard during the celebration of the feast
of Saint John the Baptist, a transgression against the statute which
requires that habits be worn in the chapel during services. To punish
this act of irreverence, de Casault required his son to kneel in his
habit before the altar of the confraternity and repeat over and over
the psalm *Miserere mei.*[55]

The fact that both these incidents took place before the mid-
seventeenth century is significant. In the sixteenth century, especially in the latter decades, the bishops of Marseille were non-
residing. In the first half of the seventeenth century, a succession of
weak men were awarded the mitre. During this period priors of
penitent confraternities found it fairly easy to continue earlier practices. It was only in the second half of the seventeenth century that
the city experienced a succession of vigorous bishops. These men
immediately set about the task of reestablishing the boundaries
between the clerical and lay estates. This is the best interpretation
of Bishop Étienne de Puget's chastisement of Lazare de Cordier
for preaching in public in 1661. Lazare de Cordier was admonished
to limit himself in the future to simple commentaries before his
confreres in their chapel with the doors locked.[56]

From this date a steady flow of episcopal proclamations
sought to deflate the pretensions of priors. These efforts reached
their culmination in the statutes of the penitents of Saint Henry
edited in 1717. The penitents of Saint Henry were the creation of

Bishop Belsunce who named them for his patron saint. He also dictated to them their original set of statues. The first statute makes clear Belsunce's ambition:

> Cette Compagnie aura toujours pour supérieur un prêtre tel que Sa Grandeur (Belsunce) voudra lui donner; elle regardera ce prêtre comme son supérieur a qui elle doit et tout ceux qui la composent un profond respect et une parfaite obéissance dans ce qui regarde les devoirs de l'oeuvre. Ce Supérieur aura la bonté au jour de l'assemblée de faire une exhortation aux confrères sur l'importance et le mérite de cette oeurve de Miséricorde, d'aminer par ses discours le tiédeur de ceux dont la zèle pourrait se ralentir, entretenir la ferveur des autres, il aura la bonté de reprendre et corriger les abus qui pourraient se glisser. Les Prieurs de la Compagnie auront soin de l'avertir de ce qu'ils remarqueront de défectieux dans la conduite de frères afin qu'ils les reprenne publiquement. Si les frères avertis deux ou trois fois en particulier ne se corrigeaient point. Si le cas échéait ce qu'a Dieu ne plaise qu'il fallait expulser quelques confrères pour les cas cy-après mentionnés. Le Directeur aura seul l'autorité de la faire, prenant sur cela le Conseil des prieurs, officiers, et des plus sages et plus prudents de la Compagnie. It veillera avec soin à ce que chaque confrère soit exact dans tous ses devoirs, que les prières et offices se recitent avec respect et dévotion, que l'on fréquente les Sacrements sur tous les jours fixés par les statuts.[57]

The recent work of Louis Chatellier on early Jesuit confraternities has shown that, like their mendicant predecessors, the Jesuits attempted to maintain complete control over the lay associations under their authority by instituting an office of clerical supervisor or, "Directeur de Conscience," over each.[58] Belsunce, a former Jesuit novice and one of the greatest episcopal defenders of the Jesuits in the eighteenth century, obviously sought to copy in the statutes of the penitents of Saint Henry the organizational structure of a Jesuit confraternity. But in his ambition to create a model of what would be to him as a bishop an acceptable confraternity of penitents, he failed. Just fourteen years later in 1731, the penitents of Saint Henry reedited their statutes, the most important change being the complete disappearance of the office of clerical supervisor. The office of prior in these statutes did not regain all its traditional pretensions. The right to correct, that is, to supervise the moral behavior of the members, was taken away and given to the governing council.[59] As for the prior, the statutes admonished him "maintenir . . . ferveur, plutôt par le bon exemple et le douceur, que par les exhortations et les corrections."[60]

Although after 1650 the sacerdotal pretensions of priors became a target of reforming bishops, bishops were not completely successful in eradicating them. Rather, these pretensions became a point of contention between confraternities and bishops. In this regard it is interesting to consider the 1814 statutes of the reestablished pénitents Carmélins, which presumably reflect practices at the end of the eighteenth century. The statute explains as follows:

> Le père Recteur sera aussi fort diligent avertir tous les frères, par des billets fait à la main, le jour devant les Vendredis des quartre temps, le jour de l'Invention et Exaltation de la Sainte Croix, le premier jour de l'année et le premier dimanche de Carême, afin qu'ils se puissent trouver un grand nombre à la chapelle sur les six heures du soir pour chanter l'office de la passion de Jesus Christ, et faire toutes les oeuvres de piété et devotion que nous sommes obligés de faire aux susdits jours dans notre susdite chapelle, comme encore tous les dimanches et fêtes le père Rectuer ou le sous Rectuer liront l'évangile en forme de méditation, en animant tous les frères par leur exemple, de bien méditer le parole de dieu non seulement pendant la Sainte Messe, mais encore pendant le jour.[61]

It is clear from this description that the pseudo-sacerdotal pretensions of priors were gone. There is no mention of the expectation that priors preach or make "corrections." But still the office is granted a relatively active role in the spiritual lives of confreres, albeit primarily one of cheerleading. Perhaps this implies a compromise between bishops and confraternities reached by the end of the eighteenth century. In that era of skepticism and anti-clericalism bishops perhaps found it useful to allow laymen to actively "animate" the faith of others. Despite episcopal efforts to the contrary, the office of prior retained much of its quasi-sacerdotal allure.

From Prior to Rector to Prior

The spiritual powers of the prior started high and gradually declined as a result of clerical opposition. The temporal powers of the office went in the opposite direction. The growing economic dependency of confraternities on the purses of those elected as priors translated into the expansion of that office's control over confraternal affairs. This expansion is discernable in two areas: the decline of the powers of the Banque vis-à-vis those of the office of prior and the growth in status of the office of prior-syndic.

From the beginning the Banque was a passive political body, a forum through which the prior could have his decisions and initiatives affirmed. The statutes of the penitents of the Holy Spirit of 1558 state only that the prior should govern "avec les conseilles des recteurs." Yet it is important that in the same statutes the new prior did not control the election of the members of the Banque. Four of the twelve positions were to be filled automatically by the exiting prior, sub-prior and two sacristans, the other eight were to be elected from a slate of candidates chosen by a committee composed of the new prior and sub-prior, the old prior and the exiting Banque. The Banque at this point was independent of the authority of the prior.

By 1611 this had changed. In their statutes of that year the penitents of Saint Lazarus decreed that half of the eight available positions on the Banque were to be filled by the new prior, while the other half were to be filled by the prior leaving office. Apparently not all the confraternities adopted the practice of having the new prior simply appoint the Banque for his year in office. In their 1679 statutes the penitents of Saint Anthony continued the older practice of appointing a committee to select candidates for the available positions. But even here the new prior gained the right to select the replacements for the absent members of the exiting Banque which, with the old and new priors, made up the nominating committee. In the eighteenth-century editions of their statutes, both the pénitents Bourras and the pénitents Carmélins allowed the new prior to select men for all the available positions on the Banque.

Still, there would always be at least four men—the exiting prior, sub-prior and sacristans—who did not owe their position on the Banque to the prior. Since a régiment could not take place unless the full Banque was present, one way to neutralize the efforts of the prior was to absent oneself from the monthly meeting. By the seventeenth century, however, the practice of permitting priors to select substitute banquiers from the other members present in the chapel was begun. In the registers of deliberations of both the pénitents Carmélins and the penitents of Saint Anthony, the term *subrogé* often appears next to a banquier's name, indicating that he was not an official member of the Banque, but a substitute chosen by the prior. In the case of the pénitents Carmélins, six of the fourteen banquiers had subrogé noted after their names in the régiment held June 7, 1629. In 1664 when the Banque had increased to sixteen, eight of the banquiers listed for the July 13 régiment were substitutes. The penitents of Saint Anthony had to substitute for absent banquiers in the same proportion. For the régiment held September 8, 1671, nine substitutes for absent banquiers from the eighteen-member Banque had to be found.[62] That the reigning prior was able to substitute for absent banquiers meant that there was no way any of these individuals could stop one of his initiatives. In sum, by the seventeenth century any force the Banque possessed as a counterweight to the authority of the prior had disappeared. It served simply as a rubber-stamp to his plans.

One of the people who lost out under this arrangement was the prior-syndic, who saw disappear his ability to affect the actions of his successor. But while his power in this area declined, his authority and influence in other areas of confraternal life grew. In general, growth can be discerned in either of two areas: liturgy/ ceremony or administration. In the statutes of the penitents of Saint Anthony, for example, the syndics were the only officers, other than the masters of ceremonies, permitted to carry batons in processions. The confraternity maintained a secondary altar to its patron, Saint Anthony, and yearly appointed four priors to maintain it. Two of these priors were always the prior- and sub-prior-syndics.[63] In a régiment from 1656 the confraternity decreed that henceforth each of the syndics had the right to march in all the confraternity's processions, "sans habit penitens, avec son manteau."[64] This right would seem to contradict everything known about confraternities and their concern for secrecy. But perhaps it was simply an exception which proved the rule: the fact that no other confrere could reveal himself publicly made this right such a singular honor.

It was one of the obligations of the confraternity to console ill or dying confreres. To this purpose usually two brothers at a time were sent to sit by the sick member's bedside. Coordinating this effort was a time-consuming task, usually reserved for the prior or sub-prior. But both the pénitents Bourras and the penitents of Saint Anthony made it a duty of the prior-syndic.[65] Another minor administrative task taken over by the syndics, at least in the case of the penitents of the Trinité vieille was that of auditor of accounts.[66]

Over the course of the seventeenth century the office of prior progressively exerted more control over the life of the confraternity. The men who came to occupy the office had known too much power to relinquish it the year after their administration, indulging in the basically honorary duties granted to the first régidour. There being few essential activities left to claim, they expanded the office in all directions available. Thus the development of the office of syndic made election to the office of prior a two- and in some cases a three-year proposition, the first year being the actual year of leadership, the second and third something of a "cool down" period devoted largely to minor but necessary tasks.

The first efforts at curbing the growth in power of the office of prior came from the founders of reformed confraternities. Because they aspired to an older, more collegiate ideal of confraternal life, these men structured their organization in such a way as to prohibit the possibility of dominance by an elected head. The most concrete way in which they sought to achieve this effect was by taking final authority out of the prior's hands and placing it in the hands of the

senior members of the confraternity. The statutes of both the pénitents Bourras and the pénitents Carmélins originally established
above their elected head a group of individuals known as the
Fondateurs. Election to the office was based on seniority and,
distinct from all other offices, was for life. The primary function of
the Fondateurs was to watch over and maintain the statutes in all
their integrity. They were the final judges in all disputes within the
confraternity and were expected to come together in session to
debate any infraction against the statutes they perceived in the
actions of the rector, vice-rector or members of the Banque. Once
an infraction had been confirmed, the Fondateurs had the option
of demanding its correction, or if the infraction indicated a need to
change the statutes, to bring the case before a general assembly of
all the members.[67]

With the pénitents Bourras the powers of the Fondateurs
went even further. On the Feast of Saint Simon and Saint Jude
(October 28) each year, these men sat in session and every member
of the confraternity, beginning with the prior, had to appear before
them or pay a fine of one-half liter of wax. Once before the
Fondateurs, each member's behavior for the past year was scrupu-
lously examined, the individual having the right to defend himself.
The Fondateurs then had the power to impose whatever penance
or punishment they deemed justified including, should the statutes
mandate it, expulsion from the confraternity. In the case of the
pénitents Bourras even the power to make corrections was taken
from the rector's hands and placed in those of the senior members.

It appears, then, that there was some significance to the
change of name from *prior* to *rector*. In late medieval church Latin,
the term *prior* usually signified the head of a religious body, while
the term *rector* indicated a person in charge of a church and its
material well-being.[68] By the 1590s when the first reformed confraternity appeared, the term "recteur" was already in use in several
of the existing confraternities to denote members of the Banque.
The word had connotations similar to those of the word "trustee"
in modern English, that is, an advisor or counselor on the material
well-being of a corporation or institution. Thus, to the founders of
reformed confraternities the elected head should be more of a
trustee than an executive.

How effective this reform was is difficult to determine. The institution of the Fondateurs lasted only a generation in the confraternity of pénitents Bourras. In 1623 it was suppressed, according to Jullien, because newer members resented the Fondateurs' efforts to correct their spiritual lives. The powers of the office were given to the Banque (whether this included the powers to correct other members is not known), and the term in office for members of the Banque lengthened from one to three years.[69] With the pénitents Carmélins, however, the Fondateurs were still active in the affairs of the confraternity in 1660. Forty years after the start of the confraternity they are mentioned in almost every régiment. But beyond indicating that the Fondateurs were still active, perhaps it also indicates that they were too active. They appear to have become an upper division of the Banque, meddlesome, but with little power. It does not appear from the confraternity's register of deliberations that they acted in any way as a counterweight to the office of rector, which, like the office of prior, had the right to substitute for absent banquiers. Still, in the 1739 edition of the Carmélins' statutes the office is mentioned with its original powers intact.

The second effort to control the office came from bishops. In 1698 Bishop Charles de Vintimille, seeking to control the confraternities through control of their expenditure, prohibited all confraternities from making any expenditure over five livres without the advice and consent of the parish priest, any expenditure over fifty livres without the advice and consent of the diocesan office. This ordinance was later confirmed and expanded by Bishop Belsunce who required all confraternities to keep an accurate account of revenue and expenditure and to present it for approval to the curé at the end of the accounting year.

Here also the original statutes of the penitents of Saint Henry reveal Belsunce's ideas of reform. Given that his office of spiritual director had the same authority and performed the same functions as the Fondateurs, his decision to return to the title of "prior" has to be read as a conscious rejection of the reforms attempted by reformed confraternities. As conceived by him, the duty of the prior was to serve as the lay assistant to the spiritual director. In this capacity, he and the officers he chose to serve with him were to be in office for two years. One of the more fascinating aspects of the original statutes of the penitents of Saint Henry is the absence of the offices of prior- and sub-prior-syndic. The confraternity was to have a council composed of the prior, sub-prior and four conseillers, nominated by the prior, but voted in by the assembled confreres. To this council the prior had the option, when he thought it necessary, to add two or four "des plus ancien et prudents" of the confreres to help reach a decision. Both the Banque and the individuals who served as its nominal heads were gone.

By 1731 they were back, and it was the office of spiritual director that had disappeared. Yet it would be wrong to assume that the confraternity had returned to the *status-quo-ante*. Few of the powers possessed by the prior of the earlier confraternities were claimed by the prior of the penitents of Saint Henry. Instead, through a complete restructuring of the organization and procedure of the council, once again the governing council had the controlling hand in confraternal affairs. The confraternity still elected four at-large counselors, but they were joined at the régiments by the prior, sub-prior, two syndics, secretary, treasurer and master of novices—in other words, the officers actually responsible for running the confraternity. In the 1717 statutes, the sub-prior, secretary, treasurer and master of novices had all been appointed by the prior-elect. In the 1731 statutes, each of these officers was elected by the assembled brothers from two candidates nominated by the previous holder of the office. Further, to combat the problem of absenteeism from the monthly meetings, the innovation of a quorum was adopted. The council was in session when seven of the eleven members, including either the prior or sub-prior, were present. In case the requisite seven members were not present, the prior could substitute for them only from the former priors or former members of the council present. The council had the final say in all matters affecting the confraternity, even, as noted above, the correction of the morals and behavior of the confreres.

As regards the prior-syndic, while he reclaimed his seat on the governing council, the powers of his office went no further. The status of this reconstituted office is indicated by the rule establishing the line of succession when both the prior and sub-prior were absent. The usual practice was for the prior-syndic to lead the service. But in the case of the penitents of Saint Henry, the "plus ancien" of the four counselors, followed by the other three counselors, had the right to lead the service. Only if all the counselors were absent did the "prieur sorti de charge ou le plus ancien confrere" take over.

The organizational reforms implemented by the penitents of Saint Henry seem to have had some influence on reformed confraternities. Contemporaneous with the establishment of the confraternity of Saint Henry, the confraternity of pénitents Bourras endured a bitter internal conflict that resulted in the prior losing the right to select replacements for absent members of the Banque.[70] It also appears that at some point in the eighteenth century the Bourras entertained the idea of a quorum, seven members of the Banque and one of the syndics judged sufficient to make a régiment valid. The other five members of the régiment were to be chosen presumably by the rector. This was superseded in the 1739 statutes by the requirement that, in case seven régents had not appeared, replacements for them would be made according to the seniority of the other members present. The rector then had the right to fill the remaining empty seats from the "plus capable" of the members present in the chapel. And while in the 1739 edition of the statutes of the pénitents Carmélins the Banque still existed, in the 1814 edition it had disappeared, presumably replaced by an arrangement similar to that of the penitents of Saint Henry.[71] Available evidence suggests, then, that at least reformed confraternities were moving in the directions pioneered by the penitents of St. Henry.

From "prior" to "rector" to "prior," the change in the name of the elected head indicates an evolution in the organizational structure of penitent confraternities centered around the question of final authority. To a great extent this process can be seen as an example of bureaucratic formalization. In the original confraternities the limits to the authority of the office of prior were simply understood. Each year one member would win the opportunity to play spiritual guide for his brethren, subject to the advice and consent of the Banque, which made sure his ideas coincided with the general direction and goals of the association. When the chapels filled with men who did not, or could not, understand the rules, and could never aspire to be leaders but who by necessity remained followers, the situation changed. The founders of reformed confraternities attempted to correct the imbalance by erecting another council upon the existing structure. But the economic dependency of confraternities on the men elected prior soon neutralized this reform. Belsunce's solution, a return to clerical control, proved unattractive to lay memberships. Finally, in the 1731 statutes of the penitents of Saint Henry, the problem was attacked at its source. A balance of power between the office of prior and the governing council, implicit in the original confraternities, is explicitly maintained by the rules regulating the powers of the office of prior and of the council.

OTHER DIRECTIONS OF ORGANIZATIONAL CHANGE

For the penitents of Saint Anthony it is possible to assess bureaucratic change for the years 1629–90; for the penitents of Saint Lazarus, for the years 1611–84. Using the bureaucracy outlined in the statutes of the penitents of the Holy Spirit as the starting point and that outlined in the statutes of the penitents of Saint Henry as the terminus, these lists provide some sense of how confraternal bureaucracies evolved beyond encephalization.

In their statutes of 1558 the penitents of the Holy Spirit put in place a bureaucratic structure consisting of a prior and sub-prior, a treasurer and secretary, two sacristans, and twelve banquiers. The same set of officers are mentioned in the 1578 statutes of the penitents of Saint Lazarus.[72] This simple structure can be compared to those presented in figure 3D for the penitents of Saint Anthony for the years 1629 and 1690, and those presented in figure 3E for the penitents of Saint Lazarus for the years 1611 and 1684.[73]

Already in the earlier lists it is possible to see that the Banque experienced the greatest relative growth. By 1611 the Banque for the penitents of Saint Lazarus had reached its ultimate size of twenty-four members. In 1629 the Banque for the penitents of Saint Anthony had fourteen members (including the two régidours). By 1694 it had grown to twenty members. The motive behind this development probably had less to do with a desire for more effective government than for the creation of more positions

Figure 3D: Change and Development in the Government
Structure of the Confraternity of Pénitents gris of Saint
Antoine*

Officer List for 1629

Prieur	Sous Prieur
Premier Régidour	Second Régidour
Banque (6)	Banque (6)
Sacristains (2)	Porteurs de Croix (2)
Coristes (2)	Aumonier de la Compagnie
Escripuain	Aumonier de Saint Esprit
Tabullaire	
Maîtres des Cérémonies (2)	

Officer List for 1690

Prieur	Sous Prieur
Premier Sindic	Second Sindic
Banque (10)	Banque (10)
Tresorier	Coristes (2)
Sacristains (2)	Secretaire
Visiteurs des Malades (4)	Maîtres des Novices (2)
Auditeurs des Comptes (2)	Survaillans (2)
Porteurs de Croix (2)	Serviteurs de Messe (2)
Trésorier de la boitte	Porteurs de la Bannierre (2)
des frères deffunts pour	Porteurs (2)
leur faire dire trois messe	
de jour de leur decess	

*Note: Offices are listed in order they appear in register.

with which to honor conscientious members. Supporting this conclusion is the expectation, apparent in the officer lists for the penitents of Saint Lazarus, that newly elected members pay all their
back dues before assuming office.[74] The enormous sizes to which
confraternities grew put election to high office out of the reach of
many members. One way to solve this dilemma was to increase the
number of high offices. Since the two offices of prior and the
offices of master of ceremonies, chorist and sacristan all had expectations of personal affluence attached, and since offices such as
treasurer and secretary presumed certain skills, the only office
where this could realistically take place was that of banquier.

The second area of relative expansion was liturgy and cere-

Figure 3E: Change and Development in the Government
Structure of the Confraternity of Pénitents blancs of Saint
Lazarus*

Officer List for 1611

Prieur	Sous Prieur
Banque droite haute (6)	Banque gauche haute (6)
Banque droite basse (6)	Banque gauche basse (6)
Trésorier de la Compagnie	Trésorier de la Mort
Secretaire de la Compagnie	Secretaire de la Mort
Sacristains (2)	Coristes

Officer List for 1684

Prieur	Sous Prieur
Banque droite haute (6)	Banque gauche haute (6)
Banque droite basse (6)	Banque gauche basse (6)
Trésorier de la Compagnie	Coristes (2)
Secretaire de la Compagnie	Auditeurs des Comptes (2)
Sacristains (2)	Visiteurs des Malades (2)
Maîtres des Cérémonies (2)	Surveillants des Morts (2)
Maîtres des Novices (2)	Prieurs de Saint Roch (4)
Portiers (2)	

*Note: Offices are listed in order they appear in register.

mony. By 1611 two chorists had appeared among the officers
elected by the penitents of Saint Lazarus. Seventy years later, as of
1684, these men had been joined by two masters of ceremonies,
four priors of the secondary altar to Saint Roch, and two masters
of novices. To the *coristes, maîtres des cérémonies* and *porteurs de
Croix* noted in the 1629 list, the penitents of Saint Anthony later
added four priors of a secondary altar to Saint Anthony (who also
doubled as visitors of the sick), two *serviteurs de messe*, two
porteurs de la Bannière, and two *maîtres des novices*. Especially
during the seventeenth century, confraternities incorporated into
their liturgies new devotions such as that of the Forty Hours and
took on new obligations, such as participating in processions and
revivals. The complexity of their devotional activities increased to
the point that by the end of that century most confraternities were
electing officers specifically concerned with organizing and directing ceremonies.

Michel Vovelle has coined the expression "baroque piety" to

denote the elaboration of liturgy and ceremony that occurred in southern French Catholicism during the seventeenth and eighteenth centuries.[75] Almost certainly the increase in the number of officers concerned with ceremony in penitent confraternities reflects this phenomenon. But it would be wrong to assume that the impetus came completely from outside the confraternities. The staging of these new devotions cost money and according to the statutes of the penitents of Saint Anthony, those men wealthy enough to be elected prior or master of ceremony would cover this expense. So while the general spiritual climate provides one explanation for the appearance of officers concerned with liturgy and ceremony, at least an equal force behind this development was the willingness of affluent members to pay the cost of incorporating these new devotional values into confraternal life.

Another area of expansion was finance. Both confraternities, for example, added two *auditeurs des comptes,* whose duties were to check the accounts every three months. An explanation for the necessity of this office is provided by the *Déliberations* of the penitents of Saint Lazarus. In a general assembly dated May 3, 1658, frère Jean Curet, prior during the year 1655–56, was called before the confraternity for failing to present an account of revenue and expenditure for his year in office. Curet explained that during his year he had not bothered with keeping an account because he assumed that either his sub-prior or secretary was doing it. The assembly proved unsympathetic to this response, understandably enough since during his year in office Curet had borrowed money from the confraternity which he had yet to repay. Curet was enjoined to prepare and present an account for his year. The assembly further decided that henceforth the confraternity would annually elect two auditeurs des comptes to check the accounts.[76]

The institution of the office of auditeur des comptes, then, emerges as yet another effort at regulating the powers of the prior. In the statutes of the confraternities of the Holy Spirit and of Saint Lazarus, one of the duties of the prior and banquiers was to check the accounts of the treasurer every three months. One hundred years later the situation had changed. The financial dependence on the prior had grown to the point where he was responsible for controlling cash flow. Not all the men given this responsibility were equal to the task.

Along with auditeurs des comptes, the later list for the penitents of Saint Anthony reveals their election of a "trésorier de la biotte des frères deffunts pour leur faire dire trois messes de jour de leur décès." Most confraternities maintained separate collection boxes for their various charitable enterprises. It was only in the late seventeenth century, however, that they began to appoint treasurers to oversee these accounts. Why is not clear. Given the financial difficulties confraternities experienced in the seventeenth and eighteenth centuries, it seems unlikely that the intake of funds was so great that it was necessary to appoint a new officer to handle them. Priors also had control of charitable activities, so this also may have been a stratagem for keeping them honest. Still another possibility is that the change in the nature of charitable activity during the Counter-Reformation may have generated a need for an officer specifically in charge of confraternal charitable efforts.

To a certain extent reformed confraternities participated in these developments. The Bourras for example, began to elect a *Trésorier de la Miséricorde* to keep account of the monies received for charitable enterprises, while the Carmélins increased the size of their Banque to twenty. But the statutes of these two associations mostly moved toward assigning new duties to existing officers. The chorists for the Bourras doubled as masters of ceremonies as well as masters of novices. The syndics in the 1814 statutes of the Carmélins likewise served as masters of ceremonies.

What is fascinating is that the bureaucratic structure Bishop Belsunce sought to impose on the penitents of Saint Henry in 1717 removed the various accretions of the previous century. To Belsunce's mind, a confraternity needed only ten officers—a prior and sub-prior, four counselors, a treasurer, a secretary, and two sacristans—in other words, the same bureaucratic structure displayed in sixteenth-century associations. All other needs were to be dealt with on an ad hoc basis by the prior. The reformulated statutes of 1731 returned to the past, but only minimally. Seven new offices were established in 1731, including those of prior- and sub-prior-syndic; a master of novices and four porters made up the other five.

Still, the organizational structure of the confraternity of penitents of Saint Henry was radically different from those of its predecessors. A concern for honor and status had been part of the motivation behind the increase in the number of official positions in earlier confraternities. Thus confraternities had increased the size of their Banques and had taken to noting previously ad hoc positions such as cenaire in their annual lists. The penitents of Saint Anthony had even granted their syndics the right to appear in public processions with their identities revealed. Belsunce can be credited with reintroducing the concept of efficiency into confraternal administration. And it is a telling statement that when they reformulated their statutes in 1731, the lay leaders of the confraternity retained this concept.

In summary, progressive financial dependency on the wealth of individual members was the determining force behind most of the change in bureaucratic structure. As suggested above, growth in the size of the Banque is best explained as a result of the bifurcation of memberships into those who had financial wherewithal to serve in key offices and those who did not. In many confraternities the Banque may have lost any real political import, but it still could serve as a reward for assiduous participation for members who could not aspire to higher posts. The appearance of auditeurs des comptes reflected an effort to curb the freedom of priors to exploit confraternal finances during their year in office. Superficially, changes in ceremonial and liturgical practices might seem to have been autonomous of financial developments. Even here, however, behind the emergence of the offices of chorist and master of ceremonies, was the willingness and ability of rich members to pay for the devotions they would have their confreres perform.

NOTES

1. Robert Nisbet, *The Social Bond: An Introduction to the Study of Society* (New York, 1970), 89.

2. For comparison see Agulhon's discussion of confraternal finances, *Pénitents et Francs-Maçons,* 99–101.

3. For a more detailed discussion of the duties of chaplains, see chapter 7 below.

4. For the pénitents bleus of the Trinité Nouvelle see Collection Fontanier, 24F-128; for the pénitents blancs of Saint Catherine, see Abbé Dasprès, *Notice Historique sur l'Église et la Pavoisse Saint Laurent* (Marseille, 1867), 6; on the pénitents blancs of the Holy Spirit, see *Livre des Pénitents blancs du Saint Esprit,* Archives départmentales des Bouches-du-Rhône, 6H-54, for the year 1662 (hereafter cited as *Livre du Saint Esprit*).

5. SPSA, arts. 28, 29.

6. It is clear that the leaders of *reformed* confraternities were aware of the savings to be gained by limiting the number of processions. A pact was initiated by the penitents of the Holy Cross with the confraternity of Notre Dame de Bon Rencontre of Notre Dame des Accoules parish in 1717 in which the former agreed to march in the procession of the latter, held on the Monday after Pentecost, in exchange for the latter supplying all the candles and torches to be used by the former in the procession. See the *Livre de la Sainte Croix,* manuscript 1191, ff. 217–18.

7. In later accounts this individual was also called the *bedot* or *bedeau,* i.e., beadle.

8. The best evidence of this is that although we know such a person existed, there is no mention of him in most accounts. Another confirmation of this practice comes from Jullien, who states that in 1790 the Bourras agreed that responsibility for the salary of the sub-sacristan would be divided between the sacristans and mandataires. See Alexandre Jullien, *Chronique historique de l'Archiconfrérie des Pénitents Disciplinés sous le titre du Saint Nom de Jésus (dits Bourras) de la Ville de Marseille* (Marseille, 1865), 114.

9. Examples can be seen in the accounts of the penitents of Saint Lazarus and the penitents of Saint John the Baptist. Also see Jullien, passim.

10. DSA, f. 67; on the Bourras see Collection Fontanier, 24F-66, account for 1763.

11. On dues paying in general see Jullien and Fontanier, *Pénitents noirs,* passim. On the penitents of Notre Dame de Pitié (Saint Martin parish) see Collection Fontanier, 24F-111; on the pénitents Bourras see Collection Fontanier, 24F-66.

12. Collection Fontanier, 24F-35.

13. *Livre des Cotes St. Lazare.*

14. Collection Fontanier, 24F-66.

15. Lucien Fontanier, *Notes sur les pénitents bleus de Notre Dame de Pitié*, Collection Fontanier, 24F-116.

16. See the régiments of the pénitents Carmélins, DC-B, ff. 26–28; for the penitents of Saint Anthony, see DSA, f. 126; on the penitents of Saint Lazarus see *Livre des Cotes Saint Lazare*, particularly the account for 1646.

17. Collection Fontanier, 24F-35; on gifts to confraternities see Jullien, 71.

18. Collection Fontanier, 24F-132, ff. 41–42.

19. Charles Gaspar Guillaume de Vintimille, *Ordonnances de Monseigneur l'Évêque de Marseille* (Marseille, 1698), 21. See Agulhon, 107–12; Michel Vovelle, *Piété baroque et déchristianisation en Provence au XVIIIe siècle* (Paris, 1973), 93–94. For the pénitents Carmélins see DC-B, ff. 87–88.

20. *Livre des Cotes St. Lazare.*

21. On the later division of the obligation see Collection Fontanier, 24F-66 and SPSA, art. 38.

22. SPSA, arts. 25–31.

23. *Livre de Saint Lazare.*

24. Hoffman, *Church and Community;* Kathyrin Norberg, *Rich and Poor in Grenoble* (Berkeley, 1985).

25. DSA, f. 126.

26. Dasprès, 7.

27. For the diocesan report see Archives départmentales des Bouches-du-Rhône, 5G-862, 863; for the two reports to the Parlement de Provence, see Archives Communale de Marseille, GG 80; for the confraternities of Our Lady of Compassion, see Lucien Fontanier, *Notes sur les pénitents bleus de Notre Dame de Pitié.*

28. As far as we can establish, the loans of the other confraternities were external. Most, in fact, were pensions for widows, children, and public institutions. In 1762, for example, the penitents of the Holy Spirit had loans of 2000 livres to the heirs of Dlle. Marie Anne Chantreaux, 800 livres from the Hôpital du Saint Esprit, and 789 livres from the "enfants de la Veuve Fornier."

29. Collection Fontanier, 24F-11.

30. Dasprès, 23; also see Archives Communale de Marseille, GG 80.

31. Vovelle, *Piété baroque,* 210–12.

32. The relevant statutes for the study of the office of prior are: Statutes of the Penitents of the Holy Spirit, art. "La façon comme l'on doibt eslire le Prieur et Recteurs" (hereafter cited as SPHS); *Statutes of the Pénitents Bourras,* chap. 4, art. 1 (hereafter cited as SPB); *Statutes of the Penitents of Saint Lazarus–1687,* arts. 1, 21, 37 (hereafter cited as SPSL); SPSL–1773, art. 14; *Statutes of the Pénitents Carmélins–1739,* art. 1 (hereafter cited as SPC); SPC–1814, arts. 1–5; SPSA, arts. 3, 9, 40, 42–44; *Statutes of the Penitents of Saint Henry–1717,* art. "Des officiers" (hereafter cited as SPSH); SPHS–1731, chap. 5, art. Du Prieur. (The above statutes can be found in the Collection Fontanier.)

33. On the penitents of Saint Anthony, see SPSA, art. 39; on the penitents of Saint Henry, see SPSH–1717, art. "Des Devoirs des Confrères."

34. On the Carmélins see SPC–1814, arts. 2–3; on the penitents of Saint Anthony see SPSA, art. 39; on the penitents of Saint Henry see SPSH–1717, art. "Des Devoirs des Confrères." For the penitents of Saint Anthony see SPSA, art. 41; for the penitents of Saint Henry see SPSH–1717, art. Des Officiers; for the penitents of Saint Lazarus see SPSL–1773, art. 14.

35. For the penitents of Saint Anthony see SPSA, art. 41; for the penitents of Saint Henry see SPSH–1717, art. "Des Officiers"; for the penitents of Saint Lazarus see SPSL–1773, art. 14. Relevant statutes for the office of sub-prior are the same as those for the prior. See also SPSH–1731, art. Du Sous-Prieur.

36. See chapter 4 below.

37. Two continuous records on confraternal life exist for the seventeenth century, the aforementioned Déliberations of the pénitents Carmélins (1621–1672) and the pénitents gris of Saint Anthony (1629–1695). In both it is possible to date the change from the terms first and second *régidour* or *recteur* to *sindic.* With the penitents of Saint Anthony it occurred during the early 1670s. With the pénitents Carmélins the term *sindic* appears much earlier, in 1638, but continues to be used interchangeably with the term *régidour* until the end of the register.

38. A search of the Latin definitions of the term *syndicus* turns up nothing of use. Monti, in his perusal of the types of offices

which existed in Italian confraternities, mentions the term as the title of an office, but gives no indication that there was any significance to it. See G. M. Monti, *Confraternité medievali dell'Alta e Media Italia*, 2 vols. (Venice, 1927), 2: 31–40. The relevant statutes for the study of the office of syndic are: SPHS, art. "La façon comme l'on doibt eslire le Prieur et Recteurs"; SPC–1814, art. 6; SPSA, arts. 21, 30–31; see also for the Bourras, Jullien, 17.

39. Confraternities varied in the terms they used to denote individual members of the Banque. The pénitents Bourras called the members of their Banque, *régents* or *régents-banquiers*. The pénitents of the Holy Spirit and the penitents of Saint Lazarus called theirs *recteurs;* those of Saint Henry called theirs *conseillers*. The other confraternities called the members of their Banque *régidours*. In all instances, however, the term *banquier* was an accepted synonym.

40. For an example of the office of the treasurer in a fifteenth-century confraternity of disciplinati, see G. Tammi, "Lo statuto dei disciplinati di Santa Maria Maddalena," in *Il Movimento dei disciplinati nel Settimo Centario del suo Inizio* (Perugia, 1962), 260–61. On the office of treasurer in confraternities of penitents see Agulhon, 94.

41. For the penitents of the Holy Spirit and the pénitents Carmélins the relevant statute on the office of secretary is the same as for the treasurer. For the Bourras see SPB, chap. 4, art. 5; for the penitents of Saint Henry see SPSH–1731, chap. 5, art. "Du Secrétaire."

42. SPSA, art. 23.

43. Support for this impression can be inferred from the statute of the penitents of Saint Anthony that prohibited the masters of ceremonies from granting their batons to any other members to lead the processions, "accompagnant des morts et aux réceptions des frères ou autre functions." SPSA, art. 20.

44. The relevant statutes for the office of master of novices remain the same as for the office of chorist with the pénitents Bourras. Only one other description of the duties of this officer is available, and that is for the penitents of Saint Henry, SPSH–1731, chap. 5, art. "Du Maître des prétendents." See the descriptions of enrollment procedures in the next chapter.

45. The relevant statutes for the office of sacristan are: SPHS, art. "Ordonnance des Custodes sive Sacristains"; SPB, chap. 4, art. 6; SPC–1814, art. 8; SPSA, art. 25–26, 28; SPHS–1731, chap. 5, art. "Des Sacristains."

46. The relevant statutes for the office of porter are: SPB, chap. 5, art. 9; SPSH–1731, chap. 5, art. "Des portiers." See also Jullien, chap. 3, passim. On the role of the porter in the confraternity of pénitents Bourras also see the discussion in chapter 4 below.

47. The information on this office is also rather sparse. The relevant statutes are: SPHS, art. "Ordonnance pour la Sene"; SPSA, art. 32. For a description of this office see Jullien, 20.

48. The relevant statutes for the office of cross-bearer, standard-bearer, and pall-bearer are: SPB, chap. 4, art. 10; SPSH–1731, chap. 5, art. "Des portiers." See also Jullien, 21–23.

49. On the mandataire in general see SPB, chap. 4, art. 11; Jullien, 19–20. On the penitents of Saint Anthony see DSA, f. 60.

50. Gilles Meerseman, "Études sur les anciennes confréries dominicaines," *Archivum Fratrum Praedicatorum,* 20 (1949): 37–38.

51. This is the interpretation of Meerseman, page 38; for another example, taken from the statutes of the disciplinati of Prato, see the same article, page 72.

52. Ibid., 99–100.

53. Collection Fontanier, 24F-2,7,131.

54. *Lazare de Cordier,* bk. 1, chap. 13.

55. On the penitents of the Holy Spirit see Fontanier, *Pénitents blancs;* on the penitents of Saint John the Baptist see Ruffi, 88.

56. *Lazare de Cordier,* bk. 1, chap. 13.

57. SPSH-1717, art. "Du Directeur."

58. Louis Châtellier, *The Europe of the Devout: The Catholic Reformation and the Formation of a New Society* (Cambridge, 1989), chaps. 2–4.

59. See SPSH–1731, chap. 3, "Des Corrections et des Peines." On Belsunce see chapter 8 below.

60. SPHS–1731, chap. 5, art. "Du Prieur."

61. SPC–1814, art. 4.

62. *Délibérations of the Pénitents Carmélins, Livre A: 1621–1634,* Collection Fontanier, 24F-91, f.27 (hereafter cited as DC-A); DC-B, f. 83; DSA, f. 203.

63. SPSA, art. 19.

64. DSA, f. 107.

65. SPSA, art. 30; Jullien, 17.

66. See the officers lists of the penitents of the Trinité vieille for the years 1676 and 1677, available at the Musée de Vieux Marseille.

67. In the case of the pénitents Bourras the group was known as the *Fondateurs-régents* and composed of twelve men. With the Carmélins it was simply the *Fondateurs* and composed of thirteen men. See SPB, chap. 1, art. 16; SPC-1739, art. 24. See also Jullien, 15–16.

68. On the difference between the terms "prior" and "rector," see Albert Blaise, *Dictionnaire Latin-Français des Auteurs Chrétiens* (Paris, 1954), who simply defines prior as a "supérieur, chef"; and rector as a "chef d'église." J. F. Niermeyer, *Mediae Latinitatis Lexicon Minus* (Leiden, 1976), gives more detailed definitions.

69. Jullien, 15–16.

70. See chapter 5 below.

71. SPB, chap. 3, art. 5, and Addendum, art. 1; SPC–1739, art. 2; SPC–1814, passim.

72. For the 1578 statutes of the Penitents of Saint Lazarus see *Livre de Saint Lazare,* 1189, f. 3. Note that these statutes do not mention the number of banquiers; I am assuming that at that point there were only twelve.

73. Both lists for the penitents of Saint Anthony were taken from DSA. For the penitents of Saint Lazarus, the list for 1611 was composed from *Livre des Cotes Saint Lazare,* 1190; the list for 1684 was composed from *Livre de Saint Lazare,* 1189.

74. In the confraternity of Saint Lazarus, for example, many men paying several years of back dues were elected to the Banque.

75. Vovelle, *Piété baroque.*

76. *Livre de Saint Lazare,* 1189, ff. 198–99.

Chapter 4

THE MAINTENANCE OF INTERNAL ORDER

INTRODUCTION

According to modern sociological theory, voluntary organizations such as penitent confraternities should have begun to decline once their original members began to disappear.[1] The confraternities of Marseille continued in existence for centuries, primarily because of their openness to new groups. The enthusiasm of wave after wave of new groups, eager to use existing organizations as vehicles for the expression of their devotional ideas, is what kept the confraternities young. The trade-off for this ongoing rejuvenation was competition for control and dissension over policies, which became major sources of organizational instability. As a result conflict resolution became a primary organizational goal.

All confraternities had statutes that required members to respect the authority of elected officials. Statutes also outline procedures to be followed in electing and installing officers and enrolling and expelling members. Descriptions of these procedures are useful for determining the expectations confraternities had of their members. Since erring members could be expelled only by an act of the governing council, régiments also provide some indications of conflict regulation and resolution. Last, enrollment data available for the pénitents Bourras offer some suggestion of the organizational utility of expulsions. Together these sources provide sufficient substance for a discussion of how confraternities sought to regulate internal conflict and how the effort changed over time.

ELECTIONS AND INSTALLATIONS

In unreformed companies the elections took place annually on the second feast of (the Monday following) Easter. Later confraternities held elections on the Sunday preceding the feast of their

113

patron saint. In his treatise Lazare de Cordier distinguishes between reformed confraternities who elected their officers by *sort* (i.e., by use of lots) and earlier confraternities who elected their officers by voice.[2] This section describes the election procedures of the penitents of Saint Anthony as representative of unreformed confraternities, those of the pénitents Bourras as representative of reformed companies, and those of the penitents of Saint Henry as an example both of episcopal efforts to rationalize the procedure and of later lay efforts at reform.

Penitents of Saint Anthony

According to their 1671 statutes, on the second feast of Easter the penitents of Saint Anthony assembled in their chapel after mass. During the previous week each confrere had received a *billet* brought to his door by the *sous-sacristain* announcing the election. The chorists began the process with the singing of the hymn "Veni Sancte Spiritus." The secretary next read the roll of the members of the Banque, the prior substituting for those absent.[3] Beyond the sixteen banquiers the confraternity selected ten other confreres to serve as ad hoc members of the nominating committee; six of these men were selected by the prior and four by the sub-prior. In the event that the prior did not appear for the election, the sub-prior alone had the right to make the selections of the nominating committee. If the sub-prior did not appear, then the *premier régidour* (prior-syndic) had that right; if the premier régidour did not appear, the responsibility fell to the next ranking banquier, and so on down the list.

After the nominating committee had been selected, the masters of ceremonies led it up to the *secret,* the meeting room above the chapel. There two members of the committee were selected as *surveillants*—one each by the prior and sub-prior—to stand watch on either side of the secretary. The prior and sub-prior each nominated nine men he felt could replace him. The members of the nominating committee by voice vote announced their choices among the nine nominees for prior and nine nominees for sub-prior, and the three nominees with the highest number of votes in both categories went on to the next round.

That round began when the nominating committee returned to the main chapel where the general assembly continued to sit. The prior announced the three nominees for prior. The secretary at that point called the roll of members and checked their choice among the three, the surveillants observing to make sure he made no mistakes. The nominee with the highest number of votes became the next prior. The process was repeated for the selection of the sub-prior after which the members broke for lunch.

The same day, "environ une heure après midi," the brothers reconvened. Again a committee was formed, this time for the nominations for the new Banque. The committee was composed of the old and new priors and the exiting Banque. The only stipulation on the composition of the new Banque was that four seats were reserved for the existing prior, sub-prior, and two sacristans. After electing the new Banque, the committee proceeded to select individuals to fill the other offices. Each of these nominees was in his turn approved by the assembled brothers by a "pluralité des suffrages," a voice vote with the secretary calling the role and the surveillants verifying the count.[4]

The election procedures of the penitents of Saint Anthony were much more elaborate than the known procedures for either the penitents of Saint Lazarus or the penitents of the Holy Spirit, perhaps an indication of the types of election-day trouble that unreformed confraternities began to encounter and the types of solutions they adopted.[5] Election day was often the occasion for disputes, and even violence, between opposing factions. The procedures adopted by the penitents of Saint Anthony represent an attempt to alleviate election day tensions by allowing more than one group a say in the selection of the next slate of officials. The autonomous role of the sub-prior as well as the use of an enlarged nominating committee militated against one faction controlling the nominating process. The use of surveillants insured against the possibility of the secretary altering the vote count in favor of one sub-group.[6]

Pénitents Bourras

On the morning of December 26, after the mass had been said, the sacristans of the confraternity of pénitents Bourras placed a table with a cross and two lit candles on it in front of the altar. One of the chorists stamped his baton to call the members to order. The members placed themselves on their knees and followed the rector in reciting the hymn "Veni Creator Spiritus." The rector, the rector-syndic, and the secretary took seats around the table; the vice-rector remained at his seat to observe order in the chapel. The secretary next called the roll of confreres in order of rank. Each confrere upon hearing his name, called out, "Sit nomen Jesus benedictum," then stepped forward to place in an urn on the table a sealed envelope (*bulletin fermé*) containing the name of the individual he would like to serve as rector for the upcoming year. When all the members had voted, the secretary opened the envelopes and counted the results. The names of the three confreres having the greatest number of votes then were placed in small metallic balls dedicated specifically to that purpose. The three balls were placed in a metal urn and shaken. An aperture in the base of the urn was opened and the confrere whose name was on the first ball that came through this opening was declared the new rector. The exiting rector mounted the altar to announce the name of his successor to which the members cried out in unison, "Pour l'amour de Dieu, soit." The vice-rector was elected following the same procedure. The rector-elect and the exiting rector then got together and selected members for the vacant seats on the Banque. These nominees were approved in whole or in part by another ballot. The new governing council chose the remaining officers for the next year.[7]

The use of lots does not seem to have been as successful for the other reformed confraternities as they were for the Bourras. Both the penitents of the Holy Cross and the pénitents Carmélins eventually modified the procedure or ceased to use lots in electing officers. The rationale for discontinuation of the practice by the pénitents Carmélins was that it led to confusion. When in 1660 several members complained that the confraternity had ceased to follow the method of electing officers by lots as stated in the statutes, it was pointed out to them that by this method, frères Honoré Cabaison and Elias Dechevaux—neither of whom could read—had been elected rector and vice-rector respectively in the year 1645. Moreover, since the company had been founded, this method had been used only "four or five times." The confraternity at this point changed the election procedure, replacing the selection-by-lot stage with a run-off election between the three most popular choices for rector.[8] The problem with the practice, as perceived by the penitents of the Holy Cross, was that often there were not three legitimate candidates for the office of rector. In a general assembly held in February, 1742, they cited the following: The original statutes stipulated that the three members with the highest number of votes be put on to the *ballote;* if two members split the majority of the votes, and the third highest vote totaled two, the member with two votes should not be included in the lottery. The confraternity in 1618 had attempted to address this problem by stipulating that only members with at least six votes could be part of the lottery. In 1643 this was increased to twelve. At this point a long court battle ensued among the membership, which resulted in a return to the six vote minimum of 1618. This was short-lived, for soon they reverted to the twelve-vote requirement. Finally, under authorization from Bishop Belsunce, the twelve-vote minimum was established in 1743. It was further stated that if only two members had more than twelve votes, then those two would go on the ballote; if only one member had twelve or more votes, he would be elected rector; if no member had twelve votes or more, the minimum would be lowered to six and the procedure repeated.[9]

The reason election by lot worked for the pénitents Bourras may well have been their unique organizational structure that allowed cliques to influence policy decisions in ways other than establishing control of the rectorship.[10] All in all, however, the method of letting the Holy Spirit decide who, among the three most popular choices, would be the rector for any given year does not seem to have been a successful innovation.

Penitents of Saint Henry

A radical change in the procedure by which officers were elected occurred between the 1717 and the 1731 editions of the statutes of the penitents of Saint Henry. Following the 1717 statutes, after the spiritual director had opened the session with the hymn "Veni Creator Spiritus," the prior proposed three confreres to replace him. The secretary divided a piece of paper into three columns, and in each of the columns wrote the name of one of the nominees. The confreres, beginning with the prior, filed past the secretary and gave their choice of the three. At the end the secretary tallied the votes and announced the winner. His name was then written in the register. The new prior next named his sub-prior and sacristans who were then approved by the assembly. Next, each of the four *conseillers* nominated two confreres to replace himself, and the above procedure was repeated. Finally the prior-elect nominated two frères for each of the positions of treasurer and secretary, and these two offices were then filled by the same procedure. In these statutes, the offices of prior, sub-prior, sacristan, and counselor were chosen for two year terms. The offices of treasurer and secretary might each be held for up to six years by the same individual.[11]

It is hard not to believe that the casual attitude with which these elections took place, as well as the lengthy terms of office, were not contrivances by Belsunce to downplay the role of officers to the benefit of the spiritual director. These elections were instituted from the top down, with members having no alternatives to the choices proposed by the prior and other officers.

These suspicions stand out all the more in comparison with the 1731 statutes. In the first stage of the election process here, the governing council asserted control. In session, each member of the governing council, from the prior downward, proposed two confreres as a replacement for himself. The council then discussed each candidate and his qualifications for the office. Should a candidate be found lacking, the council allowed the original nominator to propose a replacement. Should the nominator propose another unqualified candidate, or if he was steadfast in his support of his first nominee, he lost his privilege to nominate, and the council decided on an acceptable replacement. Once the council finished composing a slate of candidates, they returned to the general assembly. The secretary announced the names of the two candidates for prior and wrote the names on pieces of paper, which he attached to different-colored locked boxes. These boxes were placed in the sacristy off the main chapel. Each confrere was given a *jeton* (a small coin) and beginning with the prior, the rest of the council, then all the other members according to their rank, each placed his coin in the box of his choice. Once the voting was completed, the secretary opened the boxes, counted the coins, tallied them with the number of members who actually voted, and announced the winner. The procedure was repeated for all the officers except for the two sacristans and four porters, who were selected by the new prior on the day of his installation.

If any among those assembled could justify a complaint against one of the candidates, the council returned to secret session and selected another candidate. If any of the members of the council were absent from the nominating session, the prior had the right to nominate two candidates in his place.

It seems reasonable to view the penitents of Saint Henry's return to the use of a nominating committee to select candidates for office as the solution to the problem of assuring qualified candidates for every office. Reformed confraternities had dropped this stage in the election process with negative results. But in returning to the older practice, the penitents of Saint Henry made it more effective and efficient. The elaborate contingency plans of the penitents of Saint Anthony gave way to a simple process: a council was in session once a quorum was present; an absent member's nomination of replacements was made by the prior. Evidently, in one case, there had been disputes in the nominating procedure. The penitents of Saint Henry sought to solve this problem by giving officers two chances to nominate candidates before giving the task to the council acting as nominating committee.

The penitents of Saint Henry did continue one practice of the reformed confraternities—they too made use of the secret ballot instead of the voice vote.[12] In sum, they established a practical procedure that combined the most positive characteristics of the two types of older confraternities.

One last point about the election process should be made. Almost all the confraternities had a statute requiring that a member accept any office to which he was elected, or be expelled. Occasionally, however, an individual did choose to refuse an office. In 1665 the penitents of Saint Lazarus elected frère P. Gardane as sub-prior, although he was absent from the assembly. Several members were assigned to bring him to the chapel to accept this honor. He "joyously and contentedly" accepted, thanking, "ledit régiment de l'honneur que l'on lui avait faict du choisir de sa personne," and went along with the prior to announce their election to the bishop, the honorary prior of the confraternity. That night it was the custom of the confraternity to have services after vespers. Frère Gardane did not appear, and after delaying the services for him, the prior-syndic was sent to investigate his absence. The prior syndic learned from Gardane that he had had second thoughts about accepting the position. The confraternity unsuccessfully attempted to convince him to change his mind, but besides Gardane's doubts, his wife was adamant that he not accept the position. The confraternity met in general session, expelled him, and elected a new sub-prior.[13] In 1695 both the prior and the sub-prior elect of the penitents of Saint Anthony refused to accept the posts offered. After general assembly the confraternity decided to reelect in their places the prior and sub-prior syndics. It was not stated in the minutes whether the two members who refused office were expelled from the confraternity.[14]

The penitents of Saint Henry were the one company without such a statute, and perhaps again they indicate a trend. As their 1731 statutes state, any member elected to office had five days to explain to the council why he could not accept the office. Should the council accept his reasons, on the next Sunday the company held a special election to replace him.[15]

Installation of Officers

Not much descriptive material on the installation ceremonies exists for unreformed confraternities, but this may be because the ceremony was so brief as not to be regulated. In the 1558 statutes of the penitents of the Holy Spirit, the ceremony consisted of the entering prior and sub-prior placing their hands within the hands of the retiring prior and sub-prior, promising to govern loyally and intelligently with the assistance of the Banque and to punish the disobedient according to the form and nature of the statutes.[16]

Jullien describes how the pénitents Bourras elaborated on this basic ceremony. Their installation ceremony took place on the first of the year, the *fête patronale* of the confraternity. After the office had been said, one of the chorists moved to the front of the chapel and stamped the floor with his baton to signal silence. At the back of the chapel the lantern-bearer stood with his lantern; next to him the cross-bearer stood with his cross, and flanking these two men, the two most recently enrolled members stood with torches from which hung the banners of the confraternity. Upon a signal from the chorist, these men marched toward the front of the chapel. Once they reached the altar, the retiring rector and vice-rector immediately stepped down from their official seats at the back of the chapel, approached their successors, presumably seated elsewhere in the chapel, and took them by the hands. At the chorist's next signal, they marched slowly forward to the altar. Upon reaching the altar, again at a signal from the chorist, they fell on their knees, followed by the rest of the assembly. The retiring rector began to recite the hymn "Veni Creator" which was continued by the rest of the assembly. Once this was finished, the chorist signaled the rectors to march slowly back to the official seats at the rear of the chapel, where the retiring rector invited his successor to take the seat. He then presented him with an open copy of the statutes and asked, "Father Rector, do you promise to maintain and have [others] maintain these statutes?" to which the new rector replied, "I do with the grace of God." At this point the assembled brethren shouted, "God grant him the grace!" The new rector then preached a short sermon, after which a "Te Deum" was sung and the members congratulated him and reminded him "Memento mori." After the congratulations, the prior syndic closed the ceremony by reciting the two prayers, "Clementissime Pater" and "Omnipotens Clementissime Deus."[17]

Whether any other confraternity had a ceremony as eleborate as this is not known. For the pénitents Carmélins it seems likely. Their new officers entered office on July 16, the main feast of the confraternity and the day on which the company made their main procession. Because the officers did not have enough time to prepare for their installation on July 16, a régiment was held to request that the confraternity hold their elections on an earlier date.[18]

The penitents of Saint Henry returned to a much simpler installation ceremony. As described in the 1731 statutes:

Le seconde dimanche de Juilliet les pénitents générale-
ment assemblés l'après midy, installerant les nouveaux
élus, après quoy le Prieur entrant en charge nommera
deux Sacristains et quatre Portiers, qui été approuvés par
l'assemblée entrerant le même jour en exercise. Les an-
ciens officiers remettront à leurs successeurs ce dont ils
avaient été chargés respectivement, de quoy le secrétaire
dressera une délibération, signée par les parties et par le
plus grand nombre des assistants.[19]

It may be observed that the penitents of Saint Henry con-
sciously aspired to "defraternalize" the installation ceremony. The
installation ceremony in the 1717 statutes was more elaborate, with
each exiting officer walking to his successor and then escorting him
to his new place. The penitents of Saint Henry prided themselves
on their social involvement, especially on their efforts to aid the
poor and sick of the Hôpital de Saint Esprit. Consistently in their
statutes they illustrate a desire to prevent fraternalism from obscur-
ing this goal. This commitment apparently went to the point of
suppressing the display of fraternal pride other confraternities permitted on the day of the installation of officers.

THE PROCEDURES AND RITUALS FOR JOINING
A CONFRATERNITY OF PENITENTS

According to the statutes of the penitents of the Holy Spirit,
the penitents of Saint Lazarus, and the penitents of Saint Anthony,
if a man desired to be enrolled as a member of one of the earlier
unreformed confraternities, he went to the chapel of the confraternity on Sunday morning with a written request for membership,
which he passed to the porter. The porter passed the request to the
prior who, after the services, announced the names of those seeking enrollment. The prior appointed two members to investigate
the past of each applicant. They were to establish whether he had
reached the proper age (in most statutes eighteen years), had
proper means of support, was of sound Catholic faith, and had
previously been a member of another confraternity of penitents. If
the latter, he had to explain why he left his old confraternity. If the

applicant fulfilled all of these conditions, at some point during the week the two appointed members made known to him that his request had been accepted. The following Sunday he was to appear at the chapel with his habit, chapbook, enrollment fee, and a written note attesting to his having recently confessed. After the services, he was brought forward to the altar. There the statutes of the confraternity were read to him by the prior, after which the applicant fell to his knees and recited the "Veni Creator" and the "Te Deum laudamus" and repeated the words to several prayers, part of the liturgy of that confraternity, that were spoken to him. Once he had finished the prayers, he rose, now a member of the confraternity. He was then made welcome by the prior, sub-prior, and all the brethren. The last act of his enrollment was the inscription of his name in the membership book.[20]

Reformed confraternities made the procedure more complex. Because of limited enrollments, confraternities could not accede to all admission requests and were forced to establish waiting lists. And as explained in the statutes of the pénitents Bourras, when a place fell vacant in the confraternity, it was filled not by the person with the longest time on the list, but by the best qualified person on the list.[21] Also with the Bourras, an individual needed a patron among the active members in order to be received. Whether a patron was necessary for admission to the other confraternities is not known.

Reformed confraternities further complicated the enrollment procedure by establishing a waiting period of three weeks between the time the candidate made known his request for membership and the time this request was accepted or rejected. During the waiting period any members could step forward and protest an application. (Otherwise the confraternity depended upon the report of the committee elected to investigate the candidate's background.) While the investigation progressed, candidates attended services, but sat in tiny rooms called *cabinets* built into the side of the chapel. After services, it was the master of novices' job to explain to them the various customs and rituals of the confraternity. After services on the second Sunday, candidates deemed acceptable were taken from their cabinets and escorted to the secret where the rector sat waiting for them. They were invited to participate in the singing of the hymn "Veni Sancte Spiritus" and the reading of the statutes that constituted the reception procedure of unreformed confraternities. At the end of these acts candidates were asked by the rector if they desired admission to the confraternity. Upon their answers of yes they were told to return to the chapel the following Sunday, having confessed and having received communion, and with habits, chap books, sandals, and two half-pound candles.

The rite used for the reception of new members by reformed confraternities made more explicit the religious and fraternal dimensions of the reception process. The ceremonies began immediately after services the following Sunday. As described by Jullien for the pénitents Bourras, first the chorist went to the cabinet of novices, escorted the new member to the vestry, and explained to him the upcoming ceremony while he dressed. Once the new member was suitably attired, the chorist escorted him back to the chapel door. The chorist tapped on the door with his baton; from inside the porter opened the door, the assembled confreres at that moment shouting, "Frater, memento mori." On the inside stood two torchbearers with their torches alight. The chorist took the candles the new member carried in either hand and lit them from the torches, returning one to the new member and taking the other to the new member's patron (the old member who had recommended his candidacy). Next the novice, candle in hand, marched slowly to the altar and fell to his knees. The rector and other members began to recite the Miserere. The rector followed alone with the short prayer, Dilectissimi fratres:

> *My dear sweet brothers, let us pray to our lord Jesus Christ for his servant here who has chosen to leave the vanities of this world for the love of God. Let us pray to the Lord to grant him the Holy Spirit, to grant him the Holy Spirit that he might be inflamed with zeal in observing the Commandments of God and the rules of our institution, to grant him the Holy Spirit that this Spirit might watch over his heart, and guard it against the temptations of the world, and all the vain desires of the earth. And since in entering this confraternity he is renewed on the*

*outside by the habit which he must wear, let us pray to the
Lord, that he aid him with his powerful hand in the practice of good, that he preserve his heart from all spiritual
blindness, and that he deigns in the end to accord him the
ineffable light of his eternity. This we pray to him who
reigns and God the father and the Holy Spirit forever and
ever. Amen.*

Once the rector had finished, the master of ceremonies and
the torch bearers marched to the altar, then with the novices in tow
marched back to the rectoral see at the back of the chapel. The
novices again fell to their knees. While in this position the master
of novices took off their habits and placed them on prayer stand
before the rectoral see. The rector looked down at the novices and
asked:

Rector: Brother(s), what do you ask?

*Novices: The Mercy of God and the peace of all the
brethren.*

*Rector: It is necessary to hope that God has granted you
mercy since he has inspired you to want to serve in this
holy confraternity, and you will receive the plentitude of
his graces if you observe his commandments, those of the
church, and those of this holy confraternity.*

Novices: I promise it with the aid of God.

Assembled confreres: God grant the Grace.

At the end of the dialogue all of the assembled kneeled and
recited the "Veni Creator Spiritus." The rector took the habits
from the prayer stand and with the help of the master of novices
redressed the novices, saying, "Thus God redresses you as new
men created in accordance with him." The brethren completed his
sentence with "In justitia et sanctitate et veritate."

Once the novices again were dressed in their habits, the final part of the ceremony began with the rector giving a short speech on the history of the confraternity and the symbology of the various parts of the habit. Last, the rector recited the short prayer *ad esto:*

> *Lord, hear our prayers and deign to bless your servant, to whom we have come to confer the habit of holy purity, that by your grace he will obtain life, by Jesus Christ, our lord.*

The rector embraced the new confreres, welcoming them into the confraternity. Then while a "Te Deum" was being sung, the master of novices escorted the new members around to the others who welcomed them into the chapel. As the final act of the ceremony, the new members were led to their places on the uppermost benches.[22]

Earlier it was noted that the penitents of Saint Henry restructured the election procedure to make it more efficient, while simultaneously stripping the ceremonies attached to the installation of new officers of most of their symbolic import. Something similar occurred in their procedures for admitting new members. In unreformed confraternities the idea of a novitiate did not exist, although new members were called novices. Lazare de Cordier distinguishes between the reception of novices by confraternities of penitents and the reception of novices by religious orders. According to him there was no year-long trial period for membership in the latter, many members in fact joining when they were children.[23] Reformed confraternities did, however, add the mandatory three-week waiting period between the request for admission and actual matriculation; and for the first three months of membership, the novice was watched and judged. Neither of these procedures tested commitment to the confraternity, a problem which attracted episcopal concern. Belsunce, determined to frighten the less than serious away, built into the admission process for the penitents of Saint Henry a novitiate modeled on that of the Jesuit order.

An individual interested in joining the penitents of Saint Henry first arranged to have his name proposed to the council of the confraternity. The prior then appointed two officers to investigate the individual's background. Should he be found acceptable, he was sent a note that told him to come on a given day to the Hôpital Saint Esprit, which housed the chapel of the penitents of Saint Henry. At the hospital the individual, now known as a *postulant,* began the first month of his novitiate, which consisted of helping to clean and feed the sick of the hospital. If a postulant performed satisfactorily during this first month, he was allowed to enter the second stage of the novitiate and become a *prétendant.* As it was explained in the statutes, the prétendants "seront employés avec prudence aux offices des plus pénibles et plus humiliants, principalement à secourir les malades et ensevelir les morts." A man remained a prétendant for at least four months. Presumably during this time he was taught the various customs and ceremonies of the confraternity. At the point when the council decided to accept him as a member, he was advised by the master of novices to buy his habit and sandals.

Several things are worth noting about the novitiate of the penitents of Saint Henry. The first is that it combines and extends the two periods of the novitiate used by reformed confraternities— the waiting period by one week and the trial period by one month—and then places them both before the formal reception of the new member. In all it took a man at least five months to join the penitents of Saint Henry.

Second, the criteria for being accepted as a member shifted from piety to service. Of course Belsunce would have argued that men were still being judged for their aptitude for the pious activities of the confraternity. But in the case of the penitents of Saint Henry, the criteria had shifted from the ability to pursue a fraternal effort for salvation, to the ability to follow orders in performing humiliating tasks. The penitents of Saint Henry were so successful that in their second set of statutes they limited their size, evidence that their novitiate must not have been preceived as too extreme by contemporaries. The success of the penitents of Saint Henry in recruiting members is in fact one of the strongest indications that by the early eighteenth century, lay devotional sensibilities in Marseille had moved toward the Counter-Reformation glorification of the piety of social activism.

After the arduous novitiate, the reception ceremony was a simplified version, not of the ceremony of reformed confraternities, but of unreformed confraternities. The new member simply appeared on the day of his reception. After the services his habit was blessed according to the prayers "marquées dans le ritual romain." Then the member pronounced the following oath:

> I (name) promise before God and the Holy altar to observe faithfully and with all my powers the statutes and rules of the Company established under title by Saint Henry, and especially to assist sick paupers in their last moments and to carry them to their final resting place when such is ordered of me. If God will grant me grace.

All that remained was for the new member to sign his name in the membership book.[24]

EXPULSIONS AND THE MAINTENANCE OF INTERNAL ORDER

The ultimate penalty available to confraternities for the regulation of internal order was expulsion. Even the most flagrant violations of the statutes, however, were not dealt with summarily, but were argued before the governing council. The council minutes for some of these cases for several confraternities are available. They, along with the statutes themselves, provide a good sense of the social norms confraternities sought to maintain. To provide background, the first topic considered will be the kinds of infractions dealt with in the statutes.

Statutes Regulating Internal Order

Statutes that regulated internal order can be separated into two groups: those that sought to regulate the relationship of members to authority within the confraternity and those that sought to regulate the relationships between members. Every confraternity had at least one statute that established the necessity of members following blindly (*aveuglément*) the orders of elected leaders in all things pertaining to the confraternity. As was stated in the synopsis of their statutes that the penitents of Saint Lazarus prepared for novices in 1673, "L'importance de ce chapitre est si grand qu'il en est parlé en trois differents statuts sous peine d'estre chassé."[25] In case of the absence of both priors or rectors, these statutes also established the line of succession through the premier régidour or recteur (prior syndic) and then the other banquiers in order of seniority. Failure to recognize such authority led to expulsion.[26] Related to this, each confraternity also had a statute that required that all members who threatened to raise "cabales" be expelled.[27] Because members sometimes resented their election to a given post, it was common to have a statute that required members to accept whatever office they were assigned or be expelled from the confraternity (though as mentioned above, this statute was not always enforced).[28]

Secrecy was a major concern in the statutes that dealt with internal order. In part this was a question of authority. No outsider was ever to be allowed to enter the chapel without the permission of the prior or the rector. It was the duty of the porters in some confraternities, and the chorists in others, to stand at the chapel door and block the entrance of any outsider until the prior granted permission for them to enter. Any other person who took it upon himself to admit outsiders was expelled.[29] In part such stringency reflected a concern about the leaking of confraternal affairs to the outside world. Each confraternity had a statute that warned confreres against speaking to outsiders about confraternal matters. Likewise, confreres were warned against speaking to each other about confraternal affairs outside the chapel walls. The penalty for either infraction was expulsion. Yet by prohibiting brothers from speaking about confraternal affairs outside the chapel walls, confraternities were also, in effect, prohibiting brothers from coming together to discuss their grievances and decide on collective action. So the concern for secrecy in part also represents an effort to place a roadblock in the way of dissenting confreres who threatened to hire lawyers and take their cases to court. In the 1731 statutes of the penitents of Saint Henry, an effort was made to deal with the problem of dissension by stopping disagreements in the council from spreading to the confraternity as a whole. Any member of the council who divulged the substance of council meetings to other confreres risked being stripped of his office.[30]

As for the statutes that sought to regulate relations between members, their major concern was controlling arguments between confreres. Something of an evolution is discernible in the procedure for dealing with the problem. In the earliest set of extant statutes, those of the penitents of the Holy Spirit, a ritualistic procedure was followed. On the eve of the four mandatory confessions the confreres made each year, each confrere was required, before the assembled confraternity, first to reconcile himself with all other confreres, and then, on his knees before the prior, subprior and banquiers, to beg pardon from God for his transgressions. This he was expected to do in the spirit of, "vraye et fraternelle amytie." Any member who refused to perform these acts was expelled. In the latest set of extant statutes, those of the penitents of Saint Henry, all disputes were to be resolved by the appointment of two ad hoc adjudicators who sought to find common ground between the disputants. The statutes from the interim period leave the task of adjudication to prior and rectors who presumably used the threat of expulsion to pressure the disputants into reconciliation.[31]

Along with trying to adjudicate conflict between confreres, confraternities sought to establish minimal levels of fraternal obligation. The statutes of the penitents of Saint Henry waxed eloquent on this theme, recommending to confreres that they watch out for each other, perform small courtesies for each other, keep each other out of quarrels, and inform the prior should one of their brethren fall sick or stray from the flock. It is interesting that, beyond the ritual described above, the statutes of the penitents of the Holy Spirit have nothing to say on this theme. As I have argued elsewhere, the penitents of Saint Henry's verbosity on this point actually may be indicative of a decline in fraternal spirit. Because confraternities were so large, and because the rituals that might have bonded the brothers together were no longer being practiced, fraternal spirit was difficult to maintain in the later years.[32]

Three levels of penalties are described in the statutes. For lesser infractions, or for the initial occurrence of some of the major ones, confreres were usually assessed a fine. The penitents of the Holy Spirit tended toward money fines only, assessing members, for example, five sous for breaking the silence of the service, one sou for taking off their habit without the permission of the prior, or three sous for failure to participate in the burial procession of a confrere. The pénitents Bourras had similar fines for similar infractions. For slightly graver infractions, however, the Bourras assessed fines in wax. For example, failure to be at the chapel at twelve noon precisely on Mardi Gras, in order to avoid the "dissolutions escandalles et mondanites quy ce commectant ce jour là," brought the fine of a half livre of wax. Failure to announce beforehand trips of more than one month's duration to the rector, or failure to present the rector with a ticket certifying that one had made confession in preparation for the trip, brought a fine of a half livre of wax. Failure to participate in the periodic cycle of rites of confession, penance by use of discipline, and communion was punished the first time with a fine of five sous, the second time by a fine of a half livre of wax, and the third time by expulsion from the confraternity.[33]

Expulsion was the second type of penalty. While it is not readily apparent in the statutes, there were actually two kinds of expulsion. In the register of members of the pénitents Carmélins from 1685–1792, a distinction was made between those men who were *chassé* from the confraternity, and those who were *rayé* from the confraternity. The verb *chasser* is the one most readily used to signify expulsion. Available records, however, indicate that *chassé* members could be readmitted. Whereas to be expelled as in chassé seems to have meant expulsion with the possibility of readmission, to be expelled as in rayé seems to imply expulsion from the group and expungement of one's name from the book of the confraternity. The significance rests in the fact that penitent confraternities, like all other types of confraternities, were premised on a belief in the efficacy of collective prayer for the salvation of their members' souls. To be rayé from a confraternity meant not only to be expelled, but also to be denied access to whatever spiritual treasure it might have accumulated, or might come to accumulate. The statutes of the penitents of the Holy Spirit made a distinction between being chassé and being chassé in the sense of being "perpetuellement mys hors de la présente fraternité et compagnie." It seems likely that this distinction later became the distinction between chasser and rayer, and that rayer signified expulsion without any hope of readmission.[34]

In the extant statutes corporal punishment was mentioned only twice, both times by the pénitents Bourras. The first instance was in the statute on the obligation to visit sick confreres. Failure to do this the first time brought a fine of one half livre of white wax. Failure to do this the second time brought, at the advice of the Banque régiment, corporal punishment. Failure to do so the third time brought expulsion. The second instance occurred in the statutes on fighting. According to this statute, should quarrels between confreres lead to fighting, in the chapel or elsewhere, but not be grave or atrocious enough to merit *peine corporelle,* then the régiment was obliged to attempt to adjudicate the conflict. Whether this penalty was ever applied is not known, but it is interesting that it was recommended only for infractions against the statutes regulating behavior between confreres.[35]

Some Examples of Expulsions

From various sources it is possible to develop some impressions of the kinds of offenses deemed serious enough to merit expulsion. Consider a 1643 régiment called by the pénitents Carmélins against three of their members. The first case was that of frère Estienne Vignon. Vignon was one of the sacristans for the confraternity that year, and the greatest charge against him appears to have been laxity in the performance of his office. Several times he had not appeared at the scheduled time to open the chapel, thereby delaying services. Several times also he had failed to buy oil and candles for the chapel, which was part of his responsibilities. When the rector attempted to correct him, "fraternally," Vignon compounded his crime with an act of "arrogance." He boasted to the rector that complaints against his performance did not concern him since he was still legally a member of the penitents of Notre Dame de Pitié (Carmelites)—he had promised to resign from the confraternity when he enrolled in the Carmélins, but never did—and preferred their company to that of the Carmélins.

Another case was that of the Feraudz brothers, Dominique and Honnoré. Each brother was faced with his own list of infractions. Among Dominique's numerous crimes were: He continued his membership in the confraternity of penitents of Notre Dame de

Pitié (Carmelites), though he had promised to resign from that confraternity when he enrolled as a member of the Carmélins; he had never bought a habit; he had left town for more than a month without informing the confraternity; and he had missed "plusieurs confessions et dissiplines [sic]." His brother Honnoré had evidently been in town, yet failed to come to services. Added to this, he too had missed "diversses confessions, dissiplines [sic], et processions." Finally he had been caught attempting to steal a habit by smuggling it out under his clothes.

The judgment of the régiment on the Feraudz brothers is clear and certain. They were "chassés et. . .rayés de la table et des libvres." The judgment on Vignon is much cloudier. Vignon was warned that if he did not want to be, "chassé comme lesdits Feraudz sans espoir de jamais restablly par aucun Recteur," he had to pay a fine of two livres of new wax and resign within two weeks from the penitents of Notre Dame de Pitié and bring a certificate of his resignation to the rector. The régiment went on to declare that in the event he actually did this, the confraternity would be willing to allow him to continue in his office to the end of his term.

All of the confraternities had statutes prohibiting membership in more than one confraternity of penitents at the same time. But cases like those described above do not appear to have been an isolated phenomenon. According to Guibert, Marseille's confraternities of penitents were unique in that, as with religious orders, men were allowed to move from confraternities with lenient rules to those with more rigorous ones.[36] Neither of the above two cases seems to have occurred for religious reasons. It is also interesting that in both instances the move was from one chapel associated with the Carmelite monastery to another.[37] The fact that Dominique Feraudz never owned a habit is illuminating. The statutes of the confraternities stressed the necessity of possessing a habit. But Feraudz had obviously been in the pénitents Carmélins for quite some time without one. With paupers and so many young boys on their membership roles, perhaps the confraternities ceased to enforce this requirement rigorously. The penitents of Saint Anthony in one statute prohibited participation in services without a habit, yet in another statute gave new members a year to purchase one.[38]

Last, both the Feraudz brothers had had long unexplained absences from the chapel and both had missed "plusieurs confessions et dissiplines." It seems certain that neither man had participated in the confraternity and its activities for quite some time, but their lack of participation does not seem to be what triggered their expulsion. Rather it would appear that their being rayés from the books was because of the brother's attempted theft of a habit. The impression is that the confraternity bent over backward to keep members. The case of Vignon is especially revealing in this regard. The irritation and anguish he must have caused the membership with his late arrivals and his laxity in buying candles for the altar and lamps can be imagined. The régiment noted that in December, 1641 he had been enjoined to bring a certificate of his resignation from the penitents of Our Lady of Compassion by the following Easter or be expelled. Yet eighteen months later he was given two more weeks to get the certificate.

On a more general level it is possible to say that the offenses most often mentioned as causes for expulsion were fighting, insubordination, and forming a cabale, that is, taking issue with a policy decision. On April 15, 1669, election day for the penitents of Saint Anthony, for example, a fight broke out in the chapel between frères Jean Olliver and Etienne Rey. In the heat of battle Rey wounded Olliver with a knife. A special régiment was held in which it was decided that both should be expelled and their names stricken from the books. Rey later returned, however, contrite and begging for forgiveness. The confraternity forgave him and allowed him to return.[39] Similarly on election day 1664 an arguement broke out between two members of the pénitents Carmélins, frères Claude LaSoeur and Joseph Hyuert. Presumably peace was restored and the elections were concluded. As the confreres were filing out of the chapel, LaSoeur gave Hyuert a kick. In the régiment called to deal with the incident it was decided that LaSoeur be chassé and rayé, and that Hyuert be fined eight livre of wax. Both men appealed but the decisions remained unchanged.[40]

An often-mentioned cause of expulsion was blaspheming the name of Christ and the saints. A more frequent transgression, however, was vilification of the names of the leaders of the confraternity, actually a case of insubordination. To cite an example from the deliberations of the pénitents Carmélins: in 1656 frère Nicholas Boulard, accompanied by his friend frère Jean Camart, arrived late for services on one of the major feast days of the company. For some reason, while hurriedly dressing to join the others, "Boulard became embroiled in an argument which led him not only to blaspheme the name of Jesus, but to heap abuse on many of the important men of the confraternity."[41] In the régiment held on the incident, Boulard was chassé and rayé and his accomplice Camart fined four livre of wax.[42]

A third often-mentioned cause for expulsion was the raising of a cabale over some issue. One of the best examples of this comes from Jullien, who describes an occasion when in 1654 the pénitents Bourras raised their yearly dues from twelve to twenty sous and frère Raphael Brunel, "homme très versé dans la pratique des oeuvres de piété, qui avait precedément occupé plusieurs charges et dignités, même celle du recteur," protested the decision.[43] Brunel appealed first to a general assembly of the confraternity, and when that failed, to the bishop, Etienne de Puget. When Puget failed to alter the decision, Brunel appealed over his head to the metropolitan, the archbishop of Arles. This failed also, but Brunel refused to submit and pulled together a group of followers within the confraternity. When the confraternity attempted to expel him he took the case before the Parlement of Provence. Finally, in 1658, Parlement ruled in favor of the confraternity's right to raise the dues to twenty sous, and to expel Brunel. A similar but less dramatic conflict took place among the pénitents Carmélins in 1662.[44]

In characterizing offenses that led to expulsion, based on available examples, it seems fair to say that the confraternities were more concerned about offenses that threatened internal authority and order than about any other. It is curious that not one example of expulsion for a religious offense is recorded. The above case of the Feraudz brothers suggests, in fact, that confraternities simply were less rigorous in the enforcement of their religious statutes. Support for this impression comes from the data Weissman collected for the confraternity of disciplinati of San Paolo of Florence. Over the period 1434–93, that confraternity expelled 366 members. In seventy-six percent of the 161 cases in which the cause of expulsion is known, the individual was expelled for either failing to attend services, failing to participate in rites and ceremonies, or moving on to another confraternity. In only seven percent of the 161 cases was expulsion for a moral or religious infraction, and half of these cases were for sexual misconduct.[45] The fact that the San Paolo data are from the fifteenth century argues against the notion that it was the evolution of stricter modes of social conduct or the emergence of the parish as the center of the laity's religious and moral life during the Counter-Reformation that led to the comparative lack of interest in regulating moral behavior on the part of confraternities. As organizations concerned with their own survival, it makes more sense to see penitent confraternities as having come to emphasize fraternal values to the neglect of moral ones. In other words, the goal of moral regeneration of their members was transcended by the goals of organizational survival.

Expulsion in the Confraternity of Pénitents Bourras

The above discussion of expulsion suggests that expulsion was predominantly the result of two types of concerns. First, the organization wanted to remove from their group those who did not respond to the socialization process, that is, those who did not "fit in." The Feraudz brothers would be an example of this. Second, they wished to remove from the organization those who sowed discord. Since those who sowed discord were usually those upset by some action taken by the governing council, this was essentially a concern to limit the negative effects of clique infighting by expelling those who refused to accept defeat in such contests. (The case of Raphael Brunel comes to mind here.) The data on expulsions for the pénitents Bourras provide some indications of the degree to which these concerns motivated expulsions in one confraternity.

Over the course of the years 1591 to 1792, the confraternity admitted 665 men, 106, or seventeen percent, of whom were eventually expelled. The data on the expulsions presented in figure 4A have been divided into forty-year time periods. Within these time periods, expulsions have been presented according to the time from enrollment that they occurred. Thus, of the forty-seven men expelled during the confraternity's first forty years in operation, fourteen were expelled within two years of the time they enrolled, twenty between three–ten years, eleven between eleven-nineteen years, and two after twenty years in the confraternity. The information in figure 4A has been displayed graphically in figure 4B.

The justification for formatting the data as it is displayed in figure 4A is that in the absence of more direct documentation of the reasons why members were expelled, length of time in the confraternity can serve as one indicator of these motivations. The assumption is that individuals who did not fit would have been asked to leave within their first few years in a confraternity or presumably drop out on their own—like the 192 men who over the course of the eighteenth century joined the penitents of Notre Dame de Pitié (Saint Martin parish) but never paid dues—leaving it to the confraternity to exclude their names from the register. On the other hand, it would take some time to attain sufficient stature to become a political casualty, so expulsions for the latter reason would occur after a significant amount of time had been spent in the confraternity.

As the table demonstrates, over the course of years, the number and nature of expulsions within the pénitents Bourras changed dramatically. The confraternity expelled less than a third as many men in the period 1751–92 as it did in the period 1591–1630. The area where the decline is most perceptible is in expulsions that took place less than two years after enrollment. If above speculation on the connection between early expulsion and the socialization pro-

Figure 4A: Expulsions Occuring within X Number of Years from Enrollment by 40 Year Periods for the Confraternity of Pénitents Gris du Très Saint Nom de Jésus (Bourras), 1591–1792

	0 to 2	3 to 10	11 to 19	20 plus	Totals
1591–1630	14	20	11	2	47
1631–1670	1	2	2	0	5
1671–1710	0	5	6	6	17
1711–1750	0	8	9	5	22
1751–1792	2	6	3	4	15
Totals	17	41	31	17	106

Figure 4B: Percentage of Expulsions Occurring within X Number of Years from Enrollment by 40 Year Periods for the Confraternity of Pénitents Gris du Très Saint Nom de Jésus (Bourras), 1591–1792

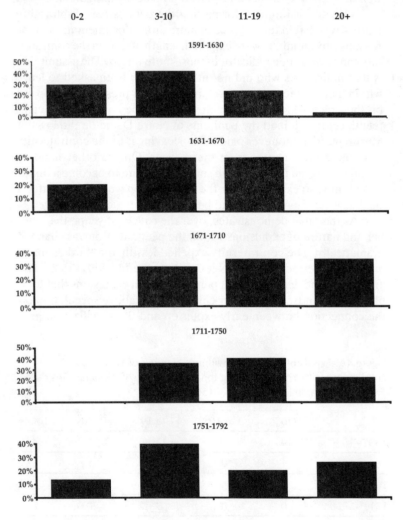

cess is correct, then in its earliest years the confraternity had a comparatively serious problem with either finding men who lived up to its expectations or with training men to live up to its expectations. Whatever the case, after that initial period the problem in this area disappeared. Over those one hundred and sixty years, seventeen men were expelled less than two years after joining. Only three of these cases occurred after 1630. While early exits from the confraternity all but disappeared, by the period 1671–1710 expulsions of men who had ten or more years as members. began to dominate. A check of the individuals expelled according to their highest rank attained in the official hierarchy provides some corroboration for the suspicion that expulsion of men with long tenures usually was the result of political infighting. Over the period 1671–1792, the period when information on office holding is fairly detailed, fifteen of thirty-three, or forty-five percent, of the members in these categories expelled had attained the rank of either rector or vice-rector. It appears that the confraternity was using expulsion as a tool for maintaining internal stability. Losers in internal conflicts were forced to look elsewhere for spiritual brotherhood or to petition for readmission and, in doing so, acknowledge the victory of their opponents. That latter conclusion is suggested by the fact that eight of the above fifteen men were later readmitted.

Some information on expulsions in the confraternity of pénitents Carmélins is also available for the period 1685–1792. Over this period the confraternity admitted 385 men of whom forty six, or twelve percent were expelled. This rate is comparable to that for the pénitents Bourras, which supports the conclusion that in the latter confraternity expulsion was also the price to be paid for failure in the political arena. It is worth speculating that the predominant motivation for recourse to expulsion in most confraternities was the maintenance of internal political stability. As suggested by the data on the penitents of Notre Dame de Pitié, most lower-level members who became disillusioned with the organization simply stopped participating in its activities. Expulsion was a procedure for dealing with active members with sufficient stature within the organization to generate discord. It is not coincidental, then, that most of the known examples of expulsions were the result of some type of political conflict. It was primarily the politically active among the brethren who were expelled, usually cases in which opposing political factions confronted each other that led to expulsions.

DIRECTIONS IN PROCEDURAL CHANGE

Over the course of the ancien régime the elected heads of penitent confraternities came to demand, and for the most part receive, almost carte blanche authority during their year in office. This made elections true contests—for the losers there was probably little hope that their plans for the confraternity would be developed or continued. It also limited the avenues of redress for those on the outside of political power. These points suggest that perhaps the most important question to answer about conflict within penitent confraternities is why it occurred so rarely and did so little damage when it did. An essential clue here is the open-admission policies pursued by most of the confraternities. Such policies acted as a sort of safety valve, holding open to dissenting confreres the option of ready admission to another association. Losers in confraternal battles did not have to accept defeat; with little effort they could simply resign, confident of gaining admission to any of several other associations. For those who cared enough to be expelled, it was probably equally accepted that after a period of self-exile commensurate with the perceived affront, they could request and be granted readmission. The distinction between chasser and rayer for contemporaries actually may have been between self-imposed exile and the termination of any prospect of further interaction. The custom of the penitents of Notre Dame de Pitié of leaving members on the books for decades after they ceased to participate as well as the custom of the pénitents Carmélins of allowing dual memberships may have reflected such practices. The former was an indication that it was not unusual for groups to return to earlier associations during their travels, the latter an indication that confraternities accepted the fact that their new enrollees often maintained commitments and attachments to previous associations.

From one perspective the freedom confraternities allowed members to join and leave as they desired might seem to make a sham of the idea of confraternities as organizations at all. This approach fails to recognize that the primary allegiance of most confreres was to their sub-group or clique. The larger organization was a facilitator of the goals of these groups. Because the importance of the organization as a vehicle for sub-group expression was recognized by all parties concerned, resignation through non-participation (because it avoided conflict) was in all probability the honorable way to accept defeat. It might also appear that a confraternity risked disaster by taking in an individual or group known to have left another association; the danger that this individual or group might be disruptive would have been balanced against his fitting in and contributing. In sum it was a worthwhile risk.

The combination of the practice of men leaving confraternities as a result of conflict and the practice of confraternities freely admitting and/or retaining men with attachments to other associations provides the best explanation for the fact that over the centuries there was very little evolution in the procedure for dealing with dissent. Given the fraternal ideal that confraternities maintained, there was little that could be done beyond the procedure described in the statutes of the penitents of the Holy Spirit. When moral coercion failed to force members to reconcile "l'un avec l'autres," there was no alternative but to expel the party deemed to be in the wrong. Once confraternities got so large and impersonal that moral coercion could not work, even that option disappeared.

Still, the creators of later types of confraternities did innovate in their approaches to the problem. Founders of reformed confraternities concluded that the source of dissent was fraternal incompatibility. Their solution was an admission procedure that established the determination of compatibility as its greatest goal, and an elaborate installation ceremony that emphasized fraternity above everything else. They recognized that conflict would occur but assumed that the presence of the Fondateurs as a sort of court of final authority would take most of the venom out of confrontations. The question of who was right and who was wrong, however, was not at the bottom of most conflicts. The result of the innovations put in place by reformed confraternities was an intensification of feelings of fraternity among clique members, which meant that sometimes whole cliques, instead of just one or two leaders, had to be expelled.[46]

It appears, though, that the statutes of the penitents of Saint Henry followed the lead of the statutes of reformed confraternities in attempting to adjudicate conflict, rather than the statutes of the penitents of the Holy Spirit in attempting to reconcile the combatants. The statutes of the confraternity of Saint Henry required that the ad hoc committee formed to deal with confrontations be empowered explicitly to "arbitrate" between the conflicting parties. Whether the penitents of Saint Henry had any luck with this approach cannot be said.

Yet in framing the statutes of the penitents of Saint Henry, Belsunce was not concerned with reforming confraternal practice by making the procedure for conflict resolution more efficient. He attributed the problem of men floating from chapel to chapel to a lack of commitment on the part of these itinerants, not just to specific associations, but to the devout life such associations presumably promoted. The solution he proposed was that evidence of commitment be provided before actual enrollment be allowed. His Jesuit-inspired five-month novitiate weeded out all but those most determined to participate. The statutes of the penitents of Saint Henry display an awareness of the many ways in which conflicts could occur and escalate. Pragmatically these statutes introduced procedures that, if followed, would limit the opportunities for misunderstandings to develop among confreres. But in these statutes, as well as in those of reformed confraternities, there seems to have been an unspoken assumption that members of a certain caliber would not carry disagreements to a point where expulsions would be necessary. For that reason framers of the statutes for both types of confraternities felt confident that the organization could intervene between disputants. The assumption had been proven false in the case of reformed confraternities. Its validity in the case of the confraternity of Saint Henry is unknown.

NOTES

1. On this point see A. E. Barnes, "Cliques and Participation in a Pre-Modern French Voluntary Association: The Pénitents

Bourras of Marseille in the Eighteenth Century," *Journal of Interdisciplinary History* 19 (Summer 1988): 25–53.

2. *Lazare de Cordier,* bk. 1, chap. 8.

3. If one of the members of the Banque was absent, the prior commandeered another confrere to take his place. If two or four banquiers were absent, the prior and sub-prior each had the right to select half of their replacements. If three banquiers were absent, the prior selected two and the sub-prior one; if five banquiers were absent, the prior selected three and the sub-prior selected two. For any number beyond five the prior selected two-thirds the number, and the sub-prior selected one-third.

4. This description of the election procedure of the penitents of Saint Anthony is taken from their statutes, SPSA, arts. 40–41; the account of the election written in their register of deliberations for 1673, from DSA, ff. 201–204.

5. For comparison see SPHS, art. "La façon comme l'on doibt eslire le Prieur et Recteurs"; SPSL-1773, art. 14.

6. On election day violence see *Lazare de Cordier,* bk. 1, chap. 5.

7. This description of the election procedure for the pénitents Bourras is taken from their statutes, SPB, chap. 3, passim, and from Jullien, 25–26.

8. DC-B, f. 80.

9. Lucien Fontanier, *Notes sur les pénitents rouges de Ste Croix,* Collection Fontanier 24F-105.

10. See chapter 5 below.

11. SPSH-1717, art., "Des Elections."

12. Though it should be pointed out that by the early eighteenth century the penitents of the Holy Cross had abandoned the secret ballot. See *Livre de la Sainte Croix,* Bibliothèque Municipale de Marseille, manuscript 1192.

13. *Livre de Saint Lazare,* 1189, ff. 247–48.

14. DSA, f. 258.

15. SPSH-1731, chap. 4, art. 6.

16. SPHS, art., "La façon comme l'on doibt eslire le Prieur et Recteurs."

17. Jullien, 26–27.

18. DC-B, f. 80.

19. SPSH–1731, chap. 4, art. 7.

20. Based primarily on the enrollment procedures described in SPSA, arts. 11–15; SPSL-1773, art. 13; SPHS, art. "Pour les novices et leurs conditions quant seront receuz."

21. SPB, chap. 1, art. 3.

22. This description is drawn from Jullien, chap. 4, passim.

23. *Lazare de Cordier,* bk. 1, chap. 5.

24. SPSH–1717, art. "La manière de recevoir les Prétendants"; SPSH-1731, chap. 9, passim.

25. SPSL-1611, art. 8.

26. SPHS, art. "Que chacun des frères soit obéissant Prieur et Recteurs"; SPC-1739, art. 13; SPSA, art. 9; SPSH-1731, chap. 2, art. 4.

27. SPB, chap. 2, art. 15, SPC-1739, art. 1; SPSH-1731, chap. 3, art. 7.

28. SPHS, art., "La façon comme l'on doibt eslire le Prieur et Recteurs"; SPSL-1773, art. 8; SPC-1739, art. 13; SPSA, art. 9; SPSH-1731, chap. 2, art. 4.

29. SPSH-1717, Introduction; SPB, chap. 1, art. 6; SPHS-1731, chap. 1, art. 5.

30. SPB, chap. 2, art. 6, SPSH-1731, chap. 3, art. 11.

31. SPHS, art., "Combien de temp de ce confesseront"; SPSH-1731, chap. 3, art. 7; SPSA, art. 51; SPB, chap. 2, art. 15.

32. A. E. Barnes, "From Ritual to Meditative Piety: Devotional Change in French Penitential Confraternities from the 16th to the 18th Century," *Journal of Ritual Studies* 1/2 (1987): 1–26.

33. For the penitents of the Holy Spirit see SPHS, Introduction. For the pénitents Bourras, see SPB, chap. 2, arts. 9, 10, 14.

34. For the register of the pénitents Carmélins see note 40 below. For the penitents of the Holy Spirit see SPHS, commentary on the ninth commandment.

35. SPB, chap. 2, arts. 12, 15.

36. Guibert, 62.

37. Fontanier also mentions a case of a member with dual membership. See Fontanier, *Pénitents noirs,* 38–39.

38. SPSA, arts. 7, 11.

39. DSA, f. 93.

40. DC-B, f. 84.

41. Ibid., f. 72.

42. Ibid.

43. Jullien, *Chronique historique,* 68–69.

44. Note that Brunel then went on to help found the penitents of Saint Maur. On the Carmélins, see DC-B, f. 65.

45. Ronald Weissman, *Ritual Brotherhood in Renaissance Florence* (New York, 1982), chap. 4.

46. For example, the register of the pénitents Bourras reveals that on December 16, 1714 five men were expelled (four of whom were eventually readmitted). On May 2, 1787 a group of six members were expelled.

Chapter 5

A CASE STUDY IN ASSOCIATIVE LIFE: THE PÉNITENTS BOURRAS IN THE EIGHTEENTH CENTURY

INTRODUCTION

In 1829 Michel Marie Bresson, an enterprising member of the reestablished confraternity of pénitents Bourras, compiled a register of all the members of the confraternity, providing as much information as was available on the dates of their enrollment and the offices they held. The record of offices held by members entering during the confraternity's first 120 years of existence unfortunately is almost blank. Information from 1710 onward, however, appears fairly complete.[1]

Bresson's register offers insight into the ways confraternities satisfied their members' needs for self-expression. With a little imagination the series of dates noted after each individual's name can shed light on the associative experience the confraternity provided, and this knowledge in turn can help illuminate the experience in other companies.

Two arguments were advanced in preceding chapters: first, that the growing financial dependency of confraternities on the wealth of their members limited access to the office of prior (rector) only to those affluent enough to pay for it and permitted the powers of the office to grow at the expense of the governing council; second, that groups of confreres banded together into cliques, and that over the centuries these cliques came to dominate chapel life. It would be helpful to know how these developments affected the dynamics of internal government. What was the relation between cliques and growth in the power of the office of prior? What was the relation between cliques and governing councils? Did informal advisory groups within cliques replace formal advisory institutions such as the Banque? As we have seen, councils lost the initiative in determining the agenda of concerns in a given year. Still, to the degree they reflected the opinion of members outside the dominant clique, governing councils retained some importance in decision-making. And while members outside the dominant clique may have acknowledged the prior's right to advocate a certain policy, acknowledgment was no guarantee of compliance. In fact, too much negative reaction to an initiative invited opposing cliques to spread dissension. Voluntary organizations, even those under autocratic governance, require some measure of consensus among members in order to function. Knowledge of the mechanisms through which consensus was obtained helps to explain both the evolution of confraternities from egalitarian to autocratic organizations and the willingness of ordinary members to acquiesce in the evolution.

A second set of questions is motivated by Agulhon's analysis of the relationship between social status outside, and political status within, confraternities. In investigating the confraternity of pénitents blancs of Brignoles in 1775, he found that the officer list perfectly mirrored the social hierarchy outside the confraternity; the rector was a royal official, the vice-rector was a member of the local bourgeoisie, the first master of ceremonies was a clerk of the sénéchaussée, and so on, down to the sacristan who was a simple cloth worker.[2] He went on to conclude that:

> Le sense hiérarchique est partout, comme on voit: non seulement dans la répartition des fonctions entre les classes mais encore dans la répartition des rangs à l'intérieur de chaque fonction lorsqu'elle est collégiale. On pourrait multiplier ces exemples; à peu près partout au XVIIe et dans le plus grande partie du XVIIIe siècle, premier et deuxième recteurs sont respectivement noble et bourgeois ou bourgeois et négociant, selon l'importance de la ville, conformément à un principe hiérarchique calqué sur celui des chaperons consulaires; le trésorier est à peu près toujours un homme du commerce, dont on utilise la compétence. Les ouvriers sont prépondérants dans les tâches matérielles de sacristains ou de porteurs de corps. . . .[3]

In Marseille personal affluence had a greater influence on political achievement within confraternities than did external social status. And tasks were not portioned out according to place in the external social hierarchy. Few laborers, for example, could afford the cost associated with serving as sacristan. Still, in a hierarchical society external social status had to play a positive role in the bid of some candidates for positions of honor and prestige—but in what ways? There is some, but not a lot of, information on the social positions of the membership of the pénitents Bourras. Fortunately, most of it is on men who either occupied or reached the highest levels of society. Using Bresson's register, it is possible to determine what may be described as these *célébrités'* careers as officers and to advance some tentative answers to the question of how external status influenced internal authority.

In the earlier discussion of the social composition of the penitents of Notre Dame de Pitié, it was established that large numbers of men from a single *métier* or *corporation* often joined a confraternity en masse.[4] One might conclude that cliques developed previous to entry into an association. Indeed, as that example suggests, the potential for control of a confraternity's organizational life may have been the prime motivation for preexisting cliques to enroll. The more exclusive enrollment procedures followed by reformed confraternities may have prompted a different dynamic.

The confraternity of pénitents Bourras was also ruled by cliques. It would be unwise to discount the possibility that these cliques reflected extra-confraternal bonds, especially in light of the continued presence over the centuries of members of the same families. But the irregularity of, the spacing between, and the small annual number of new enrollments all argue against this factor. The American social psychologist Muzafer Sherif once argued an alternative explanation of how and why cliques are formed, one that puts greater emphasis on shared experiences as the source of group bonds. Using the data in Bresson's register, it is possible to test the applicability of Sherif's theory to the social dynamics occurring in the confraternity.

Information on only approximately a third of the men listed in the register can be used with confidence.[5] This still provides a sampling of 225 men. Based on the official lives of these men, the next section will identify and analyze the hierarchy of offices and suggest some patterns in the ways in which they fit together to form careers. The section after that takes up the question of cliques, how they were formed and operated and the ways in which they aided and obstructed internal governance. The concluding section uses these findings to consider the social dimension of piety in all confraternities.

Participation, Status, and Achievement

Basic Levels of Participation

The pénitents Bourras were a small confraternity, limited by their original statutes of 1591 to seventy-two members, in honor of the seventy-two disciples of Christ. By the eighteenth century the confraternity was circumventing the regulation by making a distinction between dues-paying and non-dues-paying members (usually ecclesiastics) and by counting only those who paid dues as full members. Ten-year samplings of membership lists from 1743 to 1791 reveal an average membership of seventy-five. The confraternity had thirty-one official positions. This means that at any given time approximately forty percent of the membership should have been in office.

The number of new members admitted from year to year fluctuated wildly. Sometimes the confraternity went years without admitting any new members; other times they accepted as many as twelve. The average number of men admitted during a year for the period 1691–1792 was four. This same data tells us that members could expect, on the average, to spend twenty-one years in the confraternity. This average may be deceptively low. The pénitents Bourras, like other confraternities, may have been guilty of admitting men on their death beds in order to gain the revenues from burial fees. Over the period 1591–1792, approximately fifty-five percent of the members were in the confraternity for twenty-five years or more, seventeen percent for fifty or more. Its statutes prohibited the confraternity from accepting any new member under the age of eighteen. Again like other confraternities, however, they may have followed a policy of admitting the sons of members at an earlier age. Given that the majority of members remained in the confraternity for more than twenty-five years, it seems safe to assume that most members joined while in their late teens or early twenties.

The confraternity's small size, the long duration of member-ships, and its large official structure all help to explain the high amount of member participation. Figure 5A presents information on the number of posts assumed by the 225 men who entered the confraternity between 1711 and 1779. It indicates that over this period more than ninety percent of the members served in at least one office. Since most of those who did not serve in office were ecclesiastics, essentially every eligible member performed some task at least once. More impressive is the fact that almost half the membership served in six or more offices, while just about one-quarter served in eleven or more. The pénitents Bourras de-manded a high level of participation from their members. But given that any individual who sought to join a penitent confrater-nity had at least twelve other confraternities from which to choose, we can conclude that this obligation was part of their attraction. Men joined the pénitents Bourras because the idea of a participa-tory religious experience was attractive to them. As much as these figures reveal the willingness of the members of the confraternity to perform the tasks necessary for the maintenance of their associa-tion, they also indicate the potential of the confraternity for satisfy-ing its members' desire to serve.

Figure 5A: Levels of Participation in the Pénitents Bourras, 1711–1779 (Percentage of Members Serving in a Given Number of Offices)

Members serving in no office	8%
Members serving in at least one office	16%
Members serving in 2–5 offices	28%
Members serving in 6–10 offices	26%
Members serving in more than 10 offices	22%
Total	100%

Hierarchy and Oligarchy

Only the rector and vice-rector of the pénitents Bourras was elected by popular choice, all others being chosen by the incoming rector with the approval of first the retiring council and then the assembled confreres. Bresson's register lists thirteen offices of interest to us. The relevant information concerning these offices for the years 1711–79 has been summarized in figure 5B. Combined with the discussion in chapter 3, the last three columns in Table 5B can help establish what may be labeled the *latent* hierarchy of offices, that is, the hierarchy of offices that held the most status and wielded the most power. Two assumptions were made. First that the *exclusivity* of an office—that is, the degree to which access to it was limited—was a sign of its power and status. Second that *length of attainment*—that is, the average amount of time from enrollment to first occupancy—would likewise give an indication of an office's importance.

At the bottom of the hierarchy were the offices of pall-bearer, cenaire, mandataire, and sacristan. Seventy-eight percent of the membership served at least once as pall-bearer, and invariably this was the first office served in by a new member. This would argue for the office being something of an initiation test. A small company, the Bourras ordinarily did not have many funerals annually. But the company also buried criminals executed by the local authorities, and the pall-bearers were responsible for transporting the body from the execution site to the chapel as well as from the chapel to the burial site. Whether the confraternity owned some type of wagon to carry the caskets is not known, though this seems likely. Either way this remained a backbreaking task for only four men.

Next came the office of mandataire, another physically taxing task, requiring the individual to travel across town between twelve midnight and two in the morning each Saturday night to waken members for 3:00 a.m. services. As noted earlier, mandataires were allowed to skip services in order to rest after they had completed their rounds.

While the offices of cenaire and sacristan both required physical effort, they also required some affluence. Not only were the

Figure 5B: List of Offices and the Number of Members of the Pénitents Bourras Who Occupied Them, 1711–1779

T=225

Office	Abbreviation	Number elected at one time	Total Number Who Occupied Office	% of Total Membership	Avg. Years from Enrollment to Attainment
Pall-bearer	Pall	4	175	78%	2.4
Mandataire	Mand	2	137	61%	4.1
Cenaire	Cen	2	131	53%	5.4
Sacristan	Sac	2	135	60%	5.3
Cross-Bearer	Cr-B	1	66	29%	7
Secretary	Sec	1	63	28%	7.5
Treasurer of the Mercy	Tr-M	1	61	27%	12
Chorist	Chor	2	76	34%	11.1
Regent	Reg	4	107	48%	10.6
Vice-Rector	V-Rt	1	69	31%	11.3
Treasurer of the Chapel	Tr-C	1	43	19%	13.6
Porter	Port	1	43	19%	19.8
Rector	Rt	1	38	17%	20.8

cenaires expected to decorate the chapel for the services on Holy Thursday, they also were expected to pay for the decorations. Likewise the sacristans were responsible for the cost incurred in keeping the chapel clean and ready for services during their year in office. The fact that sixty percent of the membership served in both these offices is a good example of how a confraternity could spread the cost associated with maintaining the association throughout the membership. It is also an indication of the relative affluence of the members of the pénitents Bourras. Companies such as the penitents of Saint Lazarus, with large numbers of paupers on their rolls, could not follow such a practice.

The offices of sacristan, mandataire, and cenaire were rarely served in more than once. On the other hand, because the office required four men, service as pall-bearer was repeated by many members later in their careers. None of the four posts possessed much status; they were necessary tasks that had to be done. As will be demonstrated below, however, performance of them was an important sign of commitment. They will be labeled *minor* offices, hereafter, to distinguish them from *major* offices whose occupancy carried some connotations of prestige.

The lowest of the major offices were treasurer of the mercy, secretary, and cross-bearer. The tasks performed in these offices were more specialized than those performed in the minor offices. The sole task of the cross-bearer was to carry in procession the large wooden cross of the confraternity. Cross-bearers probably were selected for their physical strength and their conscientiousness, since the cross would have to be carried perfectly upright for long periods of time. Many confraternities simply elected the same men repeatedly to the position of secretary. The fact that so many members of the Bourras occupied this office perhaps is an indication that the membership of the confraternity was uniformly literate. The Bourras maintained a trunk (*boite*) for voluntary contributions toward the expenses incurred in the charitable enterprise of burying condemned prisoners. Thus trunk was known as the "mercy" (*miséricorde*) and the individual elected to oversee it was the "treasurer of the mercy." In the later eighteenth century the treasurer of the mercy maintained an account book separate from that for the chapel. Receipts and expenses rarely totaled more than twenty-five livres. It may be that selection for this position served as preliminary training for the office of treasurer of the chapel. But fewer than half (forty-six percent) of those elected to the former were eventually selected to the latter.

The office of chorist in the pénitents Bourras combined all the tasks involved in the offices of chorist, master of ceremonies, and master of novices in larger associations.[6] Given the elaborate liturgy of the confraternity and its book-size list of statutes, these tasks must have been fairly complex. The length of time from enrollment to selection can be determined for forty-five of the pairs who occupied the office over the course of the eighteenth century. The average difference between the two was fourteen years. In other words, in any given year one of the chorists had, on the average, fourteen more years experience in the confraternity and its ways than the other. It appears, then, that the confraternity established an apprentice system for the office of chorist in which an older member introduced a newer member to the necessary knowledge and skills associated with the position. The office for a member elected for the first time was probably viewed both as a training exercise and as a test of his capacity to perform a difficult set of tasks. Subsequent election reflected his knowledge of confraternal customs and his ability to handle the various decisions involved in maintaining the confraternity's liturgical life.

The office of vice-rector (sub-prior), theoretically the second most important office in the confraternity, was depicted earlier as possessing little real power or status.[7] Confirming evidence is provided by the confraternity of pénitents Bourras, where in terms of exclusivity and length of attainment, the office occupied a position in the middle of the hierarchy. Thirty-three of the thirty-eight men who were elected rector, first served as vice-rector. It took these men an average of 19.4 years from enrollment to be elected rector. For the five elected rectors who did not serve first as vice-rector, election to the higher post took an average of thirty years. Clearly the office of vice-rector was a rung on the ladder to the rectorship. Its primary function was to provide an apprenticeship to the duties and tasks of the higher office.

It took an average of only twelve years to be appointed to a first term as regent, or member of the governing council. This and the fact that at any given time fourteen percent of the membership held the position would argue for the office having only moderate status. That this fourteen percent was always drawn from the same pool of confreres provides a clue to the real status of the office. In fact, the office was one of the most important in the confraternity. Again, like the office of chorist, the significance of election to it a first time was different from election to it a second and third. The first time was usually both an introduction to political life in the confraternity and an opportunity for older members to evaluate a younger member's potential for leadership. Repeated selection signaled real influence.

At the top of the confraternity were the offices of rector, treasurer of the chapel, and porter. These offices were also the most exclusive and all three required an average of two decades of participation to achieve. Different from other confraternities, the pénitents Bourras expected their porter to serve as chapel police-man, door monitor, and sergeant-at-arms.[8] This effect was not achieved through any statuted authority; rather, the confraternity selected only senior men to the position, men whose personal authority was sufficient to maintain decorum.

If we change the focus of our discussion and concentrate specifically on selection for these high-level offices, some interesting patterns emerge. Let us divide the 225 men in our sample according to the highest elected office they each attained. This produces three categories: those who were elected rector, those who were elected vice-rector but not rector, and those who were never elected to either office. Next let us tabulate the number of times men in each of these groups were selected for the positions of chorist, regent, treasurer of the chapel, and porter. The resulting tabulations are displayed as percentages in the graph in figure 5C. Because these four offices were monopolized by the same men, repeated occupancy, up to the fourth time in the case of the office of regent, has been included in the figure. The graph illustrates two important points: positions at the top of the confraternity were controlled by a small group of individuals, and most of the members of this small group had at some point been chosen as rector. Read from top to bottom, each column equals 100 percent. Read

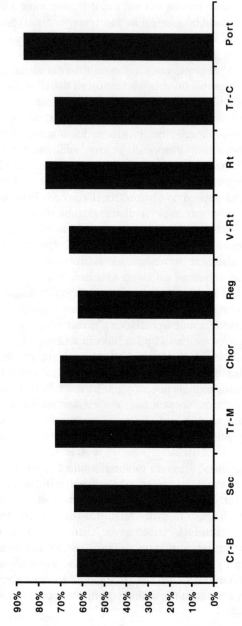

Figure 5C: Percentage of the Various Major Offices Occupied by Members of Pénitents Bourras Who Had Previously Served in All Four Minor Offices

from left to right for each office, it is possible to see former rectors asserting control. Thus, while they represented only forty percent of the members selected to the office of chorist once, they represented seventy percent of those selected twice, and 100 percent of those appointed to a third term. Likewise they formed the bulk of the members appointed to the office of regent for a third and fourth term, the offices of treasurer of the chapel and porter for a second term.

Many members of the oligarchy were appointed to the key positions of treasurer of the chapel and porter before election to the rectorship. There was nothing hard-and-fast about the relationship between election as rector and entry into the oligarchy. Is it surprising that some conclusions about who was and was not "leadership material" were formed, at least by those at the top, before the certification granted by election as rector? Individuals so perceived were chosen for positions of authority before election to the rectorship, sometimes even before election to the vice-rectorship. This would also help to explain the few individuals who never served in either rectorship and yet (as indicated in figure 5C) came to occupy positions of authority. The latter's elevation suggests that two differing criteria for achievement were in operation. Men could gain position by being popular, but also by being viewed by those at the top as competent to perform important tasks. These two criteria were not necessarily at odds. Successful performance of a difficult task might bring with it, if not popularity, at least the type of respect that could be translated into the votes necessary for election to one of the rectorships. Popular individuals who proved incompetent at important tasks probably were seldom appointed to them again.

In some confraternities the term of office for the priorship actually grew into three-year tour in the decision-making organs of government. Election as rector of the Bourras granted even greater tenure. A rector emeritus was almost always in office, serving either in a position of authority or on the governing council. Thus election as rector was only secondarily important for the specific temporary privileges it granted. Its primary importance was the entry it provided into the inner circle of members who actually ran the association.

The Path to the Top

Service in the offices of pall-bearer, cenaire, mandataire, and sacristan formed a necessary preamble to service in higher posts. To establish the importance of service in minor office for future achievement, it is again worth examining the data on the official careers of our sampling. We need to ask what impact performance of all four minor tasks involved with maintaining the confraternity had on later selection for each of the nine more prestigious positions. Eighty-five men began their careers by service in all four minor offices. If we look at each of the major offices to determine the extent each rewarded our eighty-five hard workers, we see, as figure 5C demonstrates, that none of the nine was beyond their grasp. These eighty-five men provided the majority not only of those appointed to all major positions, but of those eventually elected vice-rector and rector as well.

The importance of early conscientiousness emerges even more clearly when the careers of those never elected rector or vice-rector are considered. Let us reconsider the data presented in figure 5C on occupancy of the four key offices of chorist, regent, treasurer of the chapel, and porter from the perspective of men who never held an elective post. The resulting tabulations are presented in figure 5D. As it indicates, when a member of the oligarchy was not available, normal practice was to ask an individual who had proved his commitment through performance of all the minor chores to fill a vacant position. The path to appointment to all the higher offices ran through service in all the minor ones.

The exploitation of the offices of regent and vice-rector as "training and evaluation" exercises for future leaders also can be demonstrated. Working strictly with the data on those men who served in all four minor offices, thirty-seven of them went on to

Figure 5D: Percentage of the Various Major Offices Occupied by Members of Pénitents Bourras Who Had Previously Served in All Four Minor Offices

Cr-B	Sec	Tr-M	Chor	Reg	V-Rt	Rt	Tr-C	Port
62%	64%	72%	70%	62%	66%	76%	72%	86%

serve both as regent and as vice-rector. The sequence in which men served in the two positions does not appear to have had an effect on election to the rectorship. Two-thirds of those who served as regent and then vice-rector went on to be elected, two-thirds of those who worked as vice-rector and then spent time on the governing council went on to be elected rector. It took members in both categories an average of just over twenty years to achieve the feat.

Men were appointed to the council, but elected to the vice-rectorship. I would argue that these represented differing types of certification, and that both were significant for further advance. Appointment to the council was an indication that those at the top perceived an individual to be responsible and competent to make decisions concerning the welfare of the confraternity. Election as vice-rector indicated that an individual was popularly perceived in the same light. Individuals who fulfilled expectations in both these positions had a comparatively greater chance to be elected rector, as the fact that men who followed this route accounted for sixty-three percent of those elected rector suggests.

As to whether it was possible to determine, based upon earlier achievements, who would capture the brass ring of the rectorship, the answer must be no. Election to the rectorship after election to the vice-rectorship appears to have been a function of personal appeal and luck. The more personal appeal an individual possessed, the more often his name would appear annually among the top vote-getters. But no matter how many times he was nominated, it was luck (or the Holy Spirit) that determined his success. As for the men who climbed as far as the vice-rectorship but no further, the evidence suggests that their later years in the confraternity were characterized by gradual marginalization from the center, as newer generations of members fought for the prize.[9]

External Status and Achievement

Bresson was not the only nineteenth-century member of the confraternity who sought to memorialize the past. In 1858 frère Louis de Gonzague Jullien compiled a "necrologie," a listing by month-of-death of illustrious past members. In 1897 Lucien Fontanier, the final archivist of the confraternity, used Jullien's list and his own researches to amend Bresson's register, listing the "qualité" of as many members as possible. These lists are neither exhaustive nor definitive. But they do permit us to follow the internal careers of several members of the confraternity who had some renown in wider society.[10] Jullien divides his listing into three categories: "prêtres," "gentilhommes," and "célébrités." "Prêtres" signified any member of the 1st Estate, whether ordained or not, and "gentilhommes," any member of the 2nd Estate. What, besides bourgeois status, qualified an individual as a "célébrité" is not always given. Included under this listing were men like Elzear Lion and Jean Isouard, both former mayors of Marseille, Pierre Michel Beaujard, editor of the *Journal de Provence,* and Jean Coustan, "jurisconsulte." The reasons why others were included in the list is unclear. One such individual was François Dominique Grimaud, interesting because while he was included, his father, Pierre, one of the most powerful men in the confraternity during the eighteenth century, was not. This suggests that only individuals who had achieved some type of prestige, measured by the ethos of the age, were included in this group.

About churchmen there is not much to report;[11] therefore, the following discussion will concentrate on nobles and célébrités. Fontanier's additions to Jullien's list of nobles will be used; but because it is not clear that all the members of the 3rd Estate for whom Fontanier discovered either the occupation or profession were célébrités, only those men noted in Jullien's necrology will be considered.

Sixteen men listed by either Jullien or Fontanier as "noble" or "gentilhomme" entered the confraternity over the period 1711–79. Four of them went on to serve as vice-rector, two as rector. One of these who went on to serve as rector, Antoine Paul André de Candolle, deserves special note. De Candolle's rise in the confraternity can only be described as "meteoric." Joining in 1768, he spent the next year serving as cenaire and sacristan, the following as chorist, and the year after that as vice-rector. In 1772, four years after enrollment, he was elected to his first term as rector. Even though de Candolle was elected rector again twice, the only other office he ever served in was chorist. The other nobleman elected rector, Simon de Cauvin, followed a more traditional route, serving in all four minor offices, then as regent and as vice-rector, before being elected rector twenty years after enrollment. Unlike de Candolle, after his election he was constantly in office, serving on the council four more times, as treasurer two times, and as rector once again. If regular appointment to one of the higher offices is a valid indication of true "insider" status, then it can be argued that de Candolle, unlike de Cauvin, was an outsider. Probably older, obviously affluent, he quickly laid claim to the rectorship. But it is questionable whether he exerted any great influence on the direction of the confraternity during his three terms in office.

Twelve men from Jullien's list of célébrités joined the confraternity during the same period. Seven of them went through all four minor offices. Six of these were elected vice-rector, and three of the six were elected rector, all three serving more than once as rector. Two of these men were very active on the council, serving four times each. The other, François Grimaud, served in the offices of chorist and porter.

In contrasting the célébrités with the noblemen, it is interesting to observe that while patterns of service in minor offices are similar, the former were more active later in their careers. Few of the nobles went on to hold offices such as regent, treasurer, porter, or chorist, while the majority of the célébrités did. Why noble members proved so uninterested in playing a role in the affairs of the confraternity is a good question for which there is no answer.

External status clearly had some influence on achievement within the confraternity, but with one exception, this influence was a factor only after other requirements were met. Except for de Candolle, none of these notables made it to the rectorship without first paying the same dues as other members who sought high office. Once there, however, most became prominent members of the oligarchy. In the confraternity of pénitents Bourras there was no automatic correlation of external position with internal status.

The data on the Bourras suggest that confraternal government functioned more as a ladder that men climbed to claim a place in the oligarchy, rather than as as a mirror of external realities. Of the pool of members who had some external standing, only those who fulfilled the confraternity's expectations of leaders went on to be elected rector.

Robert Michel once postulated what he called the "iron law of oligarchy," which states that every organization eventually divides into a minority of directors and a majority of the directed. This was so for the pénitents Bourras. Was it also the case for other confraternities? Probably so, though the viciousness of election-day fighting suggests that in many of them the system of determining membership in the oligarchy was not as well developed. In 1712 Bishop Belsunce issued an ordinance, directed toward all confraternities, but probably with penitent confraternities specifically in mind, requiring them to hold annual elections for priors and other major officers.[12] The Bourras were blessed with so many affluent members that they could make their highest offices the prizes in a competition that demanded committed participation. Many confraternities could not do this. Their highest offices were available to anyone who could afford them, with the result that they were open to monopoly by men with money and ambition.

It does appear that other confraternities reserved specific offices for the training and promotion of potential leaders. Such is the inference to be drawn from the requirement that aspirants to the rectorship of the penitents of the Holy Cross serve first as mandataires and sacristans.[13] This also seems the import of the statute of the penitents of Saint Lazarus, which removed the offices of sacristan and master of ceremonies from the list of those the prior-elect could select and left them available for popular election.[14] In that confraternity these two offices were the ones which explicitly required the outlay of some funds. They were the two in which aspirants to the priorship could demonstrate both their commitment to the confraternity and their financial wherewithal. Out of concern to prohibit one clique from controlling the confraternity for an extended period of time, it made sense to remove occupancy of these offices from the control of the prior-elect.

CLIQUES AND PARTICIPATION

Co-Service and the Formation of Cliques

Study of Bresson's register reveals an interesting phenomenon. Men who entered the confraternity in close proximity appeared to have later regularly served together in office. For example, Maurice

Bremond and Dennis Pin, both of whom joined the confraternity in 1740, served together in some official capacity during the years 1748–50, 1756–60, 1763–64. During the 1748 and for the 1756–60 and 1763–64 periods, they were joined by another 1740 enrollee, Simon de Cauvin. During the 1756–60 period they were joined by Elzear Lion, yet another. During the 1748–50, and 1756–60 periods they shared direction of the association with Jean Izouard, Louis Isnard, and Antoine Isnardin, all of whom joined in 1741.

Since one of the perquisites of the rector-elect was the right to choose most of the men who served with him during his term, the regularity with which men who entered together or near each other shared government cannot be a coincidence. Clearly some form of clique formation had occurred which later expressed itself in the predilection of clique members to select each other for service in office.

Each new enrollee in the Bourras had to experience a three-month probationary period as a "novice." Yet there is no evidence that the confraternity followed an official policy of fostering sub-group, that is, clique, identification among its newest members. And the case has already been made against the possibility that group co-service was the result of bonds formed outside the confraternity. If clique formation was occurring, it was probably the result of some latent internal process.

Theories of the American social psychologist Muzafer Sherif are helpful in exploring the nature of this latent process.[15] Based on a series of experiments conducted with young boys at a summer youth camp, Sherif came to the conclusion that ordinary activities that require some degree of cooperation have the potential to bond individuals together as groups. Activities performed for what he called "superordinate goals," that is, goals all recognized as valid and from which all derived some benefit, have the potential for social bonding even given intervening factors (such as previous group affiliation). In sum, shared experiences stimulate the formation of cliques.[16]

Penitent confraternities seated new members according to date of entry on the back benches of the chapel. These new enrollees performed all confraternal activities in proximity to one another. If one imagines the little things that would make life difficult for a

fledgling confrere—correctly donning his new robe, correctly reciting the liturgy at Sunday services, learning all the customs of the
chapel—it is easy to appreciate that he would have to depend on the
men closest to him in the chapel to complete these tasks successfully.
Likewise, the experiences that he would find most rewarding—the
sermons preached by the chaplain on Sunday mornings, participation in the footwashing ceremony on Maundy Thursday, participation in the public procession and installation of new officers—were
most immediately shared with his peers. Based on Sherif's theories I
sought to evaluate the hypothesis that shared experiences, which
stemmed from proximate entrance into the confraternity, generated
group consciousness among newer members.

To confirm the soundness of my hypothesis, there had to be a
positive general correlation between nearness of entry and inci-
dence of simultaneous service in office. Figure 5F displays my evaluation of the regularity with which two individuals shared office and
the results of my findings relevant here. In order to determine the
regularity of simultaneous service, I matched each individual's career against that of each other individual who joined the confraternity after him. The computer program was instructed to count as "1"
each instance in which two individuals were in office during the
same year. These instances were then tabulated and the mean was
computed for each pair according to their year of entry. In other
words, as figure 5E illustrates, the program was instructed to calcu-
late the average number of times pairs of individuals who entered
the confraternity during the same year later served in major office.
The program then calculated the average number of times pairs of
individuals who entered one year (then two years, three years, etc.)
apart served in office together. The results of the procedure suggest
that, indeed, proximity of entry did have an effect on later co-
service in office. Pairs formed by individuals who entered the
confraternity within two years, and who, as I will explain next, spent
some time in minor office together, later served together in major
office, on average, close to three times. Pairs formed by individuals
who entered further apart, and/or did not serve together in minor
office, served together on a less regular basis. Inside the confraternity of pénitents Bourras, the experiences shared by new members
had a latent potential for stimulating clique formation.

Figure 5E: Co-Service in Office Among Members of the Pénitents Bourras, 1711–1779, Based on Entry, Interval and Previous Co-Service in Minor Office

Criteria for Pairing	Pairs Who Did Not Co-Serve in Minor Office before Co-Serving in Major Office			Pairs Who Did Co-Serve in Minor Office before Co-Serving in Major Office			Total Number of Pairs Co-Serving in Major Office	
	N	%	Mean Number of Times	N	%	Mean Number of Times	N	%
Same Year Entry	82	63%	2.4	49	37%	3	131	100%
One-Year Interval	177	82%	2.4	39	18%	2.9	216	100%
Two-Year Interval	188	85%	2.3	33	15%	3.1	221	100%
Three-Year Interval	178	94%	2.6	11	6%	1.7	189	100%
Four-Year Interval	115	93%	2.4	5	7%	2.3	124	100%
Six-Year Interval	121	98%	2.2	2	2%	1	123	100%
Eight-Year Interval	133	98%	2.3	3	2%	2	136	100%
Ten-Year Interval	134	99%	2	1	1%	1	135	100%

Figure 5F: Co-Service in Minor Office as Determinant of Co-Service in Major Office among Members of the Pénitents Bourras, 1711–1779

Criteria for Pairing	Pairs Who Did Not Co-Serve in Minor Office			Pairs Who Did Co-Serve in Minor Office		
	Total Number of Pairs	Pairs Who Went on to Co-Serve in Major Office		Total Number of Pairs	Pairs Who Went on to Co-Serve in Major Office	
		N	% of Total		N	% of Total
Same Year Entry	322	82	26%	105	49	47%
One-Year Interval	621	177	29%	99	39	39%
Two-Year Interval	600	188	31%	49	33	67%

I next tried to determine more specifically which of the experiences shared during the earliest years caused cliques to form. Worth remembering is that the confraternity of pénitents Bourras was a rigorously devout religious association, one that demanded an above-normal amount of new members' time and attention. One possibility is that surviving the three-month novitiate and first years under scrutiny may have required sufficient cooperation among new confreres to stimulate group bonds. As seen above, the four minor offices were usually reserved for newer members. All these offices demanded cooperation and interdependence among their occupants. Thus the four pall-bearers elected yearly had to work together to fullfill their duties. Likewise the two sacristans had to cooperate to have all candles lit and the chapel prepared for Sunday morning services.

Another possibility is that it was the specific effect of service together in minor office that brought about clique formation. The need for cooperation among the occupants of minor offices, however, was something confraternity leaders would have recognized from their own experience. In all likelihood they would have selected individuals to these positions who gave evidence of success in getting along. Thus the selection for minor office of men who entered near each other may have been a tacit recognition on the part of the confraternity that clique formation had already occurred. This last possibility represents a combination of the two previous ones. The experiences shared by men who entered the confraternity at approximately the same time generated bonds of friendship. The experience of service together in minor office solidified these friendships into cliques.

Figure 5E summarizes the correlation of simultaneous service in minor office with group formation and subsequent simultaneous service in major office; the first had a definite, positive effect on the latter. Pairs formed by men entering the confraternity in the same year, but who did not take service together in minor office, were in major office during the same year an average of 2.4 times. Pairs who had served together in minor office were in major office during the same year an average of 3.0 times.

Figure 5F presents one last series of numbers to validate my argument. It has been demonstrated that co-service in minor office was the best predictor of later co-service in major office. Figure 5F indicates that the key determinant of co-service in minor office was proximity of entry. Service in minor office together usually took place only among men who joined the confraternity within two years of each other. To return to the discussion of the possible causes of the formation of cliques, I would suggest that shared experiences at the time of entry created only fairly weak group bonds. On this level the fledgling group was in competition with the confraternity as a whole. These group bonds, however, were strong enough to lead to co-service in minor office. In other words, confraternal leaders took notice of emerging friendships along the back rows of the chapel and assigned tasks to newer members according to these observations. This more specific experience reinforced existing bonds and stimulated the rise of cliques. Consequently, when group members entered the mainstream of confraternal life as holders of major office, they often sought out other members of their group to hold office with them.

The Nature of Clique Co-Service

It would appear that the socialization process instituted by the pénitents Bourras effectively neutralized the influence of external bonds on members' internal commitments. Based on the above research, I propose that, though not conscious of why, confraternal leaders recognized that assigning new members tasks that made them work together helped cement commitment to the confraternity. The confraternity did not get rid of cliques, it internalized their information. This internalization helps explain the confraternity's low rate of attrition—its cliques were uniquely tied to the organization.

In other associations, however, the option of moving to another confraternity functioned as a safety valve regulating clique conflict. The absence of this option in the confraternity of pénitents Bourras allowed conflict to become especially intense. The internalization of clique formation may also explain why over the course of the eighteenth century the confraternity purged so many former rectors and vice-rectors.[17]

The pertinent question may be not why they expelled so many, but given the dangers posed to the organization by clique conflict, why they expelled so few. Most of the co-service took place in the offices of regent and rector.[18] The group of men entering in 1740–41 is a good example of this. When Lion was elected rector in 1754, he chose Bremond and Isnard to serve on the governing council. When Isnard was elected in 1757, he returned the compliment, selecting Lion as well as Pin and de Cauvin to serve as regents. When de Cauvin became rector in 1760, he selected Bremond and Isnard to serve on the council. Thus, clique co-service had its greatest effect on the decision-making apparatus.

Organizational dynamics within the confraternity of pénitents Bourras promoted the rise of cliques with an intense loyalty to the confraternity as an association. But these cliques also competed for control of the decision-making apparatus of the confraternity, which, taken to its furthest extreme, might have destroyed the confraternity. Arguably, however, the innovation adopted by the confraternity to avoid this contingency was both its greatest organizational achievement and the true source of its comparative organizational success. Each year the incoming rector selected candidates for all empty spaces on the council. The term for each of these offices was three years. This meant that the rector was able to influence confraternal decision-making for at least three years and that the three-year term of the governing council allowed for the institutionalization of a type of power-sharing among cliques. An incoming rector could bring other members of his group into office with him to serve on the council, and once there, they could establish their own agenda. But there would always be other men on the council from other groups; one clique would have the initiative, but no one clique could dominate.

The story of the biggest internal conflict the confraternity experienced in the eighteenth century illustrates the centrality of the council to the vitality of the organization. In 1718 frère François Lieutard, rector for the year, upset over the low attendance at the monthly meeting of the governing council, called a special assembly of all confreres. Arguing that since the statutes required that all regents be present for the council's decisions to be valid, and that poor attendance made it impossible to get anything done, Lieutard moved that the rector be allowed to substitute other members for missing regents and to penalize with a fine of three hundred livres dissent from a decision reached by a meeting so constituted. These propositions were duly ratified by the members present.

The announcement of these decisions at the end of chapel services the following Sunday triggered a major protest led by frère Alexis Moulard, rector during the previous year and the probable cause for the absent regents. According to Moulard, Lieutard had gone beyond his statuted powers and thereby had sacrificed his right to the rectorship. Henceforth Moulard would only recognize the authority of the vice-rector, frère Jacques Coustan. Lieutard's challenge to Moulard was the announcement of a meeting of the governing council for the following Sunday. On that day Moulard and his followers caused such a tumult that the meeting was postponed until the following Sunday. That day only four regents appeared. Unfortunately for Lieutard, one of them was Moulard (who, as the previous rector, automatically received a seat on the governing council). When Lieutard attempted to select eight substitute regents, Moulard once again excited his followers to riot, this time shouting, "Down with the rector!"

The incident split the confraternity almost down the middle, thirty-four members following Moulard's lead in establishing a breakaway group with Coustan as rector. The ensuing conflict lasted over two years. Lieutard discovered some financial improprieties committed by Moulard during his term as rector and used this to disqualify him from his position on the governing council. Moulard for his part determined to take Lieutard before the Parlement of Provence, the highest regional court, for transgressing the confraternity's statutes. In 1721, just before the case was to be heard before the court, Moulard, concerned about the scandal being brought upon the confraternity, finally backed down and arranged a compromise with Lieutard. Each side agreed to forgive the other, and the confraternity was reconstituted. On the issue of replacements for absent regents at council meetings, the decision was made to appoint the members with the most seniority among those present to take their places.[19]

What makes the incident extraordinary is the fact that the right of rectors to select replacements for absent members of governing councils had been claimed by the leaders of Marseille's other penitent confraternities for more than fifty years.[20] By trying to keep the council free of the rector's control, the pénitents Bourras were seeking an avenue for participation for members not part of the prevailing clique. Here the governing council was a mechanism that allowed other cliques to have their say. As rector in 1717 Moulard could select at least two members of the council and thus have influence over decisions for three years. His decision to use this influence in order to neutralize the plans of his successor caused the conflict. His failure only serves as an illustration that the efforts of an ambitious man to maintain control could destroy neither the confraternity nor the commitment of the members to the kind of power sharing that occurred on the council.

The sociologist William Foote Whyte, in a discussion of the dynamics of organized activity, has made the point that "the individual is not a member of a single group within a larger structure. Rather, he typically interacts within a variety of settings within the organization."[21] In *Street Corner Society,* his classic study of social life among Italian immigrants in Boston's North End, Whyte analyzes the organizational processes in the Cornerville Social and Athletic Club, a voluntary association of approximately sixty members organized primarily for recreational activities. He describes organization within the club not so much as a hierarchy of individuals, but as a hierarchy of cliques, each with its leaders, lieutenants, and subordinates. Ideas moved up and down the ladder of the cliques, subordinates making input through lieutenants, lieutenants then conveying the information to the leaders. Politics on the club level occurred among clique leaders, each leader staking out a position, then manipulating his lines of influence to get support from his followers, and with luck, those of others.[22] In these terms, Moulard's efforts to prohibit Lieutard's selection of replacements for absent regents can be understood as the result of a fear that Lieutard would replace Moulard's absent lieutenants with his own followers. When these efforts failed, it was Coustan, presumably an up-and-coming lieutenant in a clique other than Lieutard's, that enabled Moulard to lead away half the membership. And throughout the conflict both Lieutard and Moulard used various followers to make the case for the illegitimacy of his opponent's claims.

Moulard's dependence on Coustan suggests that co-service

between cliques members is more evident between leaders and lieutenants than between individuals of equal stature. Only the best and the brightest of affluent confreres made it to the top rungs of confraternal government. And as the examples from the entry years 1740–41 illustrated above, the clique members that a newly elected rector brought with him to co-serve on the council were those who could exert influence in their own right. The leader was thus provided with a means of generating popular support for his ideas. Following this line of reasoning, cliques provided the mechanism through which oligarchies ruled.

In the pénitents Bourras cliques also provided the vehicle through which entry into the oligarchy was gained. Candidates for the rectorship made it to the lottery stage through nomination by their clique. Presumably individual cliques were not large enough to guarantee nomination. The penitents of the Holy Cross, it will be remembered, attempted to enforce a rule that at least twelve votes be required for entry into the lottery stage—a requirement that makes sense only as a stratagem aimed at reducing the possibility of one clique consistently presenting the same candidate. The penitents of the Holy Cross saw the nomination process as an opportunity for coalition building. They wanted to put pressure on candidates to develop an appeal that went beyond their own circle. Election to the rectorship was to present something more than the triumph of a clique, it was to signal recognition by others that an individual had something to give not simply to his group but to an entire organization. In the confraternity of pénitents Bourras former rectors served primarily in the offices of treasurer of the chapel, porter, member of the Banque, and chorist. By appointing these men to these offices, the confraternity was attempting to designate certain offices as beyond clique partisanship, though as the Lieutard/Moulard incident indicates, the attempt was not always successful.

In Whyte's Cornerville, cliques provided a means for individuals of low status to communicate with individuals of high status, that is, for subordinates to communicate with members of the oligarchy. This was also the case with the pénitents Bourras. The means used by Lieutard to disqualify Moulard from the governing council was a complaint by an ordinary member, Pierre Giraud, who protested that he had given Moulard during his rectorship several candles to be used in the burial procession of Giraud's father, Claude. Moulard had evidently used the candles for some other purpose. Through Lieutard, Giraud was able to state his complaint before the entire confraternity.

The pénitents Bourras were unique in the amount of power they gave to their governing council. Yet by granting the council so much power, and secondarily, by allowing it to become the prime locus of interaction between cliques, they created a situation where cliques had to work together in order for the confraternity to survive. Thus the greater good of the confraternity became for the cliques what Sherif would call the superordinate goal that broke down barriers between groups and welded them into one. Moulard took his vendetta with Lieutard so far, but stopped short of the point where it would destroy the confraternity.

This argument can be taken one stage further. Agulhon has coined the term "sociabilité méridionale," to denote the behavioral tendency of Mediterranean males to express their social and religious selves within the context of fraternal organizations.[23] My research on the confraternities of Marseille suggests the existence of such behavioral tendencies on the sub-organizational level of informal groups or cliques. Sociabilité méridionale can also be described as a tendency of Mediterranean males to seek the pleasures of participation in associative organizations within the context of smaller groups. As demonstrated here, it was also through such smaller groups that they sought to affect decision-making within the larger organization.

It seems safe to conclude that the relationship between cliques and oligarchy that existed in the pénitents Bourras also existed in the other reformed confraternities. The procedure of direct election followed by unreformed confraternities, however, allowed cliques easier access to the reins of power. How they used or abused this power is hard to say. But surely contemporaries were aware of the ease with which a penitent confraternity could be directed toward a group's devotional agenda. This was an essential part of the confraternities' appeal.

THE SOCIAL DIMENSION OF PIETY

During an ordinary week a conscientious member of the péni-tents Bourras spent an average of three to five hours involved in devotional activities at the chapel. During Holy Week and other high points of the liturgical year this amount of time would be several times greater. A member's involvement, however, was not subsumed in devotional acts. Other hours would be spent at the chapel, perhaps at his home, or more probably at his office or shop, discussing the latest decisions of the rector, handicapping the next election, or presenting his ideas about possible devotional events. It would be wrong to distinguish these latter concerns as distinct from explicitly devotional ones. To paraphrase William Christian, Jr., only "religion as prescribed" is transcendent; "reli-gion as practiced" is mundane.[24] For members of the confraternity, the realization of organizational agendas was an integral part of the devotional experience. It was the Holy Spirit, after all, that de-cided which clique would achieve its plans for the coming year.

The intrinsic importance of the social dimension of the piety of penitent confraternities emerges most clearly in the complaints directed toward them by Monseigneur Belsunce in 1751. Belsunce, in line with the reforms mandated at the Council of Trent, had attempted to break down the autonomy of the confraternities and to redirect the religious energies of their members toward the parishes. How had the members of confraternities repaid his ef-forts? In Belsunce's words by "no longer performing their Easter observances and contentedly passing many years without fulfilling this obligation."[25] In other words, from the church's viewpoint, members of confraternities had ceased to fulfill even the nominal obligations of being Christians.

Belsunce's complaint highlights the significance for confreres of the organizational context of devotional life. It was the potential for fusing their social and devotional worlds that drew men to chapels. Once that potential was removed, the devotions them-selves were not sufficiently attractive to motivate men to perform them. It is in this sense that chapels of penitents can be likened to congregations of Protestant sectaries for, like such congregations, the essential dialectic within chapels contrasted a social world whose raison d'être was religious, with a religious world that existed only as a consequence of social participation. To put it more simply, to members of confraternities the act of participation was an ongoing validation of faith.

This point needs to be emphasized because otherwise the attraction of confraternities to pious laymen will continue to elude the historian's scrutiny. Henry III once characterized confraternities of penitents as "escolles de piété." But the piety these schools taught had very little in common with the piety appreciated by the Counter-Reformation clergy. Rather, it harkened back to a faith promoted in an earlier time by a different set of clerics. And it gave rise to a different definition of a good work, a definition which rewarded with the greatest amount of grace the act of loving one's neighbor as one's brother. This is not to suggest that the piety of penitent brotherhoods was medieval. And it is pushing the boundaries of the term "anachronistic" to use it to label a faith that continued to be vital for centuries. The piety of French penitent confraternities is best described as having evolved from an older set of devotional premises than those popular in the Erasmian world of sixteenth-century Catholicism. It should be remembered that penitent confraternities attracted a tremendous amount of attention from the Catholic avant-garde during the Wars of Religion. The promotion of penitent devotions during the civil war era brought confraternal piety in alignment with the spiritual sensibilities of the age, without demanding that it assimilate the values which gave rise to these sensibilities. From the civil war era onward, confraternal piety grew at its own pace, pushed forward primarily by the social and cultural parameters of their participants' organizational interaction.

The piety that eighteenth-century bishops sought to suppress was just as modern as that offered at the parish church, but with the distinction that it continued to sanctify the act of laymen (as confreres) participating in a collective pursuit of salvation. This effort, it bears repeating, involved realizing the ideal of brotherhood. And instead of condemning contemporary laymen for translating this ideal into the promotion of the organizational and devotional agendas of their particular cliques, we who live in a different era, with different spiritual values, ought to appreciate the nature and powers of the spiritual values of an earlier form of Christianity.

NOTES

1. *Registre Matricule de la Confrairie des Pénitents du Bon Jésus dit Bourras de Marseille;* see note 13, chapter 2.

2. Agulhon, 153.

3. Ibid., 154.

4. See chapter 2 above.

5. Because the data, especially on early activity, is inconsistent for the period before 1710, analysis will begin with the men who entered in 1711. Likewise, because the dissolution of the confraternity in 1792 had a negative impact on the behavior of men who entered during the last years of the century, the analysis will end with the men entering in 1779.

6. For a description of these offices see chapter 3 above.

7. See chapter 3 above.

8. For comparison see chapter 3 above.

9. Taking as an indication of authority, time from enrollment to later appointments to the governing council, it is worth noting that former rectors averaged thirty-four years from enrollment to their fourth term on the Banque, thirty-nine for their fifth term. For former vice-rectors, it took thirty-nine years for selection to a fourth term, forty-four for a fifth.

10. Jullien's "nécrologie," with Fontanier's additions, can be found in Collection Fontanier, 24F-55.

11. Over the period 1711–78, sixteen clergymen joined the confraternity. Most did not serve in office; however, four served as mandataire, five as regent, all for only one term, and one as vice-rector. There appears to have been no correlation between service in minor office and service on either the council or in the vice-rectorship. These later posts were purely honorary.

12. See chapter 7 below.

13. Fontanier, *Notes sur les pénitents rouges,* Collection Fontanier.

14. See chapter 3 above.

15. See Barnes, "Cliques and Participation: Organization Dynamics in the Pénitents Bourras."

16. Muzafer Sherif's experiments, conducted in the 1940s, are summarized in his *In Common Predicament: Social Psy-*

chology of Intergroup Conflict and Cooperation (Boston, 1960), 71–93.

17. See chapter 4 above.

18. Barnes, "Cliques and Participation," 42–46.

19. Jullien, *Chronique historique,* 73–80.

20. See chapter 3 above.

21. William Foote Whyte, "Small Groups and the Larger Organizations," in *Social Psychology at the Crossroads,* ed. John Rohrer and Muzafer Sherif (New York, 1951), 297–312, particularly 301–305. Leonard Sayles provides a summary in "The Behavior of Work Groups," in *The Government of Associations: Selections from the Behavioral Sciences,* ed. William Glaser and David Sills (Totowa, N.J., 1966), 137.

22. William Foote Whyte, *Street Corner Society,* 3rd ed. (Chicago, 1983), 146–93; 260–63. Also see his "Corner Boys: A Study in Clique Behavior," *American Journal of Sociology* 46 (1941), 647–64.

23. Agulhon, part 4.

24. See chapter 6 below.

25. "Ne faire point de Pâques, et passer ensuite tranquillement plusieurs années sans s'aquitter de ce devoir." Collection Fontanier, 24F–121.

Chapter 6
DEVOTIONAL LIFE

DEVOTIONAL PRACTICES AND ORGANIZATIONAL GOALS

The Wars of Religion helped popularize the practice of self-flagellation, but the social context in which the rite was performed provided the basis for the confraternities' success. Social context in turn was affected by the type and nature of devotions performed. The replacement of the collective practice of the rite of self-flagellation by the practice of more contemporary devotions kept penitent confraternities in tune with changing spiritual sensibilities, but ultimately it also had a negative impact on their vitality as organizations. Self-flagellation was among those rituals that celebrated fellowship, and as such, helped neutralize the divisiveness cliques brought to confraternal life; yet these types of rituals were exactly the ones confraternities discarded. The formalization of procedures for regulating internal conflict discussed in earlier chapters reflected the increasing absence of ritual mechanisms for maintaining concord. These rational procedures did not reward the experience of participation to the same degree. Thus, one of the factors behind member apathy may have been, ironically, the absence of much psychic reward for participation.

Chapter 1 provides a brief review of the history of Christian lay brotherhoods. Such a review is useful here also, this time from the perspective of how confraternal devotional practices and organizational goals interacted. William Christian, in his *Local Religion in Sixteenth Century Spain,* argues that analysis of devotional phenomena should commence with recognition of the distinction between "religion as practiced" and "religion as prescribed." By "religion as practiced" Christian means votive piety, the offering of ritual adoration to a heavenly patron in exchange for earthly intercession. Such piety is the essence of the religious experience of the vast majority of people, both past and present. "Religion as prescribed" describes the devotional experience of those individuals who are "translocal" in their sensibilities, that is, those whose loyalties "are only vestigially with their home place." Translocal individuals, "because they were idea makers, literary as well as literate. . .are most like the translocal idea-makers who write history."[1] As such, they become the subjects of the latter's researches while the devotions of practitioners of local religion are dismissed as superstitious.

What Christian describes as "religion as prescribed" has been characterized by A. D. Wright as a Neoplatonism refracted through the mind of Augustine of Hippo and by Carlos Eire as a Neoplatonism refracted through the mind of Erasmus.[2] Whatever its lineage, Platonic "transcendentalism," to use Eire's term, saw true religion as that which led the spirit away from the flesh and toward God. Since from this perspective most ritualistic devotions were preceived as leading the spirit toward a corporal sense of satisfaction, they were at best superstitious, at worst idolatrous. Because it sought to eradicate the tendency toward the ritualization of devotion, Platonic transcendentalism was prescriptive. More positively, this transcendentalism glorified the intellectual act of belief and the mental discipline the act required. God is willing to help us if only we turn our minds toward him. The mental devotions that would produce the latter effect were the substance of the translocal religiosity to which Christian alludes.

Christian seems to be arguing that very few transcendent themes figure into the devotional lives of most humans, that most of the contact initiated by them with the divine has as its goal, relief from some specific anxiety. It is the clergy, to the extent that it represents translocal sensibilities, that has insisted that transcendent themes—from fairly complex ideas such as the composition of the Trinity to simpler ones such as the concept of universal brotherhood—be contemplated as the solution to these anxieties.

To some extent the laity has accepted that faith in the Holy Trinity will help cure their sick cow, that loving their neighbor will help find the money to repair a leaky roof; but the laity has remained more comfortable with its chances before the shrine of the local incarnation of the Virgin or her son. Perhaps the greatest value of Christian's argument is that it spotlights the importance of the goals of devotional acts. As he shows, very often devotions have remained the same while the motivations for their performance have changed.

I part company with Christian when he concludes that "religion as practiced" is exclusively votive. The pursuit of salvation is also an aspect of "religion as practiced," and actions taken in this pursuit cannot be placed in the same category as those taken in pursuit of more specifically temporal concerns. Death is the one transcendent anxiety with which Christians have to be concerned. And consistently throughout Western history this anxiety has provided the opening through which the clergy has reached to grab the attentions of the laity. Some part of the devotions performed by Christians has always been penitential, that is, has always had as its object the placation of heaven specifically for the sins of the performer, despite the regularity with which the clergy repeats the notion that the way to assuage God's ire is through *caritas* or the spread of love. Part of the appeal of associative organizations like confraternities has been that they permit Christians to realize the latter goal while officially in pursuit of the former. In this sense perhaps it was not purely incidental that Christianity was first promoted through burial societies.

According to Duhr the widespread conviction that collective prayer could assist in the salvation of all participants developed during the central Middle Ages. At that time Benedictine monasteries first allowed to circulate the idea that the grace generated by the shared devotions of their members could be exploited by nonmembers for the benefit of the latters' souls. Duhr emphasized that the Benedictines first popularized the term *confraternitas,* which previously had meant something akin to the modern concept of "brotherly love." The price paid for popularization was a corruption of the original notion into the idea that the grace gained from the prayers of the monks could be exploited by outsiders.[3] Barbara Rosenwein's work on Cluniac liturgy suggests that the Cluniacs were much more explicit about the spiritual benefits of their prayers than Duhr appreciated. The notion of confraternitas the Cluniacs promoted was not a transcendent concept. As understood by contemporaries, it had to do with the spiritual prestige of Cluny and its affiliates, a prestige of sufficient strength to make a tangible difference in the effort for salvation for any and all who had access to it.[4]

Meerseman concluded that voluntary associations had a pre-Christian existence in Germanic as well as Roman society and that the development of confraternities reflected the christianizing of the idea of association in lands where Germanic cultural influence held sway. Contrary to Duhr, he sees the history of confraternities moving toward the further evangelization of the laity, as opposed to the corruption of the clergy. Meerseman presents far too much evidence to be disregarded; however, his explanation does not provide an answer to the question of why after so many centuries such an evangelical initiative suddenly began to receive a positive response. The value here of Duhr's explanation is its implications about the spread of confraternities—that the impetus behind this spread was Benedictine success in convincing the laity that there was spiritual benefit to organizing themselves into associations. Whether the laity needed much convincing is less important than the fact that the Benedictine idea of confraternitas satisfied both the clergy's and the laity's understanding of events in the emergence of lay associations as vehicles of evangelization.[5]

Still, Meerseman perceived the force behind the spread of confraternities as coming from the mendicant orders which appropriately keeps the focus on the clergy's role in the process. By the time the Benedictines had begun to decline, lay confraternities had already taken from the monasteries the idea that the grace gained from collective devotions could be a powerful aid to individual salvation. Lay associations stopped short, however, of assimilating the idea that these collective devotions had to be performed by the clergy. Only an intense and extensive effort by the medicants succeeded in persuading the laity to accept the continuing superiority of clerical sanctity. With the medicants the practice of confraternitas for the first time involved a transcendence of local or particularistic anxieties toward more universalistic concerns. The mendicant orders were the first clerical groups to support the use of self-flagellation among their lay followers. Equally important is the fact that they had their followers perform the rite as penance for prevailing political conflict or religious schism. The salvation of these followers was to come indirectly through the realization of goals identified by the mendicants as holy.

It will be recalled that the original Italian confraternities of disciplinati were under the supervision of correttore—members of the mendicant orders appointed to watch over the confreres and correct their faults. As the fourteenth century gave way to the fifteenth, these correttores gave way to lay priors. Implicit in this transition was a reaction by confreres against the universalistic concerns of the mendicants toward an elevation of their own spiritual salvation as their collective raison d'être. This elevation involved a concentration on the operation of the confraternities as organizations.[6]

Pullan took as a sign of the decline of the fifteenth century *scuola de battuti* of Venice the fact that only the poorer members practiced self-flagellation. Only from the perspective of what the clergy was teaching, however, does the bifurcation of these associations into those who flagellated and those who did not signal decadence. Those who could dispense charity did so, while those who could only receive charity mortified themselves. From the vantage point of the brothers, this prompted greater harmony in the chapel, since it gave every member a real role to play in the association's survival.[7]

A similar point can be made about Guibert's condemnation of the tendency on the part of eighteenth-century French penitent confraternities to direct most of their charity toward internal poor relief. From the perspective of the laymen within these confraternities, self-centeredness was a sign of vitality. For them it was perfectly rational to direct their charitable efforts toward making themselves stronger as associations, since it was as associations that they hoped to play a role in their members' salvation.[8]

I would suggest that the instinct on the part of confraternity members to see their associations as the prime locus of their salvation should be considered as the constant, while the clergy's success in getting confreres to see their salvation as part of the greater effort of the church was the variable. If this is correct, then what has been understood as periods of decline in the history of confraternities, such as occurred in Italy in the fourteenth and fifteenth centuries, and in France in the seventeenth and eighteenth, may more accurately be described as periods when the laity succeeded in asserting its ideas about collective salvation over clerical complaints.

This conclusion does not take into account the motivations of the clergy, either in promoting confraternities, or in acquiescing to their later independence. In his book, *The First Urban Christians: The Social World of the Apostle Paul,* Wayne Meeks makes it clear that for the earliest Christians, charity started at home and then spread abroad, that caritas as understood by the original Christian laity had to do with loving fellow Christians found in the groups in which one participated. The economic and social change western Europe experienced, beginning in the twelfth century, created the conditions for the appearance of what may be called the "second urban Christians."

What is striking is the conscious way in which this second urban laity idealized the religious experience undergone by the first. This is most evident in the pursuit of the *vita apostolica,* that is, the pursuit of a clercial life that idealized the itinerant Christian missionary of the first and second centuries A.D. It is also evident in the multiplication of pious associations and prayer groups around men who realized the new spiritual ideals. As Meeks demonstrates, in the very beginning itinerant churchmen moved from city to city, preaching to, and being supported by, small formal and informal groups.[9] The decline of the city during the late Empire as well as the earlier centuries of the Middle Ages brought with it a decline in the prayer associations and burial societies through which Christianity first developed. They only began to reappear with the emergence of the new cities of the western European Middle Ages. Significantly, this reappearance was managed by a new itinerant clergy, the mendicant orders.[10] Just as the groups Meeks studied were proto-congregations, so were the lay associations created by the mendicants. And just as the internal dynamics of the earlier groups aided in their evangelization, so too did those of mendicant confraternities make the task of missionizing easier.

When, however, internal conflict and the involvement in church affairs sapped the mendicant orders' enthusiasm for pastoral work, the constant spiritual challenges confreres put forward eventually proved beyond the orders' capacity to answer. Clerical evangelists, arguably from the Benedictines onward, turned to confraternities because confraternities provided the most efficient vehicles for the delivery of their messages. While these messages were still fresh, the chapels in the churches of the evangelists were filled with lay followers eager for instruction. But nothing brought home the fact that a message had gone stale better than the lack of response to the clergy's injunctions displayed by later generations of occupants of these same chapels. As long as the clergy's message appealed to the laity, there were laymen willing to listen—less, perhaps, because of the intrinsic worth of the message, than out of a conviction that whoever could speak such worthy words must have some access to God's favor.

When clerical authority declined, the devotions performed by confraternities did not necessarily change. Rather, lay member-ships increasingly took the initiative in interpreting what those devotions meant. Since they were no longer confident about their clerical sponsors' ability to intercede for them before God, these memberships increasingly came to emphasize that the salvation of individual members was tied to the vitality of the confraternity as an organization. Not suprisingly, they reinterpreted their devotions to reinforce the point.

At this juncture fifteenth-century confraternities of disciplinati realized a comparative advantage. Not all devotions performed by the laity are equal; some are perceived as more efficacious than others. Methods of spiritual perfection have come and gone, but clerics to this day continue to mortify themselves as an act of pen-ance. Could the laity be faulted for concluding that the most effec-tive way to appeal to God's mercy was through self-flagellation? Of the host of devotions promoted by the mendicants, with perhaps one exception (that of the Rosary), the only one to flourish when the religious orders themselves began to decline was self-flagellation.

It may be that the mendicants exploited the appeal of self-flagellation among the laity for their own benefit. In return, how-ever, they gave the rite an associative context which eventually proved irresistible to masculine Mediterranean sensibilities. The free-standing chapels, habits and hoods, and elaborate liturgies rich in symbolism were fused by the mendicants to the practice of self-flagellation. In the thirteenth and fourteenth centuries, when lay self-flagellation came under assault by various clerical authori-ties for being heretical, it was the mendicants who continued to insist that participants in flagellant associations were not simply orthodox, but an elite among the laity.

The popularity flagellant associations experienced after the mendicants began to decline should be viewed from this perspective. The confrontations that occurred in Italian associations suggest that the price in commitment to transcendent ideals the mendicants charged for participation in their confraternities was too steep for most of the laity. Once the mendicants were no longer strong enough to keep the focus on these values, and devotional life within chapels had mutated into a lay-conceptualized campaign for collective salvation, Mediterranean laities outside Italy proved quite eager to establish similar associations.[11]

As argued in chapter 1, the initial appeal of penitent confraternities was probably as burial societies. Later, clerical groups began to assist in their foundations, motivated by the potential of confraternities to assist in their liturgical and devotional activities. The earliest associations were exclusively concerned with the salvation of their members, which was to be effected through the devotions they performed. With these sorts of goals, early penitent associations did not attract much interest outside certain devout circles.

The development of sectarian conflict changed that. Just as with the early mendicant confraternities, civil-war era associations in France became vehicles for the realization of transcendent goals that had to do only secondarily with the salvation of their members. Unlike the earlier period, no clerical group(s) was behind this development, though various political authorities did attempt to manipulate the spread of the confraternities for their own ends. Rather, what distinguished the penitent confraternities of late sixteenth-century France was the degree to which they embodied lay responses to religious strife. Penitent confraternities during the Wars of Religion were primarily concerned with the defeat of Protestantism and the salvation of Catholic society, goals that made them popular across France. These newer goals emerged suddenly, before the organizational structure of existing associations could encompass them. An organizational crisis developed that stimulated the evolution of the reformed and unreformed confraternities discussed in previous chapters. As Catholicism regained ascendency in France, however, the need for penitent confraternities as a bulwark against Protestant inroads declined. By the late seventeenth century, more and more French confraternities were beginning to resemble fifteenth-century Italian confraternities in their self-centered concern for organizational vitality. Maintenance of a sense of brotherhood became the object of almost all legislation. As for the devotions performed by confraternities, they ceased to be a celebration of Catholic fidelity and became once more good works aimed at increasing the corporate grace of the association. Self-flagellation was a casualty of this development—the end of sectarian conflict ended its career as a popular symbol of Catholic defiance and it became again an act of faith with an appeal only for the devout. Meanwhile confraternities were busy sampling the new devotions of the Counter-Reformation.

The Constituent Elements of Devotional Life

Devotional life in penitent confraternities consisted of three different elements. Members of confraternities wore their habits for all devotions, and all their activities started, even if they did not finish, at the chapel. The material culture of penitent associations was not part of their appeal, but an essential element of their devotions. Confraternities of penitents, like other lay associations, spent most of their devotional time performing regular Sunday and feast day offices, and the rest participating in activities sponsored by religious orders and other lay groups. The rites and ceremonies of the liturgical year make up the second element of confraternal devotional life. The third element was penitential devotions, that is, devotions performed specifically as penance for sins committed. The first two elements did not change much across the centuries, which explains the fact that, while the third element changed completely, no one questioned that the eighteenth-century associations were the heirs of those of the sixteenth.

The Material Culture of Confraternal Chapels

CHAPELS

A confraternity's chapel was the *locale* for its devotions. As Froeschlé-Chopard observed, "La chapelle et la confrérie sont indissociables, à tel point que lorsque la premiére est déstruite, il semble que la seconde n'existe plus."[12] The chapel was the focal point of all a confraternity's activities: At least once a week members would pass through its doors for religious services, and all processions and ceremonial activities began at the chapel, even if they were to take place elsewhere in the city. In fact, because they were secret societies, confraternities were not supposed to exist outside their chapels, at least not as a tangible part of their members' daily lives. They came to life only when their members, as a collectivity, crossed the threshold of the chapel doors.[13]

Chapels were special places outside of ordinary space and times.[14] Immediately upon entering a chapel a member had to take off his coat and then sprinkle himself with holy water, simultaneously reciting an Ave Maria. Hearing the prayer, those near him were to respond, Gratia plena. Having cleansed himself, he knelt before the altar and recited five times each the Pater noster, the Ave Maria, and the Gloria patria. Last, he went before the seat of the prior to seek his acknowledgment, then kissed the feet of the crucifix immediately in front of the prior's seat. Finished, he went quietly to his seat and put on his habit.[15]

The chapel of a confraternity was a special semi-sacred world in which a member was expected to be concerned exclusively with the confreres' collective salvation. To break the silence of the chapel brought a fine. To break the silence for some mundane matter brought an even stiffer fine. To leave the chapel before gaining permission from the prior brought expulsion. Once within the chapel, a member ceased to be his own self. Rather, once within his robe and hood, he took on a special persona as a soul doing penance for its sins, as a participant in a corporate effort to supplicate the mercy of God.[16]

Since by law all chapels were sold and either demolished or converted to other use in 1793, no example of a pre-Revolution chapel still exists in Marseille. From Venard's description of chapels in Avignon, and various other sources, however, it is possible to sketch the layout of a typical chapel. While most were independent structures, they still might share a common wall with a church. In this wall a doorway was made in order for the chaplain to enter the chapel to say mass, and for the confreres to enter the church to hear other services. These doors were built with two locks, one on either side. The key to the lock on the chapel side of the door was held by one of the sacristans of the confraternity. The key to the lock on the other side was held by one of the officials of the church.

The typical chapel had at least three different rooms: the *antichapelle,* the sacristy, and the chapel proper. The antichapelle was a multipurpose room that contained the external entrance to the chapel, as well as the vestiary where the brothers changed their clothes. According to Venard, the companies of penitents of Avignon sometimes built this room to serve also as a general assembly room. In the chapel of the penitents of Saint Anthony of Marseille, the antichapelle was used also to house the secondary altar of the confraternity's patron, Saint Anthony.[17] The sacristy was a small room off to the side of the altar of the chapel proper in which a confraternity stored its religious possessions, such as relics and clerical vestments, as well as its ceremonial paraphernalia such as batons, torches, etc.

The chapel proper was arranged on the plan of a monastic choir, with the benches set up in parallel descending rows along the two side walls perpendicular to the altar. Under this arrangement the confreres could, in their chanting, better respond to the antiphons of the prior. Also, the wide aisle created in the center of the chapel could be used for preaching and for staging various ceremonies.[18]

In the smaller companies the first six spaces on the lowest bench closest to the altar on either side were reserved for the banquiers. In the larger companies it was the first six spaces on the lowest two benches that were reserved. The prior and sub-prior did not sit on the benches but on their own *sees* before the altar.

For the altar and other furnishings of the chapel there exists one excellent contemporary description. In 1793 two municipal officials came to the chapel of the confraternity of pénitents bleus of Notre Dame de Pitié (Carmelites) to make an inventory of the effects of the confraternity so that they might be sold. As the two men reported:

> In the chapel there was an altar of gilded wood with its halo inlaid with marble and gold (*sa gloire marbre et doré*), and an altar piece representing the Mater Pietatis.

The chapel itself was paneled in wood with the paneling along the front wall being gilded. Near the altar there was a wooden preaching chair (*chaire à prêcher*) painted to appear like marble, and an old lectern of gilded white wood. On the walls were eleven different paintings on canvas representing diverse mysteries. Around the front of the altar ran a communion table made of iron.[19]

Chapels occasionally also possessed two other types of rooms. First was a council room for the meeting of the Banque. This room was called the "secret" and ideally was built above the chapel proper. The penitents of Saint Anthony had such a room, as did the penitents of Notre Dame de Pitié (Carmelites). The pénitents Bourras desired such a room and in 1615 began to build one. The Trinitarians next door, however, successfully went to court to halt the enterprise.[20]

The pénitents Bourras were successful, though, in having built two cabinets for novices. These were tiny rooms into the wall of the chapel. The front of these cabinets had windows of frosted glass and an opening through which the novice could receive communion. Inside each of the cabinets was a chair, a lamp, and a chap book in order that the novice might follow the services.

HABITS

Habits were composed of two garments: the *chape,* or robe, and the *cagoule,* or hood. The robe was body length with long sleeves. In its back was a hole large enough that the penitent might use the discipline. Another piece of cloth was attached over this. The hood was a pointed piece of cloth with two holes cut for eyes. The Bourras went against this fashion by having rounded tops to their hoods, which according to one historian, was singular enough to be the real source of their popular nickname (Bourras from *bout ras*).[21] Around the waist of the costume went a belt made of knotted cord. Attached to the belt were crosses, chap books, and on occasion, whips. On their feet penitents were allowed to wear leather sandals. A final part of the habit in many confraternities was a pair of gloves, worn during procession so that people on the streets could not recognize particular members by their hands. In general, earlier confraternities chose white or blue habits, while later groups chose grey ones. There was not sufficient consistency to this rule to relate it to a reformed versus unreformed orientation. An argument has been made that black habits signaled an aristocratic lineage.[22] While the companies of penitents in cities like Limoges wore a diversity of colored habits, in Marseille only the pénitents rouges of the Holy Cross went against the traditional colors. In 1704 they changed the color of their habits to white.[23]

OTHER PARAPHERNALIA

Other than the altar furnishings already mentioned, the one other type of paraphernalia possessed by most confraternities was that relating to processions. Most confraternities had at least four batons—massive wooden sticks with artistic renderings of the devotions of the confraternity carved on, or attached to, their tops—to be carried by the syndics and masters of ceremonies. Each also owned at least one processional crucifix and probably several banners. The penitents of Saint Anthony chanted, following music booklets furnished by their chorists. Many confraternities possessed statues of the Virgin; some possessed relics. From one of Bishop Belsunce's earlier ordinances, it can be gathered that at one time confraternities also carried bouquets and made use of "violons et autres instruments" in their processions, a practice Belsunce promptly halted.[24]

The Observances and Celebrations of the Liturgical Year

SUNDAY SERVICES

Members of penitent confraternities were expected to pray daily, usually five Pater Nosters and five Ave Marias. They were also expected to fast at least once a week, usually either Wednesday or Saturday. If they did not fulfill these obligations, it was left to them to offer an alm in compensation. The foundation of their religious obligations was attendance at chapel services on Sundays. If they failed to attend for a specific number of consecutive Sundays, they were expelled. Reformed companies began their Sunday services at two or three in the morning; unreformed, at five or six. Officers were expected to be at the chapel earlier than the other confreres.[25]

The set of hymns sung at Sunday services by lay associations were known collectively as the "office." Lazare de Cordier suggests that the shifting social composition of the confraternities in the mid-seventeenth century was the cause behind the change by several companies from the Roman breviary, the set of offices in Latin sung by clerics, to the Office of the Holy Virgin, a set of offices sung in the vernacular. Confraternities were becoming associations of artisans, he claimed, and artisans could not read Latin. He explains this claim by relating the story of Bishop Turicella's pastoral visit to the various chapels of penitents in the earlier part of the seventeenth century. Because Turicella was Italian and could not speak the local dialect, the penitents conversed with him in Latin.[26]

In telling this story Lazare de Cordier no doubt exaggerated. By the early seventeenth century confraternities had already become popular in membership. Perhaps only the officers, drawn primarily from the upper class, could read Latin. But if we remember the situation in the confraternity of pénitents Carmélins in 1645, when neither the rector nor the vice-rector could read, we may better see that the change in social composition probably did cause the change in liturgy.

In another place in his treatise, Lazare de Cordier categorizes the various liturgies according to their degree of mournfulness (*lugubre*). According to him the liturgies of reformed confraternities were the most mournful. Less sad, but slow and staccato (*saccade*), was the chanting of the reformed confraternity of the Holy Cross. The least mournful was the liturgy of the unreformed confraternities, which was based on Gregorian chant.[27]

The singing of the office was the first part of Sunday services. The second part was a low mass performed by the chaplain, and the third was the fulfillment of monthly obligations. Once a month the ten commandments were read and explained to the members. Once a month the names of dead confreres were recited, and living confreres obliged to attend a requiem mass in their honor. A third monthly obligation was the reading of the statutes themselves.

Finally, once a month the confraternity was obliged to have a council meeting.

FEASTS AND OTHER EVENTS

To their regular Sunday observances, confraternities added other series of activities. Confraternities closely bonded to a religious order often had their liturgical calendars dictated by that of their clerical sponsors. The penitents of the Holy Cross, tertiaries to the Minims, celebrated not only the feasts of the Invention and Exaltation of the Holy Cross, the two main feasts of their patronal devotion, but also all major feasts of the order of the Minims. The pénitents Carmélins, auxiliaries to the confraternity of Our Lady of Mount Carmel, took as their secondary patron, Saint Joseph, the secondary patron of the Carmelites.[28] The penitents of Saint Catherine were dedicated to Saint Catherine of Alexandria and held their major procession on her feast day. But they also celebrated in their chapel with indulgences and benedictions all the major feasts of the Virgin Mary.[29]

As Lazare de Cordier sadly informs us, penitent associations were not completely immune to folk influences. He lists several of the dubious customs into which some had fallen. Aside from the practice of baking cakes for Good Thursday, he mentions the practice of dressing up the chapel with flowers and of giving each member of the confraternity a bouquet of flowers to carry during May Day ceremonies. He also mentions the custom some confraternities had of serving a funeral meal on All Souls Day (*Jour des Morts*), a meal which often preceded bouts of drunkenness. Some confraternities sang Christmas songs in French and Provençal and offered a cake to the prior and sub-prior in celebration of the event. Last, he speaks of some confraternities electing a mock prior six or seven years of age on the Feast of the Holy Innocents.[30] Lazare de Cordier wrote in the 1650s; how long after that such practices continued is not known. Neither Bishop Vintimille nor Bishop Belsunce cited such abuses in their regulatory letters, which began in the 1690s.

PROCESSIONS

According to Lazare de Cordier, each confraternity made at least four processions a year: on the day of the installation of their new officers (patronal feast), on the feast of the Assumption, on Christmas Day, and on Good Thursday. But this appears to be an overgeneralization. There is evidence that every confraternity performed a lenten procession, but processions on the other occasions involved at best three or four associations.[31] The processions on the feast of the Assumption, Christmas Day and Good Thursday were not general processions. Each confraternity marched from its chapel past the major churches of the city and then returned to its chapel. Lazare de Cordier tells how originally during the Christmas Day processions all the confraternities passed in front of the church of the Dominicans at the same time. This caused such confusion that in 1582 a council of the priors of the various confraternities decided to reorganize the celebrations, granting one-third of the confraternities the privilege of making procession on December 25, one-third on December 26, and one-third on December 27. A similar type of arrangement was in effect for the processions on Maundy Thursday, with some of the confraternities marching in the morning and some in the afternoon.[32]

Besides mandatory processions on patronal feast days, confraternities contracted to participate in the processions of religious orders and hospitals. Those confraternities with close relationships with a particular religious order, such as the Carmélins, marched only in the processions of that religious order.[33] Confraternities also made pilgrimages, for instance, the previously mentioned pilgrimage of the penitents of the Holy Cross to Notre Dame de la Garde in 1729.[34]

When a brother died, it was the obligation of the members of his confraternity to march in his funeral procession from the church or chapel of his wake to the cemetery. In the larger confraternities, funerals could have a confraternity in the streets on a regular basis. Over the period 1646–51, the confraternity of Saint Lazarus averaged eleven funerals a year. Many of the larger confraternities adopted the practice of printing notes announcing the forthcoming burial. In reformed confraternities announcing burials was one of the duties of the mandataires. In theory, failure to respond to the announcement of a burial produced a stiff fine. In practice, the popularity of the deceased determined the turnout.[35] In the statutes of the penitents of Saint

Henry failure to participate in burial processions ceased to be penalized.[36]

Vovelle identifies penitent confraternities as an integral part of the "baroque piety" in vogue in southern France during the second half of the seventeenth century and the first half of the eighteenth. His observations are correct as a characterization of the external, publicly observable devotions of confraternities such as processions, but they do not work for the penitential devotions confraternities performed in their chapels. Reformed confraternities elaborated on the rituals used for the reception of new confreres and the installation of new officers. But these ceremonies have to be separated from the devotions performed with the goal of salvation in mind. These remained private and were increasingly de-ritualized. From the start of the sevententh century onward penitent confraternities were constantly in the streets, staging their own processions or assisting in those of others, burying their dead, and making pilgrimages. Their ubiquity was part of baroque piety. While this layer of their devotional life in many instances may have detracted from the other, more essential layer, it always remained distinct from it.

There was method also in this public display. As Caro Baroja suggests, for all medieval towns, and Phythian-Adams illustrates for medieval Coventry, the feast of Corpus Christi was for the medieval town a celebration of its corporate nature. In the Corpus Christi procession each corporate entity in the town marched, its place in the procession reflecting its place in the corporate picture of the town. On that day in Marseille only the confraternity of Saint Lazarus marched, carrying the statue of the Virgin owned by the cathedral. The absence of the other penitent confraternities from this procession deserves notice. A simple explanation is that confraternities were composed of the same men who were marching in the Corpus Christi procession as members of their guilds.[37]

This simple answer, however, leads to one more complex. Just as a city through its guilds assessed corporate responsibility for its material well-being, so a city through its confraternities of penitents assessed corporate responsibility for its spiritual well-being. To follow Turner, as amended by Weissman, guilds represented material structure, while confraternities represented spiritual anti-structure. This had not been the case originally. Confraternities were originally an escape from the strictures of the material world. But eventually this very act of escape was incorporated into the spiritual economy of the city.[38] When a bishop arrived in Marseille, he was officially received by the town leaders, the clergy, and the confraternities of penitents. When a bishop died, again it was the confraternities who marched. When religious conflict finally ended in Marseille in 1596, the confraternities of penitents marched in celebration. And when the plague was over in Marseille in 1721, the city likewise made official thanks to God through a general procession of penitent confraternities to the shrine of Notre Dame de la Garde overlooking the city. The confraternities did not march on Corpus Christi because they were the other face of the city, the spiritual face, which appeared only when the city sought to communicate with God.

LENTEN OBSERVANCES

During Lent confraternities changed from their ordinary liturgical offices to the much more intense Office of the Passion. They also made processions and participated in special devotions such as the Devotion of the Forty Hours. And during Easter week in some fashion they ritually reenacted the death and rebirth of Christ. Régis de la Colombière stated that on Holy Thursday all the confraternities marked the beginning of the Easter celebration by making a procession past the major churches of the city. The *Calendrier Spirituel of 1713* noted, however, that only the penitents of the Holy Spirit and those of Saint John the Baptist made processions that day. According to it, each confraternity made its lenten procession on the first Sunday, Monday or Tuesday of Lent. On the evening of Good Thursday each confraternity reenacted the last supper. Before the rite the cenaires placed a table before the altar and arranged it with bread, fruit, and flowers. In earlier decades several confraternities had baked little cakes to commemorate the event and even allowed outsiders to observe it. A late seventeenth-century decree of the Archbishop of Arles, the metropolitan of Marseille, put an end to both practices. In truth the table was important only as a backdrop for the performance of the footwashing ceremony.[39] In most confraternities the sub-prior assisted the prior in washing the feet of all the brethren, "according to Christ's example."[40] During the minutes that they performed the ritual, the prior and sub-prior relived one of the humblest moments of the life of Jesus, one of the highlights of their year in office.[41]

The penitents of the Holy Spirit flagellated themselves on the first Friday of Lent and on Good Friday. Beyond changing to the Office of the Passion and preparing the chapel for the Easter week celebrations, it does not appear that any of the other unreformed confraternities sought to distinguish Lent from the rest of the liturgical year. Still, the culmination of the Christian year brought great anticipation to their chapels. On the Monday following Easter they elected new officers. The Sunday following Easter, after a procession, these new officers were installed.

Reformed confraternities celebrated Lent in much more rigorous and circumspect ways. The pénitents Bourras required the members, at the penalty of a half livre of wax, to be at the chapel precisely at twelve o'clock on Mardi Gras to replace the "dissolutions, escandalles, and mondanités" of that day with recitation of the Office of the Passion, a sermon by a "docteur ecclesiastique," and the election of the two men who would serve that year as cenaires. Reformed confraternities also demarcated Lent from the rest of the year by a more regular use of the discipline. At some point in the seventeenth century the Bourras decided to discontinue their reenactment of the last supper, giving the money earmarked for this purpose instead to the Trinitarians to maintain a lamp in honor of the holy sacrament. Yet the confraternity maintained the foot-washing ceremony, an important indication of the centrality of that rite to the Easter week celebration. Reformed confraternities neither elected their officers on the Monday following Easter, nor celebrated their installation on the following Sunday. The only change they experienced was a return to their ordinary offices.[42] Though Lent was a time of comparatively intense devotion for them, they did not celebrate its end as unreformed confraternities did.

The statutes for the penitents of Saint Henry do not mention Lenten services. Both sets stipulate that confreres celebrate the three feasts of Easter week (Holy Thursday, Good Friday, and

Easter Sunday) as well as Pentecost and Christmas at their parish church.[43]

Penitential Piety

FLAGELLATION

The rite of self-flagellation took place in the chapel with all the candles extinguished save one. Throughout the rite, whose length was left to the prior's discretion, the prior or someone chosen by him read through the penitential psalms while the brothers flagellated themselves. The rite was only one of three components of penitential piety, the other two being the rites of confession and communion. The earliest available statutes, those of the confraternity of the Holy Spirit from 1558, require brothers to "take the discipline," that is, flagellate themselves, five times over the course of the liturgical year: on the first of the year, the first Sunday of Lent, Good Friday, the "cross" of May (the third of May, feast of the Invention of the Cross) and the "cross" of September (the fourteenth of September, feast of the Exaltation of the Cross). They also require brothers to confess four times yearly: during Lent, by the feast of the Pentecost (their patronal devotion), by the feast of Our Lady of Mid-August (feast of the Assumption), and by Christmas, so that brothers could receive communion on Easter and the other feasts. For unreformed confraternities the grace generated by flagellation was a corporate grace that could be exploited only through participation in the confraternity. The statutes of the penitents of the Holy Spirit informed the brothers that they should receive Easter communion at their parish church (this much they had to do to keep bishops happy). The statutes also explicitly state that the other three communions were to take place in the chapel. It was here that the effort for salvation was to be initiated.[44]

Reformed confraternities increased the number of times the discipline was taken, and synchronized the two cycles. For example, the statutes of the pénitents Bourras doubled the number of times brothers were expected to whip themselves. The Bourras took the discipline every Friday of Lent. In addition they made use of the whip on Pentecost, the feast of the Assumption, All Saints Day, and Christmas.[45] Equally important, members bracketed performance of the rite with confession before and communion afterward. Reflecting Counter-Reformation sensibilities, the rite had become an individualized act of faith. As the statutes of the Bourras explained, the brothers had the option of taking the discipline "dry or bloody according to their devotion" (*seche ou sanglante cellon leur dévoction*),[46] such volition permitting the penitent to decide to what degree he needed to perform penance.

It might be expected that the spiritual ferment that gave rise to reform confraternities also induced unreformed confraternities to increase the number of times they practiced the discipline. Available evidence suggests this was not the case. The 1578 statutes of the confraternity of Saint Lazarus require members to confess and commune four times yearly, and to take the discipline twice. In the reedition of their statutes from 1687, the devotional obligations are the same. Actually it appears that the onset of popularity led unreformed confraternities in the opposite direction. Both of the sets of statutes available for the sixteenth century mention self-flagellation, so it seems reasonable to assume that during this period all unreformed confraternities practiced the rite. Yet in the *Cayer pour les pénitents de Saint Antoine,* a missal published in 1624, and in their 1671 statutes, there is no mention of the rite of self-flagellation. The missal published for the confraternity of Notre Dame de Pitié (Saint Martin parish) in 1674 lists no procedure for taking the discipline. The missal published by the penitents of Saint John the Baptist in 1748, which evidently was also used by the confraternities of the Holy Spirit and Saint Anthony, also does not. When unreformed confraternities ceased to demand that their members practice self-flagellation is not clear, but it seems to have been so by the second half of the seventeenth century.

Reformed confraternities continued to practice the rite through at least the middle of the eighteenth century. In his history of Marseille, written in 1696, De Ruffi condemned those confraternities of penitents that "did not maintain their statutes," referring to those confraternities that did not hold brothers to the devotional obligations specified in the statutes.[47] Since self-flagellation was the one devotional obligation that distinguished penitent confraternities from other types, it seems clear that he had it in mind. All the associations exempted from this condemnation were reformed confraternities. In their statutes from 1739, both the Bourras and the Carmélins continue to list the obligation to perform the rite. Since both sets are signed by Bishop Belsunce, it seems safe to conclude that the obligation was still being honored. About the same time, the penitents of the Holy Cross were describing themselves as a confraternity of penitents "disciplinés" in their register of deliberations, a term that usually signaled the practice of self-flagellation. It is hard to reconcile the idea of them continuing the use of the discipline in conjunction with the other devotional obligations that they took on during the period however.

Why unreformed confraternities gave up on the rite of self-flagellation can not be stated with certainty, but no matter how powerful the religious symbology of the rite, it was probably very difficult to get one hundred to two hundred men to perform it on a regular basis. The presence of three reformed chapels by the middle of the seventeenth century also probably acted as a drain, funnelling away from unreformed chapels those individuals who wanted to take their devotional lives to a higher level of intensity. Self-flagellation never lost its prestige as an act of penance in early modern Marseille, but that is because it was performed on a regular basis only by a devout few. From perhaps the early seventeenth century onward, the bulk of the men under penitential garb sought salvation through other devotions.

THE DIRECTIONS OF DEVOTIONAL CHANGE

Evangelizing the lower classes of Marseille is the first direction in which penitential piety evolved. Modest as the devotional obligations of unreformed confraternities may have been, they still were far more rigorous than those ordinary laymen were used to performing. Almost certainly confraternal leaders felt pressure to lessen these obligations. That they did not respond to the pressure may be the best reflection of how unreformed confraternities internalized the spiritual ferment of the age. This may seem a trivial point, but it had tremendous import for the religious history of early modern Marseille.

Few men could live up to the devotional requirements associated with membership in a confraternity of penitents, but a significant portion of the male population of Marseille tried. Sectarian concern stimulated the popularization of the confraternities of Marseille. But at some point that concern mutated into a desire on the part of the pious men who controlled confraternities to evangelize Catholic society. In modern society we have obscured the gradations between levels of believers, but in the sixteenth century, "penitent" was still synonymous with "convert," both terms signaling a layman who had left the world in his pursuit of salvation.[48] Outside of the confraternities of penitents, few men in Marseille fit into this category. Thus the popularization of penitent confraternities was simultaneously the evangelization of Marseille's male laity. Different from the process of evangelization that later occurred under the direction of Bishops Vintimille and Belsunce, this process concentrated exclusively on the transformation of masculine piety. Before the middle of the sixteenth century it had been possible to be a devout male Christian without being a member of a confraternity of penitents. From that point through the first half of the eighteenth century it was not.

For the men who subsidized this evangelization, the act of penance became the effort to maintain the masses of those less inspired at a level of devotion above and beyond the norm. Evidence that the officers of unreformed confraternities saw themselves as missionaries can be found in the statute of the confraternity of Saint Lazarus, which required that when a member died, each of the brothers say twelve Pater Nosters and twelve Ave Marias for his soul, but when "un frère pauvre" died, each was to say fifty Pater Nosters, and fifty Ave Marias. Remember also that the same confraternity paid poorer members to carry its statutes in processions and that in 1671 it reorganized its efforts at poor relief toward granting greater assistance to indigent confreres.

The rite that replaced self-flagellation in confraternal liturgies was the Adoration of the Cross. As described in the missal of the penitents of Notre Dame de Pitié, "tous les Vendredys de Caresme, au soir après l'Office," a crucifix was to be set up before the altar, and five candles were to be lit and placed around its base. Two brothers were to be chosen to recite hymns in the background. Then:

The prior, barefooted, will go kiss the Crucifix, performing, during the time between his seat and the Crucifix,
diverse genuflections, according to his devotion. This action will be continued by each of the confreres, one after
the other.[49]

Worth noting about this rite are two things: the focus on individual articulation of faith and the expectation that articulation
take physical form. As observed in chapter 1, for Catholics the
measure of faith lay in the actions it engendered. The adoration of
the cross was a ritualized public confession of faith. Its performance confirms the image of confraternal chapels as forums of
evangelism. Yet its performance also gives a sense of how the
sensibilities of the Counter-Reformation changed life in these chapels. Before the Wars of Religion, there had not been a need for
members to make regular proof of their faith.

To do for others was the pathway to spiritual perfection celebrated during the Counter-Reformation. Counter-Reformation piety placed a premium on social activism, on the grace to be gained
by helping others. A third way penitential piety evolved was
through the incorporation of social welfare projects into collective
activities. According to Fabre, the confraternity of the Trinité
vieille did not begin to solicit donations for the Trinitarian Bureau
Pour la Rédemption des Esclaves until 1578. Once that occurred
though, the confraternity threw itself into the task, providing the
monastery not only with a sufficient amount of money to continue
its charitable enterprise, but also, as Fabre uncharitably points out,
a regular source of income for its miscellaneous expenses.[50]

Just as the Bourras set the standard with use of the discipline,
so they set the standard with charity. Upon its inception in 1591 the
confraternity took upon itself the task of burying the bodies of all
criminals executed by civil authorities. In 1592 Antoine Mascaron,
rector and founder, as well as minter for the city during its brief
period of independence, sent his son to Rome to petition the
confraternity of Saint John the Baptist of that city for access to the
indulgences they gained for performing the same service. Presumably an act of friendship to Charles de Casaulx, the man for whom
he served as minter, lay behind Mascaron's decision to share these

indulgences with the confraternity that de Casaulx led, the penitents of Saint John the Baptist.[51] The pénitents noirs retained the right to bury all condemned prisoners of noble lineage, while the Bourras buried every one else. Along with burying condemned prisoners, from the beginning the Bourras annually purchased the freedom of an individual in debtors' prison. In the eighteenth century the confraternity added to its activities the care and maintenance of the widows and children of sailors lost at sea. Toward the end of the century, this latter effort broadened into a coordinated program of poor relief jointly sponsored with the Franciscans.[52]

Throughout the seventeenth century and the first part of the eighteenth, the penitents of Notre Dame de Pitié (Saint Martin's) and their clerical sponsors, the Pères de la Merci, did battle with the Trinitarians and their confraternity over the right to solicit funds for the redemption of Christian captives. According to Fontanier, when the monastery of the Pères de la Merci was ordered closed because of indigence, the pénitents bleus began instead to bury the paupers at the Hôpital des Incurables.[53] Fontanier also tells us that the penitents "de la Charité" (Saint Maur) came into existence in 1662 with the goal of burying the paupers of Saint Martin parish. Evidently after it was reestablished by Bishop Belsunce, it expanded this service to all the parishes of the diocese.[54]

The Counter-Reformation ethos was perhaps best realized in the penitents of Saint Henry. The confraternity met at a chapel in the Hôpital du Saint Esprit where it assisted in the care and burial of the patients. According to Fontanier, this is the exact same service once performed by the penitents of the Holy Spirit in the very same chapel.[55] It is striking that the confraternity of the Holy Spirit never mentions this service in its 1558 statutes. Assuming Fontanier is correct, clearly charity work was ancillary to its other activities. The concern of the penitents of Saint Henry to regulate the brethren's performance of their task appears throughout the bulk of the 1731 statutes' ten chapters. Noteworthy also is the fact that these statutes establish monthly performance of the Office of the Dead, and more importantly, weekly participation in one half-hour of group meditation in the chapel. It was only after motivating themselves through meditation that confreres were supposed to attend to the sick.[56]

In many ways the meditative piety promoted by the confraternity of Saint Henry continued the Jesuit influence discernible in the case of reformed associations, but with this crucial distinction: reformed piety posited no conflict between ritual and meditative devotions. As the statutes of the pénitents Bourras informed members, after weekly services they were to engage in "oraison mentalle avec ferveur de coeur."[57]

The piety advanced in the statutes of the penitents of Saint Henry questioned the sanctity of any ritual performance apart from that which occurred at the parish. Grace was to be gained through action, not spurious ritual. To be sure, their statutes insisted that the brothers commune ten times a year, but this was mostly a reflection of Bishop Belsunce's commitment to the Jesuits—there is no mention of confession.[58] Beyond communion, the recitation of weekly and monthly offices, and the simplified ceremony for the installation of officers mentioned above, the statutes are silent about liturgical life. Instead of the rich ceremonial life so much a part of the attraction of older confraternities, members of the penitents of Saint Henry were expected to gain satisfaction from helping the paupers in the hospital. As the 1731 statutes explained, the brothers were to

> oversee with prudence the precious moments of the poor sufferers, within whom they should seek to inspire a tender confidence in the Father of Mercy, mixed with an extreme regret for having given him offense; to produce in them acts of faith, of hope, of love, of resignation to the sorrows of their agonies and their death, but also of their coming union with the death and Passion of Our Lord through which their sins will be expatiated.[59]

Members of unreformed confraternities also sought to reach heaven through service to the poor. But in their cases, the poor being served were inside the organization. The piety of the penitents of Saint Henry was not much different from that of the pénitents Bourras. But by the time the penitents of Saint Henry appeared, the Bourras had presented to the public mind for more than a century an association of social service with rigorous physical mortification. That the same level of love could be obtained without recourse to self-flagellation made the penitents of Saint Henry sufficiently popular that they had to limit their size in their second set of statutes.

DECADENCE OR SHIFT?

As mentioned earlier, at the end of the seventeenth century the local historian Antoine De Ruffi was condemning unreformed confraternities for not maintaining their statutes. His condemnation was misplaced. It is no coincidence that Lazare de Cordier felt the need to include in his mid-seventeenth-century study of the confraternities of Marseille a chapter distinguishing the confraternities of penitents from the processions of flagellants condemned by the church and Gerson. As he explained, the fact that confraternities practiced the rite in the privacy of their chapels freed it from any taint of heresy.[60] Already by the middle of the seventeenth century, lay practice of self-flagellation was under attack. By the end of the century, Jacques Boileau was calling into question the sanctity of the act even as performed by clerics.[61] If churchmen like Boileau questioned the orthodoxy of self-flagellation, is it so surprising that laymen shied away from it?

The 1671 reedition of the statutes of the confraternity of Saint Anthony makes no mention of the rite of self-flagellation. Without doubt here is an example of the type of confraternity about which De Ruffi was speaking. But nine years earlier in 1662, the confraternity had affiliated itself with the Dominican confraternity of the Rosary, which meant that their devotional life was taken over by the Dominicans.[62] Was the absence of self-flagellation a sign of decadence or a result of devotional evolution?

Contemporaries as well as historians have assumed that performance of self-flagellation was an accurate index of devotional fervor. Both have been too influenced by the example of reformed confraternities, who, being more exclusive, conservative, and elitist, held on to the performance of self-flagellation as a standard of commitment far longer than older associations. Penitent confraternities were eager to involve themselves in any pious activity that could bring God's favor to their chapels. At the end of the sixteenth century the rite of self-flagellation was perceived as having this capacity. Among the Catholic devotional elite it never lost its prestige—in the second half of the eighteenth century, the chapels of reformed confraternities were over-populated with both pious laymen and clerics. But in older chapels over the seventeenth century devotional life became a function of popular devotional sensibilities, confraternities incorporating and discarding devotions according to the former's appeal to their members.

Even reformed confraternities eventually began to give in to the times. Something akin to what happened with the penitents of Saint Anthony happened with the penitents of the Holy Cross in 1704. The confraternity affiliated itself with the Third Order of Saint Francis De Paul of the Minim Order, an association for both men and women. In the statutes of that association, inscribed in the register of the penitents of the Holy Cross, there is no mention of self-flagellation.[63]

Contemporaries condemned the confraternities for no longer maintaining their statutes, without taking into account that those statutes reflected religious sensibilities that were by that time anachronistic. Historians should have spotted the inconsistency in the expectation that eighteenth-century laymen be attracted to centuries-old devotions, but they likewise have insisted on seeing as decadence the real effort confraternities made to remain spiritually relevant over the course of the centuries. Yet the only thing that kept members returning to chapels was the perception that what occurred there was holy. As the idea of what was holy changed, the devotions performed by confraternities also changed. Most of the rituals performed by the earliest confraternities took place in their chapels, befitting their status as secret societies. Later sponsorship by religious orders changed the situation only slightly. The real transformtion occurred in the second half of the sixteenth century, when confraternities accepted an increasingly prominent role in local devotional life. Their evolution as part of baroque piety negatively affected their previous stance as private associations existing on the margins of Christian society. Similarly, when baroque piety began to be replaced with the interiorized piety more commonly associated with the Counter-Reformation, confraternities replaced baroque practices with activities perceived as pious by eighteenth-century Christians. Each new devotional wave took the confraternities further away from the initial idea of penance practiced in the chapels. But since this early idea was no longer relevant from the point of view of the confraternities as devotional associations, such deviation should be preceived as progressive.

DEVOTIONAL CHANGE AND ORGANIZATIONAL EVOLUTION

The discussion to this point appears to suggest that devotional change had no effect upon the confraternities as organizations. It did, but in a subtle, concealed fashion. All of the rituals performed by confraternities may be said to have promoted feelings of what the anthropologist Victor Turner labeled *communitas*. All, for the matter, may be said to have generated the sense of collective identity that according to Sherif resulted from all commonly performed tasks. I would argue, however, that the devotions and procedures that replaced them went in the opposite direction, toward the generation of a sense of self, as opposed to the group, toward the creation of a concern for individual, as opposed to collective, salvation. Psychological studies of altered states of consciousness suggest that part of the reward for participation in collective ritual, part of communitas, is an enhanced sense of union with other participants. Other participants intrude on the rewards for performance of meditation. Thus, even though confraternities like the penitents of Saint Henry tried to ritualize meditation, or at least bracket its practice with rituals, it produced no collective psychic dividends. As for the charitable activities confraternities performed, again as the statutes of the penitents of Saint Henry indicate, they were for the spiritual benefit of the brothers performing them, not the confraternity as a whole.

Members of penitent confraternities limited the performance of the rite of self-flagellation from the very beginning. Yet performance of the rite probably generated the strongest group bonds. It probably also went further than the performance of any other rite toward reinforcement of the confraternity's transcendent goals. Discontinuance of the rite did not alter the organizational structure of confraternities as much as remove one of its more important props.

Unfortunately for the confraternities, this particular prop was essential for the maintenance of internal harmony. Originally, decision-making in confraternities was by consensus, with moral and social coercion being exercised on disputants. As the statutes of the confraternity of the Holy Spirit illustrate, framers of confraternal statutes may have had no idea of the concept of communitas, but they were aware of the power of collective participation in ritual to resolve conflict.[64] As clique conflict began to predominate, the need for such a mechanism for restoring amity among warring factions only increased. But of course it was just at this moment that religious sensibilities turned against ritual performance.

In 1704, as noted, the confraternity of the Holy Cross affiliated itself to the Third Order of Saint Francis de Paul, a move which presumably signaled the discontinuation of its older ritual devotions. Twenty years later a general meeting of all confreres began with the comment:

> This meeting has been proposed by frère Jean Gris, rector, who has observed with sadness the dissension which has been developing for some years among the vast majority of the brothers, not only because of the laxity of some, but also because of the discord and division which has occurred many times as much because of the acts of brothers as because of the confusion in our statutes.[65]

The attitude expressed in these minutes is typical. The tension in the chapel was the fault of the statutes whose procedures for handling debate and dissension were not sufficiently sophisticated. The solution the confraternity adopted was also typcial. Henceforth:

> In order to satisfy the confreres and maintain good order, there will be a meeting of the governing council the first Sunday of each month in which there will be discussion of all that has happened in the chapel during the previous

month, temporal as well as spiritual, in order to prohibit the possibility of division and discord among us.[66]

Based on the elaborate procedures to avoid or resolve conflict discussed in chapter 4, it seems safe to conclude that meetings like this took place in unreformed confraternities decades earlier. In those instances also leaders did not understand that the growth of internal discord was actually a reflection of the decline of group cohesion, and the decline in group cohesion was in turn a result of the divergence from the performance of rituals that had helped preserve that cohesion. Without the reinforcement of rituals that symbolically made them all the same, confreres became too conscious of their differences. Without the psychic rewards of collective performance, members had little motivation to look beyond the goals of their immediate circle to the greater goals of the organization.

Nor, according to the spiritual values of the age, was this development such a bad thing. Laymen educated to the sensibilities of the Counter-Reformation would not let their confraternities come between them and their salvation. In the second half of the eighteenth century freemasonry flourished in southern Provence. As Agulhon recognized, freemason lodges inherited the transcendent sense of fraternalism, the secrecy, and the elaborate ritualism of the confraternities in their popular years. Agulhon concluded that when the local elite fled the chapels of decaying and declining penitent confraternities, they took with them the associative life they knew in the confraternities. I would agree that the ideal of fraternity once maintained by penitent confraternities migrated to freemason lodges. But I would argue that this migration resulted not from the decline of the confraternities but from the secularization of the ideal. In the second half of the eighteenth century it was difficult to maintain that such an ideal was Christian. Confraternities did not try. Instead their members accepted the need to create that type of fraternal world elsewhere.

Fraternalism did not disappear from confraternal chapels. It just became more focused on intermediate social groups—fellow guildsmen, family members, or friendships developed in the confraternity itself. Only in reformed confraternities such as the Bourras and Carmélins did the old values survive. Even there, though, this survival was dictated by its fusion with more contemporary devotional trends.

Beyond their continued existence, late eighteenth-century associations had few collective and few transcendent goals. That is not to say that their members had lost their concern for salvation, just that the essentiality of the confraternity in the realization of that goal had receded. As was seen with the confraternity of Notre Dame de Pitié, the most a chapel could claim to be was a context for the devotional effort, and again with the exception of the smaller, more exclusive associations, one chapel was as good as the next. What continued to make them attractive was this plasticity. In a certain sense they had once again become evangelical. A resolute circle of laymen, or even a solitary individual determined to take that first step toward salvation, probably found a confraternal chapel a more inviting place than the parish. Certainly there they or he would be complimented for making a fresh start, as opposed to being chastised for having previously lost the way. Bishops like Belsunce made it clear to members of confraternities that what happened in their chapel was acceptable only as a supplement to what happened at the parish church. No longer could the notion be maintained that the chapel was the locus of salvation; many men so resented this that they turned their backs on both their chapels and the church. Many more took solace in the long history of confraternities as vehicles for the salvation of ordinary laymen like themselves. Relative to the other lay associations that existed at the time, penitent confraternities still offered the best opportunity for laymen to take the initiative in the determination of their spiritual fate. What is important is that for Catholic laymen on the eve of the Revolution, as for their forefathers, participation in a confraternity remained in essence an act of faith.

NOTES

1. Christian, 178–79.

2. A. D. Wright, *The Counter-Reformation: Catholic Europe and the Non-Christian World* (New York, 1982); Carlos M. N. Eire,

War Against the Idols: The Reformation of Worship from Erasmus to Calvin (Cambridge, 1986).

3. J. Duhr, "La confrérie dans la vie de l'Église," *Revue d'histoire ecclésiastique* (1939); 437–78.

4. Barbara Rosenwein, "Feudal War and Monastic Peace: Cluniac Liturgy as Ritual Aggression," *Viator* 2 (1971).

5. See in general G. G. Meerseman, *Ordo Fraternitatis: Confraternite e Pieta dei Laici nel Medievo*, 3 vols. (Rome, 1980), in particular vol. 1: 8–12.

6. See chapter 3 above.

7. Brian Pullan, *Rich and Poor in Renaissance Venice: The Social Institutions of a Catholic State* (Cambridge, Mass., 1971).

8. Guibert, *Les confréries de pénitents en France.*

9. Wayne Meeks, *The First Urban Christians: The Social World of the Apostle Paul* (New Haven, 1983), 74–110. Robert L. Wilken, *The Christians as the Romans Saw Them* (New Haven, 1984), 31–47.

10. The best introduction to the religious change of the twelfth and thirteenth centuries is M. D. Chenu, "Monks, Canons, and Laymen in Search of the Apostolic Life," in his *Man, Nature, and Society in the Twelfth Century* (Chicago, 1968). See also Lester Little, "Pride Goes Before Avarice: Social Changes and the Vices in Latin Christendom," American Historical Review 76 (1971): 16–49, and his book *Religious Poverty and the Profit Economy in Medieval Europe* (London, 1978).

11. On the mendicant orders see R. Brookes, *The Coming of the Friars* (New York, 1975); F. Vernet, *Les Ordres Mendicants*, (Paris, 1933). For a useful survey of the varieties of confraternities, see E. Delaruelle, *L'Église au temps du Grande Schisme et de la crise conciliaire (1378–1449)*, vol. 14 of *Histoire de L'Église,* ed. Fliche and Martin (Paris, 1964), 670–85. On the mendicants and flagellant confraternities in particular see the two collections of articles, "Il Movimento dei Disciplinati nel Settimo Centanario del suo Inizio," *Deputazione di Storia Patria per l'Umbria, Appendice al Bollettino, numero 9* (Perugia, 1962), and "Risultate Prospettive della Ricerca sul Movimento dei Disciplinati," *Convegno Internationale di Studio, Perugia, Centro di documentazione sul movimento dei disciplinati* (Perugia, 1972).

12. Marie Froeschlé-Chopard, *La Religion Populaire en Provence Orientale au XVIIIe siècle* (Paris, 1980), 168.

13. This discussion is drawn primarily from the statutes of the various confraternities. See also Jullien, 56–58; Fontanier, *Pénitents bleus,* and his *Pénitents blancs.* Also of value here are *Notes sur les pénitents bleus* and *Notes sur les pénitents blancs;* Agulhon, 96–99; and Venard, 1581–83.

14. Weissman, 90–95.

15. SPSA, art. 1. For an analysis of the symbolic implications of similar rituals for Florentine companies of disciplinati, see Weissman, chap. 2.

16. See for comparison SPSA, arts. 4, 8; SPSL–1773, arts. 3, 12; SPHS, art. "Statute comme doibvent entrer les Frères la présente fraternité et compagnie pour dire leur office."

17. Venard, 1582; SPSA, art. 31.

18. Such was the style of confraternal chapels in Avignon. While there is no specific evidence that this was the case in Marseille, what evidence does exist supports this conclusion. See Venard, 1582.

19. Fontanier, *Pénitents bleus.*

20. For the penitents of Saint Anthony see SPSA, art. 40; for the penitents of Our Lady of Compassion see Fontanier, *Notes sur les pénitents bleus.* For the story of the Bourras and their effort across the century to build a secret see Jullien, chaps. 6–7, passim.

21. Marcel Régis de la Colombière, *Fêtes patronales et usages des corporations Marseillaises* (Paris and Marseille, 1863; reprint, Marseille, 1977), 10.

22. See Fontanier, *Pénitents noirs.*

23. On the confraternities of Limoges see Guibert, 91–173. On the penitents of the Holy Cross see Fontanier, *Pénitents rouges.*

24. Especially useful here are the statutes of the penitents of Saint Anthony. Also helpful are the various paintings of the general procession made in 1721 to Notre Dame de la Garde, photographs of which are available at the municipal archives of Marseille. See also "Objets des confréries de Pénitents limousins" by the Commandant Martignon, in the *Bulletin de la Société archéologique et historique du Limousin* (1954). For Belsunce's ordinance see Fontanier, *Pénitents noirs,* 56–58.

25. Jullien, chap. 3; *Lazare de Cordier,* bk 1, passim; and in general SPSA, arts. 20–24, and SPB, chap.4.

26. *Lazare de Cordier,* bk. 1, chaps. 5 and 9.

27. *Lazare de Cordier,* bk. 1, chap. 13.

28. For an idea of the relationship between the liturgical year of the confraternities and that of their clerical sponsors, examine the *Calendrier Spirituel de Marseille* by Père Saint Albans, S.J. (Marseille, 1713).

29. Ibid.

30. *Lazare de Cordier,* bk. 1, chaps. 20–21.

31. *Le Calendrier Spirituel de Marseille,* passim.

32. *Lazare de Cordier,* bk. 1, chap. 14.

33. Cf. the pénitents Carmélins and the penitents of the Trinité vieille, both of whom made processions with their clerical patrons.

34. For the types of processions confraternities made see Lazare de Cordier, especially book 2; see also Régis de la Colombière, *Fêtes Patronales et Usages.* For an example of the contracts between confraternities and religious institutions see that between the penitents of the Holy Cross and the Confraternity of Notre Dame de Bon Recontre summarized in Fontanier, *Pénitents rouges.* See also contracts between the penitents of Saint Anthony and the Dominicans, DSA, ff. 153–72. On the pilgrimages of penitents of Saint Anthony see the same register, f. 61.

35. DSA, ff. 60–67. Also see chapter 2 above.

36. SPSH–1731, arts. 8–10.

37. Julian Caro-Baroja, "The City and the Country: Reflections on Some Ancient Common Places," in *Mediterranean Countrymen,* ed. Julian Pitt-Rivers (Paris and The Hague, 1963), 33–34. Charles Phythian-Adams, "Ceremony and the Citizen: The Communal Year at Coventry, 1450–1550," in *The Early Modern Town,* ed. Peter Clarke (London, 1976).

38. Victor Turner, *The Ritual Process: Structure and Anti-Structure* (Ithaca, N.Y., 1969). Weissman's discussion of Turner's ideas in his *Ritual Brotherhood,* chap.1.

39. On the reenactment of the last supper and the episcopal ban against the making of cakes see Jullien, 20–21. See also *Lazare de Cordier,* bk. 1, chap. 20.

40. SPSL–1578, art. 18.

41. Weissman points out that in the latter part of the sixteenth century the confraternities of disciplinati of Florence, which were progressively becoming more elite in their social composition, responded to their members' complaints of the vile and demeaning nature of the act of foot washing by discontinuing the act. I would like to thank Professor Edward Muir for bringing this point to my attention.

42. SPB, chap. 2, arts. 10–11; SPC–1621, art. 8. Also see Jullien, 20–21. For discussion of election procedure of reformed confraternities see chap. 3, part 2.

43. SPSH–1717, art. "Des Exercices Spirituels et Prières"; SPSH–1731, chap. 1, art. 4.

44. SPHS, art. "En quel temps se prendra du discipline."

45. SPB, chap. 2, art. 8.

46. SPB, chap. 2, art. 9.

47. I have taken some liberties with the translation here. De Ruffi wrote: "Toutes ces Chapelles sont d'une sainte institution; la dévotion y regnoit autrefois, comme dans une Maison religieuse la mieux reglée; les status y etoient observés avec beaucoup d'exactitude. Cette ferveur s'est beaucoup ralantie, & ces Compagnies ont cela de commun avec les Communautés les plus austères de l'Église. Toutefois on ne droit pas mettre dans ce nombre les Chapelles du Bon Jésus, de Sainte Croix, du Mont-Carmel & de Saint Maur, parce que les status y sont gardés dans toute leur entenduë." *Histoire de la Ville de Marseille,* 2: 88–89.

48. A. E. Barnes, "On the Necessity of Shaping Men Before Forming Christians: The Institutionalization of Catholicism in Early Modern Europe and Modern Africa," *Historical Reflections/ Réflections Historiques* 16 (1989): 222–23.

49. "Le prieur s'Étant dechaussé ira baiser le Crucifix, et depuis sa place jusque là où est le Crucifix, il fera diverse genuflections, selon sa devotion, ce qui sera continué par tous les Frères, l'un après l'autre." *Heures des frères pénitents bleus fondez sous le titre de Notre-Dame de Pitié, joingant l'Église Collégiale et Paroisiale St. Martin* (Marseille, 1674), Collection Fontanier, 24F–106.

50. Augustin Fabre, *Histoire des Hôpitaux et des Institutions de Bienfaisance de Marseille* (reprint, Geneva, 1973) 300–309.

51. Jullien, 46–51; Fontanier, *Pénitents noirs,* 18.

52. Lucien Fontanier, *Le Tiers-Ordre Observantin et son Bureau d'Assistance et l'Oeuvre de la Pénitente du Bon-Jésus en faveur des Enfants des Marins Pauvres* (Aix-en-Provence, 1922).

53. Fontanier, *Notes sur les pénitents bleus.*

54. Fontanier, *Pénitents de la Charité,* Collection Fontanier.

55. Fontanier, *Pénitents blancs du Saint Esprit,* Collection Fontanier.

56. SPSH–1731, chap. 1, art. 4.

57. SPB, chap. 1, art. 4.

58. Six of these communions were to take place in the chapel. The other four, those on the first Sunday of Lent, Easter, Pentecost and Christmas, "L'on suppose qu'ils scavent qu'ils sont tant au moins obligés d'Être à leur paroisse." See SPSH–1717, "Des Exercices Spirituels et Prières"; SPSH-1731, chap. 1, art. 5.

59. "En menageant avec prudence les moments prècieux des pauvres agonisants, auxquels ils tâcheront d'inspirer une tendre confiance au Père de Miséricorde, melée de l'extrême regret de l'avoir offensé; leur faisant produire des actes de foy, d'esperance et d'amour, de résignation aux douleurs de l'agonie et à la mort même en union de la Mort et Passion de Notre Sauveur por l'expiation de leur péchés." Avis instructif aux Pénitents de Saint Henry (written by Belsunce?), art. 5, attached to SPSH-1731.

60. *Lazare de Cordier,* bk. 1, chap. 4.

61. Jacques Boileau, *Histoire des flagellans, ou l'on fait voir le bon et mauvais usage des flagellations parmi les Chrétiens* (Amsterdam, 1701).

62. DSA, ff. 128–29. See also the *Déliberations* of the Confraternity of the Holy Rosary, Bibliothèque Municipale de Marseille, manuscript 1187, f. 7. The relationship between the penitents of Saint Anthony and the Confraternity of the Rosary is further discussed in the next chapter.

63. This conclusion is based on the statutes of the latter organization, which are included in the register of the confraternity. See *Livre de la Sainte Croix,* ff. 167–69.

64. As noted in chapter 4, the confraternity of the Holy Spirit required that brothers should line up before each of the four annual communions, and then according to rank, reconcile, "les uns les autres." Those who refused were expelled.

65. "Laquelle assemblée a esté proposé par le frère Jean Gris, père Recteur, qui cest avec douleur quel voit gemier (gémir?) depuis quelques années la plus grande partie des frères non seulement pour le relâchement de quelques uns mais encore à cause de la discorde et survenue plusiers fois tant par le défaut des frères que faute d'explication nos statuts et réglements." *Livre de la Sainte Croix,* f. 120.

66. "Pour Contenier les frères et maintenir le bon ordre, il sera tenu tous les premiers dimanche du mois un Régiment particulier pour seclaircir de tous se qui sest passé dans la chapelle et parmi les frères tant pour le temporel que pour le spirituel afain deviter quil ny ait point de division ni de discorde parmi nous." Ibid., f. 121.

Chapter 7

THE CONFRATERNITIES AND THE CLERGY

THE DYNAMICS OF CONFRATERNAL-CLERICAL INTERACTION

The relationship of confraternities with the clergy can be conceived according to two different dynamics. With their clerical sponsors confraternities left the door open for direction, and because of their constant search for devotional acts to perform as penance, their initiatives could always be overriden by clerical evangelism. Although this door more often than not remained closed from the clerical side, there were several examples of religious orders fulfilling a pastoral role. From the beginning the relationship with the episcopacy was an adversarial one. In the sixteenth century and for most of the seventeenth, the confrontation was muted, few bishops having the time or the resources to take on the confraternities; but this only made later bishops more resolute in their determination to bring the confraternities in line.

These two dynamics could have competed, but they predominated in different eras. In the sixteenth century clerical groups enthusiastically supported confraternities. By the start of the religious wars, the major monasteries, as well as all four parishes, had their own associations. The one note of discord during these halcyon days was sounded in 1542 when the Carmelites expelled the penitents of *Notre Dame de Pitié* from their chapel, a decision reversed nine years later out of financial necessity. The experience of the Carmelites is an indication that by the 1540s an awareness had already developed among the clergy of the costs associated with having an independent-minded group of laymen in close proximity. It is instructive that at this point the financial reward was perceived as outweighing the nuisance.

The penitents of *Notre Dame de Pitié* (Carmelites) were a renegade group from the original confraternity. Other clerical groups probably felt that the Carmelites got their just desserts for taking them in. Certainly the monastery's experience did not in-

216

hibit other clerical groups from founding associations—between 1550 and 1580 four new confraternities came into existence. Only during the latter years of the religious wars did clerical groups become truly estranged from penitent confraternities. As recruitment centers for the Catholic Holy League, confraternities probably attracted many violent and/or politically radical individuals. And while the leaders of the league in Marseille, men like Casaulx and Mascaron, made great protestations of their faith, it is questionable whether they recognized the authority of any churchmen. Direct evidence of a decline of commitment by churchmen is available only from the early decades of the seventeenth century, but as in the case of the popularization of confraternal chapels, all indications suggest that the process actually began during the civil wars.

The seventeenth century was the period of the confraternities' greatest popular success. It was also the period when most clerical groups withdrew from any effort at pastoral supervision. There may be a causal connection here, but it is difficult to determine in which direction this occurred. It can be said that for the confraternities the retreat of clerical sponsors was more a bonus than a penalty, since it allowed them greater freedom to develop in directions most attractive to laymen.

By this time, however, the episcopacy had begun to take an interest in confraternal affairs. Thus, as direction from clerical sponsors disappeared, direction from bishops began to take shape. To borrow from Weber, the authority clerical sponsors claimed over confraternities was charismatic. Laymen followed the dictates of these churchmen because they were convinced of the latter's holiness. Bishops claimed the ultimate authority possessed by the church as an institution, seeing themselves as shepherds, and members of confraternities as their flock. And just as the good shepherd never willingly allows part of his flock to stray, so bishops refused to permit the laymen in confraternities freedom to determine their own devotional agendas. The direction bishops sought to give to confraternal life was vastly different from that clerical sponsors had sought, both in its conception of what was devout and in its expectation of compliance to this ideal. Few laymen would have taken issue with the shepherd/flock metaphor. The problem was that few felt themselves to be as sheepish as bishops insisted. The confrontation between bishops and confreres involved more than confraternal independence; it involved an assessment of the spiritual tradition behind that independence. This spiritual tradition had once been one of, as Bossy characterized it, "super-orthodoxy." But for Counter-Reformation bishops it was in its essence, as Bishop Belsunce explained, "presque profane."

CONFRATERNITIES AND THEIR CLERICAL SPONSORS

As lay associations confraternities required the service of priests for the performance of weekly mass, the rite of communion during major celebrations such as Easter or Christmas, and the feast of their patronal devotion. Almost all the confraternities also paid their chaplains to sing weekly masses in honor of their dead (although these services normally took place in the church of the chaplains). Chaplains also were expected to be available to march in funeral processions and perform burial rites. At the heart of the relationship between a confraternity and its chaplains were written contracts which explicated such services and the amount chaplains would receive in compensation. It might be expected that these contracts determined the basic level of interaction between the two groups. The evidence suggests, however, that clergy conscientiously fulfilled their contractual obligations only with those confraternities with whom they maintained an intimate pastoral relationship.

The relationships maintained by the Trinitarians with the three confraternities who looked to them for chaplains provide useful examples. Not much detailed information exists on the relationship between the Trinitarians and the penitents of the Trinité vieille, but it is clear that throughout its existence the confraternity remained very close to the religious order. The Trinitarians dressed the confraternity in white robes with their own blue and red insignia and the scapular of the Trinitarian confraternity of Notre Dame de Bonne Ayde, and assigned them the task of soliciting funds for the Bureau pour le Rédemption des Ecslaves.[1] Fabre's uncharitable assessment to the contrary, without the prestige of the Trinitarians and their Bureau the confraternity probably would not have been so successful in collecting funds. And it is to the Trinitarians' credit that the confraternity became so efficient in its appointed task. The fees paid by the confraternity to the religious order were relatively high, but the confraternity was also comparatively large with a diverse population. And when the confraternity was in need of a new chapel, the Trinitarians helped organize and run a raffle to generate the funds needed for the task. It is also worth noting that while the monastery broke its connections with the other two confraternities during the eighteenth century, it maintained its relationship with the penitents of the Trinité vieille until 1792. The relationship between the Trinitarians and the penitents of the Trinité vieille exemplified the way in which a lay organization could grow and function under the direction of a clerical group.

The relationship between the Trinitarians and the penitents of the *Trinité nouvelle* was not as cordial. Soon after its establishment the confraternity went shopping for new spiritual directors and for most of the late sixteenth century associated itself with the priests at the parish church of Notre Dame des Accoules. That relationship must have proved even less satisfying, for in 1601 the confraternity renegotiated its contract with the Trinitarians. The substance of this contract is interesting for the light it sheds on the areas of estrangement between the two parties. The Trinitarians received sixty livres yearly for providing chaplain service to the confraternity. During their first tenure the religious order evidently had been lax in the performance of their obligations, and before returning to the fold, the confraternity wanted assurance that such behavior would not be repeated. Accordingly, a clause was inserted in the renegotiated contract allowing the confraternity the right to subtract one ecu (three livres) from the sixty livres each time the member of the order appointed to provide chaplain service failed to appear for one of the confraternity's events. Since entrance to the chapel of the penitents of the Trinité nouvelle was gained through the church of the Trinitarian monastery, it was part of the duties of the Trinitarians to see that one of their members unlocked the door of the church at the times when the penitents would be using their chapel. Here also the Trinitarians had apparently been lax, so a clause in the contract allowed the penitents to force the door of the church whenever the Trinitarians failed to open it.[2]

It would be nice to say that the confraternity and the religious order settled down to a positive and mutually satisfying relationship. But again in the 1639 and 1684 the two parties signed contracts essentially enjoining the religious order to fulfill its original obligations as chaplains. And both in 1641 and 1671 the question of the chapel door again became a point of contention. The available record of contracts between the confraternity and the Trinitarians stops at the end of the seventeenth century. But it is worth noting that in 1771, because of lack of membership, the two Trinitarian monasteries in Marseille were combined. The Trinitarians made use of the occasion to free themselves from their obligations to the penitents of the Trinité nouvelle. It is not known which religious order provided the confraternity with chaplain service from that point.[3]

While the Trinitarians were less than conscientious in their relationship with the penitents of the Trinité nouvelle, they were positively antagonistic to the pénitents Bourras, the third confraternity for whom they provided chaplain service. From the time the confraternity moved into a chapel on the grounds of the monastery in 1604 until the Trinitarians summarily discontinued supplying it with chaplains in 1733, the two parties went to court against each other at least five times, not to mention the presumably numerous confrontations that did not reach this stage and thus went unrecorded.[4] In 1632 the representative of the monastery complained to the *lieutenant de la Sénéschaussée* about the chanting of the pénitents Bourras and the Trinité nouvelle during their Saturday night services. The Bourras began theirs at approximately two o'clock. The penitents of the Trinité nouvelle began theirs, as the representative of the monastery complained, about the time the Bourras finished. The Trinitarians wanted the singing stopped so that they could get some sleep. "Should the present state of affairs continue," summed up the representative, "it will be necessary to abandon the monastery!" According to Jullien, fortune rarely took the side of the Bourras in their battles with the Trinitarians, but this time it did. The lieutenant, it seems, was a relative of one of the leaders of the pénitents Bourras. He came and listened to the services of the confraternities and declared that they were not as loud as the Trinitarians complained.[5]

Perhaps this defeat was still on their minds when in 1643 the Trinitarians set out to expel the confraternity from its chapel. The religious order had originally sold land to the confraternity without the authorization of its chapter-general, which its constitution did not allow it to do. Based on this loophole, the order argued before the Parlement de Provence that they had a right to expel the Bourras from their chapel. This right the Parlement granted, with the stipulation that the Trinitarians reimburse the confraternity for its investment up to that point, a sum reckoned at three thousand livres. In a dramatic confrontation before their chapel door, the Bourras only grudgingly accepted the court order to vacate the premises. They made one last appeal of the decision to the Parlement de Provence, but the verdict remained the same. At this point, early in 1644, fortune smiled on the confraternity once more; the Trinitarians were unable to pay the three thousand livres, so after more than a year of conflict the situation remained the same.[6]

With this sort of background, it is not surprising that in 1733 the Trinitarians decided to discontinue their service as chaplains for the pénitents Bourras. This sent the Bourras off on a search for a new set of chaplains. From 1733 to 1742 an unidentified religious order served in this role. In 1742 the confraternity began a forty-year relationship with the Servites, which seems to have been the most satisfying it experienced. But in 1782, because of a lack of members, the Servite monastery in Marseille was dissolved. For the last ten years of their pre-Revolutionary existence, the Bourras had chaplain services performed by another unidentified religious order.[7]

The chapel of the penitents of the Trinité vieille was situated on the grounds of the Franciscan monastery, one reason perhaps, why the Trinitarians remained relatively close to them. As the experiences of the two confraternities whose chapels were located on their premises illustrate, the order was next to impossible as landlords. No doubt the chanting of the confraternities did disturb the sleeping monks on Saturday night; but as churchmen they should have been eager to sacrifice a few hours sleep for the opportunity to play a positive role in the spiritual development of so many souls. That they were not, that they were in fact quite resentful of the inconvenience, is a graphic indication that the Trinitarians did not perceive their contracted obligations to serve as chaplains as an opportunity to evangelize.

Evidence suggests that the Trinitarians were not unique in such behavior. Lazare de Cordier, as prior of the penitents of the Holy Spirit, made an effort to gain restitution from the priests at Notre Dame des Accoules for a similar failure to perform contracted services. As Lazare de Cordier pointed out in his letter to the priests, the penitents of the Holy Spirit had paid the parish two hundred ecus in 1582 to establish two perpetual requiem masses. These masses were to be said after matins at the main altar of the parish church every Mondy and Friday, with the priest assisted by deacon and sub-deacon. Before the masses the church bells were to be rung, and during the masses two torches were to be burned. Several times in the past, Lazare de Cordier noted, the penitents had had cause to complain about the laxity of the priests in the performance of this obligation. At this point, in 1661, he felt it necessary to request back the two hundred ecus so that the confraternity might seek to have this service fulfilled elsewhere. The outcome of the complaint is not known, but there is no record of the confraternity changing its chaplains.[8]

The search made by the penitents of the Trinité nouvelle for new chaplains soon after their establishment and the contract the penitents later signed with the Trinitarians both suggest that the religious order was negligent in the fulfillment of its duties from the very inception of the relationship. It would seem that the confraternity's prime, and perhaps only, attraction for the religious was the rent they provided for a chapel built originally for the penitents of the Trinité vieille. Certainly no sense of pastoral commitment animated the relationship between the Trinitarians and the pénitents Bourras. The simple fact is that, if the religious order could have afforded the cost, it would have washed its hands of the confraternity as early as 1643 instead of letting the relationship drift on for another seventy years. Like the Carmelites—who a century earlier had tried to dispose of their commitment to the penitents of Notre Dame de Pitié (Carmelites) only to invite the confraternity back because they needed the revenues from rents and chaplain fees— the Trinitarians were constrained to maintain their relationships with the penitents of the Trinité nouvelle and the pénitents Bourras out of economic need. It takes little imagination, however, to appreciate the lack of enthusiasm on the part of the religious order for these relationships. Can one picture anything more formal, or more perfunctory than the way the Trinitarians must have performed their duties as chaplains of the pénitents Bourras after 1643?

Relations such as existed between the Trinitarians and the penitents of the Trinité vieille were unusual but not exceptional. The Minims gradually nurtured the penitents of the Holy Cross to the point that the confraternity established itself as a third order to the religious order. The Carmélins were originally conceived of by the Carmelites as an extension of their scapular confraternity and wore the insignia of that confraternity on their outfits. While it is uncertain whether the confraternity ever lived up to the Carmelites' expectations, relations continued between the two. The penitents of Saint Anthony and the Dominicans provide an interesting example of how a relationship between a confraternity and a religious order could evolve. The penitents of Saint Anthony came into existence as protegés of the Fathers of Saint Anthony. Very early the confraternity moved its chapel, then its contract for chaplain service to the Dominicans. Gradually over the seventeenth century, the Dominicans nurtured the confraternity into accepting a role as an auxiliary of their confraternity of the Holy Rosary.[9]

In all four of the above cases the relationships were built on, or cemented by, some form of institutional connection above and beyond that of a contract. Most of the confraternities did not have such "special" relationships. Interaction with their chaplains was superficial, contractual, and if the above examples are a fair indication, at times antagonistic.

While the transformations the confraternities experienced during the civil war era were certainly one source for clerical disinterest, the example of the pénitents Bourras and the Trinitarians argues against seeing this as the sole cause. The Bourras were the model of a devout association, yet this did not stop the Trinitarians from trying to force them away. The majority of the religious orders that provided chaplain service to the confraternities had their origins in the Middle Ages. By the seventeenth century they were in a losing competition with newer Counter-Reformation orders such as the Jesuits, the Capuchins, and the Oratorians for the best and brightest of those entering the clergy. By the eighteenth century almost all were in the throes of decline.

Another factor in the withdrawal of religious orders from active supervision of confraternities must have been the gradual decline of the religious orders themselves. The eighteenth-century peregrinations of the pénitents Bourras in search of chaplains have been noted, as has the search after 1771 by the penitents of the Trinité nouvelle. The penitents of Saint John the Baptist also spent the last years before the Revolution in search of chaplains. The problems these confraternities had finding chaplains probably reflect a situation that began in the seventeenth century as the lack of new blood caused older religious orders to retreat from their commitments to the laity.[10]

Why did not the new religious orders of the Counter-Reformation step in to fill the vacuum? To a certain extent they did. The Minims, established in Marseille during the second half of the sixteenth century, founded the penitents of the Holy Cross. The Fathers of Mercy, another order that appeared in the sixteenth century, took over the chaplain duties for the penitents of Notre Dame de Pitié (Saint Martin parish) from the parish priests of Saint Martin during the seventeenth century. The Fathers of Saint Maur, a reformed Benedictine group established during the seventeenth century, played a role in the foundation of the penitents of Saint Maur. These were all minor religious groups, however. The more prominent of the new religious orders, such as the Jesuits and the Capuchins, preferred developing their own confraternities to taking over the direction of existing ones. In other parts of France the Jesuits especially were active in promoting and developing penitent confraternities. Perhaps because penitent confraternities had existed for such a long time in Marseille and had already established their niche in the local religious environment, new religious orders shied away from investing energy in their redevelopment as part of those orders own evangelical missions.[11]

The parish clergy had an important role in the implantation of the confraternities in Marseille. The clergy at Saint Martin's parish cut its connections with the penitents of Saint Martin's parish early in the seventeenth century, and we know from Lazare de Cordier's efforts that relations between the penitents of the Holy Spirit and the chapter of canons at Notre Dame des Accoules were less than friendly. And since Bishop Vintimille's plan for reforming the confraternities featured the use of the parish clergy as monitors of confraternal finance, it seems certain that by the end of the seventeenth century parish clergy related to the confraternities primarily as auxiliaries of the bishops. Thus there may be some significance to the fact that the three confraternities forced to dissolve by the royal commission sent to investigate confraternal finances in 1768 were the three remaining confraternities dependent on the parish clergy for chaplain service. By 1770 the parish clergy had completely disassociated itself from the maintenance of the city's penitent associations.

The picture of the relations between confraternities and their chaplains drawn here is stark and somewhat counter-intuitive. It is hard to believe that connections as tenuous as those described here could survive for centuries. But as suggested above, there was some economic incentive for clergymen to maintain the connections, and performance of the duties of chaplain to a penitential confraternity was not especially taxing. And from the confraternities' perspective, the inconvenience of the occasional non-appearing chaplain must have been more than outweighed by the freedom gained from clerical noninterference. It should also be remembered that laymen who wanted more spiritual direction had the option of joining a confraternity with a closer bond with its clerical mentors. The status quo for most of Marseille's confraternities for most of their existence was a situation in which their clerical sponsors exercised little influence over their organizational lives. Beginning in the second half of the seventeenth century, bishops began to change the status quo.

THE CONFRATERNITIES AND THE EPISCOPACY

During the first one hundred fifty years after their introduction into Marseille, confraternities of penitents experienced little effective episcopal supervision. During most of this period the episcopal see of Marseille was a political prize granted by the kings of France to their protégés. Of the fourteen bishops of Marseille between 1490 and 1640, four never took possession of their see, two did not reside, and the other eight, either because of other commitments or because of their inability to tame the inhabitants of the city, never established effective episcopal control.[12]

It is unclear when to date the beginnings of the effort to bring the city under effective episcopal control. The blessed Jean Baptiste Gault (1642–43) is usually credited with the introduction of the Counter-Reformation in Marseille. Brilliant and dedicated, Gault gave promise of totally reforming the spiritual life of the Marseillais. His reign was cut short by death, however, after only four months on the see. Étienne de Puget (1644–68), Gault's successor, was the first true Counter-Reformation bishop of Marseille. From Puget onward Marseille benefitted from a succession of competent, committed episcopal administrators who gradually revitalized the city's ecclesiastical organization. Not surprisingly, earlier bishops paid little attention to penitent confraternities— they had much more pressing concerns. Only with Charles de Vintimille (1684–1708) and Henri de Belsunce (1709–55) did reform of the confraternities become a priority.

The one available document which describes the relationship between the confraternities and the bishops of Marseille between 1499 and Vintimille's episcopacy dates from 1605. In it Bishop Turricella (1605–1618) agrees to renew the permission granted by his predecessor for the confraternities to receive communion in their chapels on Easter Sunday, on condition that the priest who performed the rite be delegated by the parish priest. The document goes on to explain that while the confraternities did have the right to receive communion in their chapels, a right which the parish clergy was required to recognize and honor, nevertheless the monies collected during the offering on Easter Sunday belonged to the parish, and were to be given to the priest performing the rite. Also to be given to the priest was a list of all the confreres who had received communion. This list was to be passed on to the parish clergy who presumably checked the names against the parish list. Eventually the list was to be presented to the bishop at the annual diocesan synod.[13]

Lazare de Cordier provides some background on the document. According to him, at least since the reign of Turricella's predecessor, Frédéric Ragueneau (1572–1603), confraternities had been petitioning the bishop for permission to receive Easter communion in their chapels. The parish churches were too crowded, their petitions ran, and the multitude of women present on that day offered the weaker-hearted brothers an invitation to sin. The decrees of the Council of Trent, the confraternities argued, only required that a confrere make confession at his parish, not receive communion there. Ragueneau disagreed, and required all members of confraternities of penitents to receive communion at their parish church or be excommunicated. It is doubtful, though, that this ordinance was effective. Ragueneau, a supporter of Henry III in a city very much committed to the Holy League, spent most of the 1590s in self-imposed exile in Italy.[14] He was not even the predecessor noted in the 1605 document. The earlier permission for the confraternities to receive Easter communion in their chapels had been granted in 1597, when the episcopal see was vacant, and the authorizing official was the vice-legate from Avignon.[15]

Lazare de Cordier described the 1605 agreement as a wise compromise based on an Italian precedent. Exactly what he means cannot be established because the precise substance of the 1597 document is not known. From the 1605 document it can be gleaned that parochial dissent from the practices of the confraternities had existed earlier. From Lazare de Cordier's commentary it follows that the confraternities had been so serious and so insistent in their efforts to receive communion in their chapels that Ragueneau had had to resort to the threat of excommunication as a means of forcing them to follow his ordinance. But as Lazare de Cordier goes on to say, the 1605 agreement represented a compromise which, while safeguarding the rights of the parish, also fulfilled the desires of the confraternities of penitents. It seems safe to conclude that the stipulations that the priest who performs the rite be delegated by the parish priest, that the alms collected that day were the property of the parish, and that the name of each confrere who received communion be taken down in order to be noted on parish records, were all Turricella's innovations. This would leave the simple permission for the confraternities of penitents to receive communion in their chapels as the substance of the 1597 document.

Easter communion is the central rite of the Catholic faith, the measure by which the church itself determines who is and who is not a faithful member. That the confraternities were capable of performing the rite in their chapels gives a good indication of the degree to which at the end of the sixteenth century they acted as an alternative to the parish, indeed, as the central institution in the religious lives of their members. In their defense of the practice of taking Easter communion at their chapels the confraternities made no reference to past custom. Presumably had such an argument been available, the confraternities would have used it. Their failure to do so, then, suggests that the practice was an innovation of the civil war era. One may speculate that initially most confraternities had participated in Easter rites at the churches of their chaplains or clerical sponsors, and that in the wake of the withdrawal of the clergy from active supervision of the confraternities they took the initiative in having the rites performed in their chapels. Certainly this line of reasoning makes more sense than the concept of confraternities originally receiving communion at the parish church and then unilaterally deciding to move their reception of the host to their chapels.

If these speculations are correct, then Turricella's compromise of 1605 may in fact represent a fledgling effort to bring the confraternities under some type of episcopal control. Significantly, this effort did not involve challenging the confraternities' autonomy, only neutralizing what was to the parish clergy the most threatening aspects of this autonomy. Turricella's compromise required the confraternities to respect the primacy of the parish in lay devotional life, but it did nothing to align the activities of the confraternities with the activities of the parish, the major concern of bishops a century later.

According to Lazare de Cordier, Turricella's compromise remained in effect until the 1640s, when Bishop Puget put a halt to the practice of the confraternities receiving Easter communion at their chapels, not by prohibiting the act but by refusing to recognize this communion as valid, and requiring each confrere to receive communion within two weeks at his parish.[16] It was Puget also who chastised Lazare de Cordier for presuming, as prior of the penitents of the Holy Spirit, to preach during Sunday services at the chapel. And the January 17, 1653 entry in the *Délibérations* of the penitents of Saint Anthony records that on this day, the feast of Saint Anthony, Bishop Puget came to visit the confraternity's chapel, celebrated mass with the confreres, then granted permission for the confraternity to expose the holy sacrament on that day.[17]

There is no evidence that most priors presumed to preach to their confreres, so Lazare de Cordier's actions, and Puget's reactions to it, should be read as an exceptional case. And Puget did not condemn the practice of Easter communion in the chapel as much as he declared that in the eyes of the church the rite would no longer be recognized as valid. Similarly, he did not change the practices of the penitents of Saint Anthony, only asserted his right to approve their performance. Like Turricella, Puget did not challenge the autonomy of the confraternities as much as try to curb what to him were its most obnoxious manifestations.

Another document that sheds light on the relationship between the episcopacy and the confraternities dates from 1698. Charles Gaspard de Vintimille took charge of the diocese of Marseille in 1684, although he was not invested as bishop until 1692. In 1698 he published a set of ordinances regulating the religious activities of his diocese. Four of the six were concerned with the financial administration of all confraternities and are interesting in that they placed all aspects of the financial administration of confraternities, even those associated with the churches of regulars, under the supervision of the curés. Vintimille also felt it necessary in one ordinance to impose several prohibitions on the confraternities of penitents: celebration of their offices during the time of the parochial services, the entrance of women into their chapels even during religious celebrations open to the general public, and the performance of the rite of holy communion in their chapels without his permission. In the second ordinance aimed at penitent confraternities, he prohibited the confraternities from holding any processions without his permission and from making their annual Holy Thursday processions at any time but during the morning hours. In this second ordinance he also regulated their conduct during processions and required them to be punctual in their attendance at burials of their confreres. Finally, he disallowed deviations from the normal routes followed in the burial processions and forbade confraternities from enrolling in their membership registers any person dead or at the point of dying.[18]

By the end of the seventeenth century, as waking up in the early hours of the morning lost its allure as an act of penance, many confraternities rescheduled their weekly prayer meetings at times that brought them into conflict with services being held at the local parish. Bishops could not force members of confraternities to attend services at their parishes, but they could, like Vintimille, prohibit the scheduling of simultaneous events at the chapel.[19]

More difficult to interpret is the ordinance banning the entrance of women in confraternal chapels. One of the arguments put forward by confraternities to justify receiving Easter communion in their chapels had been that the sight of women at the parish posed too much of a temptation to sin (presumably in thought and not in deed) for weaker members. This notion of women as inimical to penitential piety was still present in the eighteenth century. Agulhon reports that Archbishop Brancas of Aix-en-Provence felt it necessary in 1739 in the same set of ordinances to prohibit the confraternities of that city from holding assemblies in their chapels, "ni avant le soleil levé ni après le soleil couché," and from permitting access to "aucune personne du sexe" (though as Agulhon later points out, Brancas' prohibition against nocturnal meetings was motivated by a concern to control the dissemination of Jansenist ideas).[20] Agulhon also notes the scandal created in Aix in 1776 when a group of women singers performed before one of that city's chapels of penitents.[21] The theme of women as pollution is found nowhere else in the documentation, however. On the other hand, the statutes of the *pénitents blancs* of *Notre Dame de Gonfalon* of Lyon contain several articles regulating the behavior of women and children in the choir built above that confraternity's main chapel. It is clear that the confraternity was serving as an alternative to the parish not only for its members but for their families as well. Something similar perhaps was occurring in Marseille's confraternal chapels. Vintimille's ordinance probably was aimed at reducing the threat confraternities posed to the parish.

Vintimille was the first bishop to take the initiative in dealing with the confraternities. Unlike his predecessors he did not negotiate with the confraternities, but asserted his authority over all aspects of their activities. It is not known, however, how the confraternities responded. Bishop Vintimille left the diocese of Marseille in 1708 and was replaced by Bishop Poudeaux who died within the year. In 1709 Bishop Belsunce began his forty-six year reign over the see of Marseille. Because of the crucial role he played in the history of the confraternities, it is useful to review the salient facts of his life.

Henri François Xavier de Belsunce de Castelmoron was born in Perigord in 1674, the second son of the Baron de Castelmoron. He came from the long line of Huguenots and was baptized by a Protestant minister. In 1680 his family proclaimed itself Catholic, but later returned to the old religion.[22] Still, his father was politically astute enough to consent to his son being raised as a Catholic. Henri was trained by the Jesuits at the College Louis-le-Grand in Paris. From the first his family chose for him a career in the church, and at the age of eighteen he received the abbacy of the monastery at Reole in Bearn. To his parents' consternation he renounced this position and sought entrance into the Society of Jesus.

Though Belsunce lived past his eightieth year, he was always in poor health, and the life of a Jesuit proved too arduous for his constitution. In 1701, near death, he left the Society and returned to his parents' chateau. Recuperated, he launched an ecclesiastical career which in eight years saw him advance from parish priest on his familial estates, to vicar-general of the diocese of Agen, to bishop of Marseille.

As a bishop Belsunce well fulfilled the Counter-Reformation ideal for which Saint Charles Borromeo was the prototype. Soon after his installment he reorganized the diocesan seminary for the training of priests and made it more rigorous. During the 1730s he established the College Belsunce for the training of laymen as well as future clerics, and placed it under the supervision of the Jesuits. For the clergy of his diocese he arranged a synod in 1712 and various retreats after that. In 1722 he established a bi-monthly series of lectures on theological topics given by Jesuit scholars. During his reign seven new religious orders were established in Marseille and a fifth parish added to the existing four. Belsunce did not spend all his time in ecclesiastical administration. He was known for his many pastoral visits to the minor churches and chapels of the diocese and for his impromptu sermons made while on walking tours of the city. Soon after his arrival he wrote a new catechism, which remained in use until 1849. On his invitation the Capuchins preached countless missions in the diocese. During one of these missions, in 1734, Belsunce, despite his sixty years, preached, heard confession, and administered the sacraments for forty days in succession.

Belsunce is best remembered in the histories of Marseille for two things. First, for his refusal to leave the city during the Plague of 1720 and his resolute leadership of the city during the crisis, and second, for his forty-year battle against Jansenism. Perhaps it was the legacy of his Calvinist forebearers that made Belsunce so diligent and narrow in his defense of the bull *Unigenitus*. Then again, perhaps it was his love for the Society of Jesus and its ideals that gave such strength to his fight against the Jansenists. Either way Belsunce was among the first French prelates to recognize the bull in 1713, and in defense of it he initiated a war of words with Jansenist writers across France that continued into the 1740s. Until his death he maintained a fanatical concern to keep his diocese free of Jansenist influences.

Belsunce's first communique to the confraternities is now lost.[23] In the general ordinances for the diocese Belsunce published in 1712, however, there is a section on confraternities. For the most part, the regulations are an extension and elaboration of those of Vintimille, but with several important additions. Among the ordinances regulating confraternities in general, there is one which required that all confraternities hold yearly elections for priors and other major officers. As the ordinance explains, this was to halt the practice in some confraternities of one or more men remaining in control for several years at a time. Henceforth, confraternities had to hold elections within fifteen months of the previous election or have the powers of the officers in charge voided.[24]

Another general ordinance, seeking to prevent "des disputes scandaleuses" that developed Sunday mornings at parish churches when the various questors seeking alms competed among themselves to go first, stipulated that henceforth the questors for the Corpus Domini (i.e., the lay association responsible for parish upkeep) would take precedence over all other confraternities. This ordinance did not necessarily relieve the congestion, but it did clarify that the parish and its needs would have priority over all other charitable enterprises.[25]

In the preamble to the ordinances specifically aimed at penitent confraternities, Belsunce articulates the guiding principles in his efforts to reform them:

> Nous voudrions de tout notre coeur voir revivre de nos jours ces temps fortunés où l'esprit de piété, de ferveur, de détachment et de soumission faisant l'aimable caractère des confréries établies dans l'Église et où ceux qui les composaint, se souvenant que, séparés en quelque manière du reste du monde, ils devaient mener une vie, plus exemplaire, plus chrétienne, plus humble, plus pénitente et plus mortifiée que le commun des fidèles, retraçaient par leurs vertus et leurs exemples, la vie des premiers chrétiens. Les Institutions et les Réglements des Confréries sont toujours les mêmes, les obligations des confréries n'ont point changé: mais leur esprit s'étant peu à peu perdu, elles ne sont pas plus aujourd'hui pour la plupart que des assemblées presque profanes, où l'on voit moins de dévotion qu'ailleurs, et beaucoup plus de vanité et indépendance; et ce qui devrait servir à la santification des fidèles n'est le plus souvent qu'en vain prétexte pour les éloigner de leurs Paroisses et même pour plusieurs, une occasion de débauche.[26]

If by "soumission" Belsunce means to his authority, then it can be stated that there was never a time when the confraternities willingly accepted episcopal authority. They had suffered from "vanité" and "indépendance" from the beginning, first under the direction of their clerical sponsors, then under their own impulse. In picturing the confraternities as having declined from some previous spiritual state, however, Belsunce could clothe his innovations in the fabric of reform. In this light the most telling comment in the statement is the observation that the confraternities were only a "vain prétexte" for their members to avoid participation in religious activities at their parish. Over the next four decades Belsunce would attempt to remove this "pretext."

Not surprisingly, the first topic in the ordinances directed at penitential confraternities was parochial obligations. Unlike Vintimille, however, Belsunce sought to negotiate. Confreres were exhorted to attend Sunday services at their parish at least one out of every three Sundays. And while there was no penalty for not doing so, the ordinance went on to justify itself with the comment that the religious obligations of members of confraternities were the same as those of other members of the faithful. As long as they fulfilled their Easter obligations, there was no legal way for Belsunce to force members of confraternities to attend Sunday services, particularly if they attended services at their chapels on the same day. Belsunce tried instead to compromise: He threatened the confraternities with a rigorous interpretation of their obligations as Christians, and then cajoled them with a willingness to accept a modified form of this obligation.[27]

Belsunce also modified Vintimille's prohibition against the admission of women to the chapels of confraternities. Whenever women, as part of parochial celebrations, made a procession to one of the chapels, Belsunce now permitted them in. This modification lends support to the earlier interpretation that the motivation for excluding women from participation in activities in confraternal chapels was the danger such participation posed to religious life at the parish. In the context of parochial activity such participation was now deemed acceptable.[28]

The most important addition Belsunce made to the ordinances of Vintimille, however, was a prohibition of clerical members appearing in public in the robes and hoods of confraternity members. Henceforth, when churchmen marched in confraternal processions, they were to do so in their surplices. Furthermore, from that day forward any priest desiring to join a confraternity had to gain his permission beforehand.[29] Priests and members of religious orders had made up a significant portion of the membership of confraternities from the beginning, and under the cover of robes and hoods, mixed freely and equally with lay members. Such behavior, Belsunce argued, was contrary to priestly dignity. Left unsaid was the fact that clerical members marching in the robes and hoods of members certified the special status of penitential confraternities as different and superior to other types of lay associations.

Thus, the intent of this ordinance was not simply to establish more distance between cleric and layman. It was also to make more explicit the lay nature of penitential confraternities.

Belsunce's next set of regulations date from 1739. During the intervening years he had achieved renown throughout France for his fight against the Jansenists and fame across western Europe for his resolute leadership of Marseille during the years of the plague, 1720–21. During these years he had not ignored the confraternities. Especially in the years before the plague and before his battle with the Jansenists intensified, he busied himself in the development of the penitents of Saint Henry as a model confraternity. He also reestablished the penitents of Saint Maur under the Oratorians. In the 1720s and 1730s he came to regret the latter action as the Oratorians emerged as the coordinators of the Jansenist movement in Marseille. In 1737 Belsunce felt obliged to write the *intendant* of the province.

> Monsieur. . . . Il est encore très vrai que la chapelle des pénitents de St-Maur, qui est fort près de l'Oratoire et qui a autrefois été erigée par les pères de cette congrégation, est l'assemblage de tout ce que nous avons icy de jansénistes et que ceux qui s'engagent dans cette compagnie, étant bons et soumis catholiques, y sont bientost pervertis. Cette chapelle de St-Maur a une porte de derrière dans un lieu écarté, et c'est par cette porte et non par la grande, que les Frères Pènitents entrent et sortent ordinairement.
>
> S'ils veulent tenir des assemblées, rien ne leur est plus aisé, sous prétexte des enterrements des pauvres; il n'est guères de jours qu'il n'y ait des Pénitents qui y vont.[30]

Belsunce was concerned enough about the problem to station spies outside the chapel of the penitents of Saint Maur in an unsuccessful effort to gather evidence against them.[31]

The 1739 ordinances have a different tenor than the earlier ones. In the preamble Belsunce allows himself a note of self-congratulation in recognizing that the confraternities had come far along the road of reform that he advocated. But they had not gone far enough. Once again Belsunce chastises the confraternities for laxity in performance of their Christian obligations. Two new types of concern, however, are the focus of this set of ordinances. The more important was the problem of confreres not going to confession. To deal with this problem Belsunce granted the members of confraternities nineteen days to go to confession and bring certification of this act to the governing council of their confraternity. Failure to confess during this period would lead to the exclusion of the confrere from the activities of his confraternity. Next Belsunce proclaimed that in the future each confrere was to go to confession during Lent or suffer the same penalty. Last, he required that before a man could be accepted into a confraternity, he had to certify that he had attended confession within the last year.[32]

The second new problem was the practice of some men, upon being expelled from one confraternity, enrolling in another. This particular problem had been one of the causes behind the institution of a period of a novitiate by some confraternities. To deal with this problem, Belsunce required that the candidacy of each individual be discussed publicly within the confraternity, and that each individual seeking transfer from one confraternity to another get written permission from him beforehand.[33]

We lack the text of the next missive Belsunce sent out in 1747. But from a later reference it can be established that this missive required all confraternities to bring their missals to Belsunce to be corrected or face interdiction. In this way Belsunce hoped to establish uniformity and orthodoxy in the liturgies of the various confraternities.[34] The text of Belsunce's final ordinances regulating confraternities of penitents, written in 1751, has been preserved. Belsunce by then had been in his see for forty-one years, and a great part of this final missive is given over to theological musings as he seeks to explain to the confraternities their reason for existence. From these musings we can get a view of the state of the confraternities through the eyes of the man who had attempted to reform them for more than forty years. Belsunce was upset with the quality of the individuals the confraternities were matriculating. For him confraternities of penitents were select societies of only the most pious, committed men—an attitude that no doubt was behind the arduous novitiate of the penitents of Saint Henry. He was distressed also about the decline of discipline within the confraternities. Confreres, he noted, openly frequented "spectacles," dances, cabarets, and gambling places. But these were minor transgressions that dimmed before a greater abuse: many confreres had taken "ne faire point de Pâques, et passer ensuite tranquillement plusieurs années sans s'acquitter de ce devoir." This is the first direct mention of the confraternities and their Easter obligations in an episcopal ordinance for more than one hundred years. It provides an indication of the results of the episcopal policy, begun by Etienne de Puget a century earlier, of requiring the members of confraternities to fulfill this obligation at their parish church; the members eventually ceased to do so.[35] To meet this challenge, Belsunce adopted in the ordinances the same technique he had earlier employed in getting confreres to attend confession. Henceforth, no man could be admitted into a confraternity without a certificate from either one of the vicar generals or from his parish curé verifying that he had recently received communion. This certificate had to be copied by the confraternity "mot à mot" in its membership book, or the confraternity faced being placed under interdiction. Further, failure to receive Easter communion at the parish was established as an abuse for which the penalty was automatic expulsion from the confraternity. Laxity on the part of the confraternity in the prosecution of this abuse would lead to it being placed under interdiction.[36]

There was very little that Belsunce could do about the problem of the quality of men the confraternities were accepting. But he could stop one of the greatest abuses in this area by requiring that boys attain the age of fourteen and have the permission of their guardians before being admitted into a confraternity. Also he could put pressure on the confraternities by requiring that any member who led a "vie scandaleuse" be expelled from the confraternity. Exactly who was to decide what constituted such a life is left unsaid. Failure to follow these regulations would cause a confraternity to be placed under interdiction.[37]

Was Belsunce successful? There are no reports of confrontations between confraternities and Belsunce and no reports of a confraternity being placed under interdiction to help gauge the reception of Belsunce's reforms. But their changing focus suggests that he must have had some degree of success. Moreover, the financial reports collected in 1727 and the statutes edited in preparation for his episcopal visit in 1739 provide evidence that the confraternities recognized his authority.

Belsunce was successful in reforming the confraternities along what can be recognized as one of the main lines of the Counter-Reformation, that is, the imposition of the bishop's authority over all aspects of lay devotional life. In this sense his actions were but a culmination of the movement that began with Puget and continued with Vintimille. The types of problems these bishops sought to deal with were not new, for as we have seen, the confraternities themselves had previously developed procedures to deal with them. But either these procedures did not work, or more probably they did not work to the satisfaction of the bishops. What Belsunce did across the first half of the eighteenth century was to devise, and put the finishing touches on, a system for controlling the confraternities from above. For some matters he legislated direct intervention, as in his efforts to establish uniformity among the statutes and liturgies of the confraternities. In others he was content to place pressure on the confraternities themselves to make the necessary reforms, as with his threat of interdiction to force the confraternities to discipline members who failed to make yearly confession or take Easter communion, or who led, "vies scandaleuses."

But it would be wrong to conclude that this successful administrative reform signaled organizational transformation. How deeply Belsunce affected the esprit de corps of the confraternities is a matter about which we can only speculate. Two minor incidents give some insight into the effect Belsunce had on the confraternities. The pénitents Bourras in 1751 petitioned Belsunce to change the time of their Sunday services from 3:00 A.M. to 5:00 A.M. Belsunce rejected the request, issuing an episcopal ordinance prohibiting such change to make sure the confraternity did not go ahead without his approval. The Bourras let the matter drop until after the death of Belsunce in 1755, but in 1757 they unilaterally changed the starting time of their services to 5:00 A.M. apparently without any comment from the diocesan office.[38] Prior to this, in 1756, the confraternity had changed the starting time of its lenten Friday offices from 3:00 A.M. Friday morning to 5:00 Friday afternoon.[39] Not much can be made from these stories, but at least we can see that while Belsunce's efforts could inhibit, they could not halt the movement in the direction of laxity on the part of the confraternities.

It also appears that men simply avoided the confraternities while Belsunce was on the see. As noted in chapter 2, enrollment figures for the eighteenth century suggest that most confraternities suffered a decline in enrollments in the late 1730s, the period of Belsunce's greatest push for confraternal reform, only to rise again in the 1760s and 70s, after his death.

In sum, it seems that Belsunce's efforts to restructure the confraternities as an ancillary devotional experience were only partially successful. As he himself admitted, forcing the confraternities to close their chapels on Easter Sunday led their members to cease to participate in church rites altogether. And while the confraternities accepted his authority, this acceptance did not signal their permanent acquiescence. This was apparently Belsunce's conclusion also. It is ironic that he ended the preamble of his final set of ordinances by expressing the same sentiment with which he had begun his first set of ordinances forty years earlier:

. . . le premier esprit de vos compagnies se perd peu à peu, elles deviennent à la honte de la pénitence chrétienne, des assemblées presque profanes, ou regnant souvent la vanité, l'indépendance, la jalousie et les dissentions.[40]

After the death of Belsunce, Jean Baptiste de Belloy was granted the see of Marseille. He was to reside there until the Revolution. Where Belsunce had been fiery, he was moderate. Where Belsunce had been combative, he was conciliatory. Where Belsunce set out to force the confraternities to reform, he appears to have been willing to accept the status quo.[41] He issued no new ordinances for the regulation of confraternities of penitents. And the above stories about the pénitents Bourras suggest that he did not follow a policy of active intervention in the confraternities' affairs. He was bishop during the dissolution of the confraternities of penitents of Saint Catherine, of the Holy Spirit, and of Saint Lazarus in 1767, though we do not know what role he played in these events. Overall he does not appear to have focused much attention on the confraternities.

He did not need to. From liturgy to membership to financial administration, Belsunce had attempted to put his imprint on virtually every aspect of confraternal life. Belloy inherited a diocese in which everything that could be done to reform confraternities had been done already.

NOTES

1. Fabre, *Histoire des hôpitaux,* 2: 300–306.
2. Transactions of the Holy Trinity, 50H-48.
3. Ibid.
4. Jullien notes that over the course of the seventeenth century the two parties confronted each other in court five times, in 1615, 1632, 1642, 1643–4, and 1655.
5. Jullien, 64–65.
6. Jullien, 65–67.
7. Ibid.
8. *Livre du Saint Esprit,* 6H-54.
9. DSA, ff. 130; 246–47.
10. In 1773, the Observant and the Conventual branches of the Franciscan family were joined by papal decree. In Marseille, also, the two houses were combined. In 1779 the representative of the new monastery petitioned the bishop to have its obligations to the penitents of Saint John the Baptist reduced to one mass a month. The confraternity protested the petition in the episcopal court, but the bishop ruled in favor of the monastery. How the confraternity filled its need for other services is not known. See Fontanier, *Pénitents noirs,* 55–61.
11. On Jesuit confraternities see Louis Chatellier, *L'Europe des Dévots.* It should be pointed out, however, that neither the Jesuits nor the Capuchins had any reluctance toward incorporating penitent confraternities into their devotional exercises.
12. J. P. Palanque, *Le Diocèse de Marseille* (Paris, 1967), 116–20.
13. Taken from an extant copy in the register of the penitents of the Holy Spirit, *Livre du Saint Esprit.*

14. Given the connections between the confraternities and the Holy League, it may be that Raguenau's decision was motivated more by political than religious reasons. See Harding, "Mobilization of Confraternities," 93–95.

15. *Lazare de Cordier,* bk. 1, chap. 11.

16. Ibid.

17. *Lazare de Cordier,* bk. 1, chaps. 11, 12; DSA, especially ff. 79–81. Also see Palanque, *Diocese de Marseille,* 141–46.

18. *Ordonnances de Monseigneur l'Évêque de Marseille, leu et publiées dans son Sinode le 16 avril 1698* (Marseille, 1698).

19. Most of the confraternities in Marseille included in their statutes an admonition that members also attend mass at their parish church each Sunday morning. However, it is doubtful that the members heeded this demand or that the confraternities chastised them for ignoring it. See Agulhon, 124–28.

20. Agulhon, 125.

21. Ibid., 122.

22. What evidence I have suggests that the Castelmorons once again became Catholics after the Revocation of the Edict of Nantes. See Thomas Berengier, *La vie de Monseigneur Henri de Belsunce, évêque de Marseille* (Paris and Lyon, 1887), 1: 5–21.

23. The 1712 ordinances mentions an earlier pastoral letter. See Fontanier, *Pénitents noirs,* 41–43.

24. Ibid., n. 9.

25. Ibid.

26. See Fontanier, *Pénitents noirs,* 41–43.

27. Ibid.

28. Ibid.

29. Ibid.

30. Printed in the *Correspondence de Monseigneur de Belsunce* (Marseille, 1911), 351.

31. Paul Ardoin, *La Bulle Unigenitus dans les diocèses d'Aix, Arles, Marseille, Frejus, Toulon, 1713–1789,* 2 vols. (Marseille, 1936), 2: 85–89.

32. Fontanier, *Pénitents noirs,* 46–48.

33. Ibid.

34. Ibid., 57–58.

35. Fontanier, *Pénitents noirs,* 46–48.

36. Ibid.

37. Ibid.

38. This version of the story comes from the notes to the register of the pénitents Bourras, "Registre matricule," nn. 68, 70. Jullien offers a slightly different, but not nearly as substantiated, version. See Jullien, 87.

39. "Registre matricule," n. 69.

40. Fontanier, *Pénitents noirs,* 58.

41. Palanque, 187–91.

CONCLUSION

If penitent confraternities were religious organizations engaged in an ongoing effort to remain spiritually relevant, why were they condemned by bishops as decadent? The best response is that the type of spirituality they celebrated was, from the perspective of the post-Tridentine church, anachronistic. Confraternities provided an organizational vehicle for the pursuit of holiness through the emulation and imitation of holy men, and clerics eager to play this role always found chapels open to them. Yet this idea of Catholic religiosity was medieval. During the Counter-Reformation charisma was institutionalized. As Trent mandated, the laity was to look first and last to bishops and priests as spiritual guides. Lay piety became less a response of enthusiasm to what one saw and heard from evangelists and more an act of obedience to what one had been trained to believe.

Confraternities taught a form of obedience, but it was obedience to the idea of fraternity. Belsunce was unfair when he accused the confraternities of being "presque profane." During the Middle Ages, fraternal moral suasion, or "brotherly love," had been the most glorified form of cultural coercion. By Belsunce's time it may have lost its status to the notion of paternal correction, or "fatherly advice," but fraternalism remained part of the reward for participation in the monastic life, and as such, a valid religious instinct. Belsunce's comment is best appreciated as a desideratum. In the church he sought to create, fraternity would be recognized as a secular motivation. As the statutes of the penitents of Saint Henry indicate, ideally confreres would merely discuss the best ways to instill submission and resignation in the dying paupers under their charge. To give him his due, he was offering confreres an opportunity to share in the prevailing Christian ideal of evangelization through social activism. It may even be argued that this idea of evangelization paralleled the course to spiritual perfection pioneered by a new group of holy men, the Jesuits. But these allurements could not camouflage the absolute renunciation of fraternal-

243

ism Belsunce demanded in exchange. The second set of statutes of the penitents of Saint Henry do more than just negate the powers of the confraternity's spiritual director; they also affirm that the confraternity was a fraternal association. Fraternalism could be curtailed as an organizational goal, but it could not be suppressed.

This last point suggests that the confrontation between confraternities and bishops was inevitable. Nevertheless, it is still worth stressing that in the confrontation bishops may have been guilty of overreacting. Penitent confraternities operated for centuries as alternatives to the parish, but it is not clear how much of a threat to the parish they posed. For all of their popularity, they retained as committed members only the devout. And even in a city as resolutely Catholic as Marseille, this was only a small percentage of the male population. It would be different if the devotional programs developed at the parish had been aimed at satisfying the spiritual cravings of this group. But the thrust of post-Tridentine parochial reform was toward establishing minimum, not maximum, levels of observance. Penitent confraternities catered to those Catholics who wanted more, not less, than what was being offered at the parish.

It is amusing to speculate on what Alexis de Tocqueville, that determined enemy of *dirigisme,* would have commented on the battles between bishops and confraternities. Forced participation in yearly communion at the parish was more desirable than regular voluntary participation in communion at a confraternal chapel or a monastic church. De Tocqueville would have agreed that this conclusion was premised less on the long-term interest of the Catholic Church and more on episcopal arrogance. Belsunce was quite willing to throw the baby out with the bath water, to jettison a still vibrant older form of piety in order to insure the survival of a newer one. He did not succeed, mostly because the tradition of fraternalism upon which penitent confraternities were based could not be uprooted by bureaucratic fiat. Ironically, fifty years later, this same tradition was providing the impetus behind Catholic resistance during the Revolution. By then, of course, it was being celebrated as the essence of Catholicism.[1]

It may be, though, that in putting an end to any evangelical pretensions still being maintained by the confraternities, Belsunce was saving them from themselves. The financial costs and organizational stress involved in trying to save the underclasses had been the greatest sources of organizational instability. The lifting of these burdens may have freed confraternities to concentrate on the salvation of the men who were sufficiently committed that they regularly participated in chapel life. Available evidence points to confraternities being far more stable in the second half of the eighteenth century than in the first. One explanation for this development is that Belsunce's reforms permitted confraternities to return to what they had been in the beginning, mixed societies of devout clerics and laymen.

In this sense, what Vovelle saw as dechristianization in actuality may have been the shedding of a level of popularity that from the beginning was more inimical than beneficial to the confraternities as religious organizations. Both Agulhon and Vovelle tied their understandings of penitent confraternities too narrowly to the recreational predilections of the Provençal social elite. As such they completely misconstrued the nature of the transformations occurring during the middle of the eighteenth century. Spiritual decadence was not making penitential devotions vulnerable to secularism. An older, lay-initiated form of Counter-Reformation evangelism was breaking down under the pressure of episcopal reform.[2]

The processions and other ceremonies performed by confraternities that Vovelle associates with baroque piety must be understood in the context of how penitent confraternities evolved over the sixteenth and seventeenth centuries. As illustrated by financial accounts, the most direct form of social welfare in which the confraternities engaged was paying paupers to carry statues in processions or to prepare the chapel for ceremonies. And when it came time to distribute alms it was to indigents among the brethren that confraternal leaders turned. The task of evangelizing Marseille's underclasses was intimately tied to the celebration of baroque piety, both in the sense that it was the social elite that paid for both, and in the sense that the former gave the latter most of its religious significance. Confraternities benefitted from the popularity they gained as vehicles for the dispensing of this type of devotion. They suffered from the organizational dysfunction popularity brought with it. And they survived this dysfunction because their organizational apparatus was sufficiently adaptable to neutralize the negative effects of successive waves of goal displacement. Organizational theorists have much to learn from their story.

Agulhon argues that social elites left confraternal chapels to found freemason lodges because the confraternities had become decadent. I would argue that to the extent that social elites left, it was because bishops decreed out-of-bounds the kinds of activities in which elites wanted confraternities to engage. As Agulhon noted, many men maintained dual memberships in penitent chapels and freemason lodges. It is wrong to posit an opposition between these two forms of associations and better to think of freemason lodges as providing an outlet for fraternal instincts no longer permitted in confraternal chapels.

The popularity of the confraternities had entailed their moving into the center of the effort to evangelize Catholic society through social welfare. It should be clear that while this development could and did disrupt the organizational dynamics operating in chapels, only in a few instances did it determine the organizational dynamics there. Only three associations foundered, and in all three cases, opposition from the parish clergy who served initially as clerical sponsors was a probable contributing factor to eventual decline. A tightly regulated reformed confraternity like the Bourras never let its charitable activities get in the way of the associative experience that kept its membership so committed. Even an association as accessible as the confraternity of Notre Dame de Pitié (Saint Martin's parish) retained enough of a sense of itself as an organization that it prospered after the evangelical period. Over the course of the last decades of the eighteenth century, after almost two centuries at center stage, the confraternities again found themselves along the margins of Catholic devotional life and flourished once more.

NOTES

1. Sauzet, "Sociabilité et Militantisme"; Marie-Hélèn Froeschlé-Chopard et Régis Bertrand, "Les pénitents et la rupture révo-

lutionnaire," *Pratiques religieuses dans l'Europe Révolutionnaire (1770–1820),* Actes du Colloque Chantilly, 27–29 novembre 1986 (réunis par Paule Lerou et Raymond Dartevelle, sous la direction de Bernard Plongeron).

2. Agulhon, 120–36; Vovelle, *Piété baroque,* 100–105.

Appendix

A BRIEF HISTORICAL INTRODUCTION TO THE CONFRATERNITIES OF MARSEILLE

The following brief narratives provide introduction to the seventeen confraternities of penitents established in Marseille between 1499 and 1792. They have been compiled from various sources and are as thorough as possible.

LES PÉNITENTS BLANCS DE SAINTE CATHERINE (1499)

According to most authorities, the confraternity of pénitents blancs under the protection of Saint Catherine of Alexandria were founded during Lent in 1499.[1] Guibert states that it was the daughter company of an association under the same devotion established in Martigues in 1306,[2] a connection that helps explain the confraternity's odd choice of a patron devotion, the decision to establish its chapel at the parish church of Saint Laurent and to choose priests from that parish as chaplains.[3]

The confraternity of Saint Catherine introduced penitent devotions to Marseille, and from its membership came the founders of five of the next seven confraternities. Despite the defections it seems to have been relatively successful during its first century. In 1604 the confraternity negotiated with the parish for additional space in the garden of the rectory in order to build a bigger chapel. Lazare de Cordier describes this chapel as being of, "très belle construction, ornée de mosaïques, de marbres, et enrichée de vitraux de couleurs variées."[4] Its prosperity can be discerned also by its founding, in the same contract with the parish, a perpetual requiem mass for the deceased brethren of the confraternity, to be said by a priest with deacon and sub-deacon. A later transaction in 1611 paid for a torch to be burned during the mass.[5] By the eighteenth century, however, the confraternity had fallen on hard times. In 1727 it reported to the diocese that it was more than five hundred livres in debt.[6] By 1768 its plight had become so severe that the royal authorities forced it to combine with two other confraternities of penitents in similar straits.[7]

LES PÉNITENTS BLEUS DE NOTRE DAME DE PITIÉ (1506) (1531)

During Lent of 1506 fifteen members of the penitents of Saint Catherine separated, apparently amicably, from their brethren and marched in procession to a little chapel outside the city walls called Notre Dame de Roet. There they established themselves under the protection of Our Lady of Compassion (*Notre Dame de Pitié*), a popular devotion first preached in Marseille a century earlier by Saint Vincent Ferrer, and again according to Guibert, the patronal devotion of yet another of Martigues' flagellant confraternities.[8] Finding the chapel too remote for easy access, a few months later they moved back into town to a "crypte" under the same devotion at the Hôpital Saint Jacques de Galice in the parish of Saint Martin. In 1524 the Constable de Bourbon began an imperial invasion of France by laying seige to Marseille. The Hôpital Saint Jacques de Galice was taken over by the city of Marseille and used as a storage place for grain. The confraternity of Our Lady of Compassion was forced to give up their chapel. What happened to them from then until 1531 is not known. In 1531 they were recorded as buying "7 or 8 cannes" of land in the parish cemetery of Saint Martin near the city wall in order to build a chapel.[9]

At this point a bitter argument among the members of the confraternity—unsuccessfully adjudicated by the priors of the other confraternities of penitents—led to the decision to split in two. One group, the larger, stayed with the prior and founded the pénitents bleus of Our Lady of Compassion of Saint Martin's parish. The other group, led by the sub-prior, negotiated with the prior of the Carmelite monastery and established in the garden of this monastery the pénitents bleus of Our Lady of Compassion of the Carmelites. Following the history of the confraternities of Marseille included in the *Délibérations* of the penitents of Saint Anthony, the confraternity of Notre Dame de Pitié (Saint Martin's parish) is listed as the second confraternity of penitents, and the confraternity of Notre Dame de Pitié (Carmelites) as the sixth established in Marseille.[10]

Presumably the chapter of canons at Saint Martin parish originally provided the confraternity with chaplain service. But according to Fontanier, at some point the penitents of Notre Dame de Pitié became affiliated with the Fathers of Mercy and served as *questors* for the religious order's enterprise of purchasing and freeing Christian slaves. In honor of this they were allowed to wear the insignia of the religious order on their habits.[11]

The group of penitents who left with the sub-prior to found a chapel at the Carmelite monastery has left few records. Those that do exist indicate that from the beginning the confraternity had an uneasy relationship with its clerical landlords. In 1542 the Carmelites cited Francis I's proclamation of 1539 as justification for forcing the confraternity out of its chapel. Financial necessity, however, led the Carmelites to relent, and in 1551 they sold the chapel back to the company. But the Carmelites' real feelings about the confraternity are revealed in their decision in 1621 to establish their own confraternity of penitents.[12]

LES PÉNITENTS BLANCS DU SAINT ESPRIT (1511)

On the feast of Pentecost, May 12, 1511, fifteen members of the confraternity of Saint Catherine departed in order to establish their own confraternity. This group marched to the Hôpital Saint Esprit in the parish called Notre Dame des Accoules, or simply, "Les Accoules," where they founded a new company under the protection of the Holy Spirit. They built a chapel in the "grande salle" and dedicated themselves to serving the sick and burying the dead of the hospital. Their chaplain services were performed by canons at the parish church next door. In 1544, because their activities were causing inconvenience to the hospital's patients, they moved out of the grande salle to a chapel they had built in the cemetery.[13]

In the latter half of the sixteenth and throughout the seventeenth and early eighteenth centuries, the pénitents blancs of the Holy Spirit was one of the premier confraternities of Marseille. In

1574 the confraternity received a visit from Henry III, on route to Paris from Poland. He presented them with the gift, still extant, of a register bound in red leather with fleur-de-lys embossed in gold.[14] During the seventeenth century the confraternity evidently was a meeting place for the members of the Valbelle faction of city government.[15] Whether this had any influence on the decline of the confraternity is not known. It was the second of the three confraternities forced to dissolve in 1768. Interestingly, it was among the first confraternities reestablished after the Revolution.[16]

LES PÉNITENTS BLANCS DE NOTRE DAME DE BONNE AIDE (LA TRINITÉ VIEILLE) (1515)

The stated aim of the order of the Holy Trinity since the time they were founded in 1198 was the redemption of Christian captives enslaved by Muslims. Pious members of the laity who sought to join in this work were formed into confraternities under the protection of either the Most Holy Trinity or Our Lady of Good Help, the marian devotion associated with the Trinitarians.[17] In recognition of the assistance they gave the Trinitarians in their collection of alms, members of the confraternity were granted the right to wear a white scapular with the red cross over blue cross emblem of the Trinitarians sewn into it, as well as the right to participate in the indulgences attached to the scapulars.[18]

In 1514 the Trinitarian confraternity in Marseille, in existence since 1306, established itself also as a confraternity of penitents. According to Lazare de Cordier, their initial chapel was a subterranean one near the Porte Galle.[19] According to the historical notice of the confraternity written in the nineteenth century, however, the confraternity's initial chapel was within the monastery of the Trinitarians, and was destroyed in 1524 when the monastery was razed in preparation for the siege by the Constable de Bourbon.[20] From 1524 to 1528 the pénitents blancs of the Trinité vieille were the guests of the pénitents noirs of Saint John the Baptist at their chapel in the garden of the Observant Franciscans. They rejoined the Trinitarians in 1528 at their newly-built monastery. In 1548 the confraternity built its own chapel in the garden of the Franciscan monastery but retained the sponsorship of the Trinitarians.[21]

The fate of the penitents of the Trinité vieille was intimately tied with that of the Trinitarians and the Trinitarians' Bureau pour la Rédemption des Esclaves. This office expanded as Marseille grew to become the major French *entrepôt* on the Mediterranean. Although all other religious associations were dissolved in 1792, the Bureau's work was deemed important enough that it was allowed to continue.[22] Marseille was one of the main centers of the Trinitarian order, which knew its heyday in the seventeenth century. The confraternity of penitents that grew out of its confraternity of lay assistants benefited from this prosperity.[23]

LES PÉNITENTS NOIRS DE LA DÉCOLLATION DE SAINT JEAN BAPTISTE (1521)

The *pénitents noirs* of the Beheading of Saint John the Baptist were established June 24, the feast of Saint John the Baptist, in 1521 in the garden of the Observant Franciscans. According to Fontanier they were formed as a third order for the local monastery of the Knights of Saint John of Jerusalem. He explains that the habit of the confraternity was black—it was a modified version of that of the knights—and why the membership of the confraternity was the most consistently aristocratic of all the confraternities of penitents of Marseille. Whether his speculations are correct or not, the relationship between the confraternity and the military orders was certainly noted throughout the seventeenth century.[24] Though the confraternity may have started as a third order to the Knights of Saint John, their chaplains were the Observant Franciscans. After 1593 it shared with the confraternity of the pénitents Bourras the charitable enterprise of burying prisoners condemned by the state, the penitents of Saint John the Baptist burying all condemned nobles, and the pénitents Bourras burying all condemned commoners. For this both confraternities gained the indulgences attached to the burial of criminals belonging to the confraternity of disciplinati of Saint John Beheaded of Rome.[25]

Among the more illustrious members of this confraternity was Phillipe Emmanuel, Duc de Gondi, often in Marseille in his capacity as "Géneral des Galeries" in the early seventeenth century. The most important name on the membership list, however, was that of

Charles de Casaulx, republican leader and dictator of Marseille, 1591–96, who throughout his dictatorship served as prior of the confraternity. In fact, most of the leading men in Casaulx's faction were members of the pénitents noirs.[26] In 1602 it was forced to sell its chapel in the garden of the Observant Franciscans to the family of Pierre de Libertat, the assassin of Casaulx. The confraternity required monetary assistance from the Franciscans to help build another chapel outside, but not far from, the monastery.[27]

LES PÉNITENTS GRIS DE SAINT ANTOINE, ABBÉ (1550)

Two confraternities were established in 1550 to carry the relics of famous saints reputedly from Marseille. The relics of Saint Anthony, the founder of monasticism, were housed in the monastery of the Fathers of Saint Anthony in Marseille, and it was in this monastery that the pénitents gris were established. They did not remain there for long, moving to a garden outside the Dominican monastery in 1553 before eventually taking on the Dominicans as chaplains. The pénitents gris carried the relics of Saint Anthony in processions, particularly on his feast day, and kept the relics in their chapel. In 1637, no doubt upset that the confraternity used the Dominicans as chaplains, the religious order of Saint Anthony decided to halt the practice and petitioned the bishop to have the relics returned to its church. The bishop agreed, on condition that the relics be kept locked away in some fashion requiring two keys, one going to the penitents and the other going to the religious.[28]

The pénitents gris of Saint Anthony styled themselves a "compagnie royale." The only other confraternities claiming this distinction were the pénitents bleus of Saint Jerome of Toulouse and the pénitents blancs of Notre Dame du Gonfalon of Lyon.[29] In the two latter instances the title signaled honorary membership by French kings. There is no evidence that any French monarch ever joined the confraternity of Saint Anthony. Why the confraternity considered itself a royal confraternity remains unknown. The penitents were also known as the "Bavaires" from the old French word for "talkative," popular acknowledgement of the fountain outside their chapel that featured a statue of Saint Anthony with water spouting from his mouth.[30]

LES PÉNITENTS BLANCS DE SAINT LAZARE (1550)

Marseille celebrates Saint Lazarus as its first bishop, and his relics are housed in the cathedral known as Saint Mary Major or simply as the "Major." The pénitents blancs of Saint Lazarus was created in 1550 to carry his relics. Initially they met in the chapel recently vacated by the penitents of the Trinité vieille in the monastery of the Trinitarians. As that proved too small, in 1559 the confraternity gained permission to build a chapel in the cemetery at the Major. The canons of the cathedral chapter served as their chaplains, and they took as their charitable enterprise the maintenance of the lepers at the Hôpital Saint Lazare. The penitents of Saint Lazarus were also known as the "confraternity of the bishops" because many of the bishops of Marseille joined it and became its priors, and because they were granted the right to carry the coffins of those prelates in their funeral processions. They were the third of the confraternities disbanded in 1768.[31]

LES PÉNITENTS BLEUS DE NOTRE DAME DE MISÉRICORDE (LA TRINITÉ NOUVELLE) (1558)

According to Guibert the pénitents bleus of Our Lady of Mercy (Notre Dame de Misércorde) were the result of a further splitting of the pénitents bleus of Our Lady of Compassion of Saint Martin parish.[32] The confraternity represented a successful effort by the Trinitarians to establish a confraternity of penitents in the chapel vacated by the penitents of Notre Dame de Bonne Aide. While under the protection of Our Lady of Mercy, they were popularly called the penitents of the Trinité nouvelle to distinguish them from the first company of penitents associated with the Trinitarians. There is some disagreement on the date of the establishment of this confraternity. De Ruffi and Guibert say 1566, but the *Délibérations* of the penitents of Saint Anthony say 1570 and Lazare de Cordier says April 17, 1575.[33]

In 1578 two noble Marseillais decided to establish a non-flagellant confraternity under the devotion of Our Lady of Mercy at the parish church of Notre Dame des Accoules. They convinced the pénitents bleus to join and worship with them and to make a common procession together on December 8, the feast of the Immaculate Conception. This proposition entailed the pénitents bleus breaking their ties with the Trinitarians and accepting as chaplains the canons of the chapter at Notre Dame des Accoules. The pénitents bleus consented to the arrangement until 1602, when they decided to return to the Trinitarians for spiritual direction, even though this meant remaining in the shadows of the penitents of the Trinité vielle and the Bureau pour la Rédemption des Esclaves. Toward the end of the eighteenth century, the ties between the confraternity and the religious order were once again broken, this time by the religious order. In 1771 the Trinitarians paid off their contract with the confraternity and left it to fend for itself.[34]

THE CIVIL WAR CONFRATERNITIES

Three confraternities of penitents existed only for a short time during the spiritually charged periods of the Wars of Religion. The only source of information on them is De Ruffi's *Histoire de Marseille*.

Les Pénitents de la Transfiguration de Notre Seigneur (1569)

The penitents of the Transfiguration of Our Lord were established in 1569. They seem to have been connected with the Benedictine nuns of the Abbey Saint Sauveur. The nuns granted the company the use of the church of Saint Thomas as a chapel, in exchange for an annual payment of eight florins and the expectation that the company say seven masses upon the death of one of their sisters (which suggests that the confraternity might have been composed of priests).[35]

Les Pénitents Noirs de l'Annonciation de la très-Sainte Vierge (date unknown)

Inspired by a pilgrimage to Notre Dame de Lorette, Fabio de Casaulx, the son of Charles de Casaulx, established this confraternity. As he was already a member of the pénitents noirs of Saint John Baptist, he chose for his confraternity a habit of the same color. The company built its chapel next to the monastery of the Servites. The confraternity of the Annunciation of Our Lady was perceived as little more than a group of followers of Charles de Casaulx, and as such, it was dissolved in 1596 when Casaulx was assassinated.[36]

Les Pénitents Blancs de Notre Dame de l'Annonciation (1592)

In 1592 establishment of a confraternity with almost the same name was allowed by the diocese. Guibert suggests that its foundation was probably the result of the diffusion southward of the confraternity of the same name established ten years before by Henry III in Paris.[37] The unique feature of the confraternity was that it accepted members only between the ages of ten and twenty years, and thus was conceived as a sort of training school for the adult confraternities. Twenty young men comprised the initial membership. They were given a chapel next to the Hôpital Saint Jacques de Galice, but evidently soon were disbanded.[38]

LES PÉNITENTS GRIS DU TRÈS-SAINT ET TRÈS-AUGUST NOM DE JÉSUS (LES PÉNITENTS BOURRAS) (1591)

In 1591 Antoine Mascaron, minter and member of the council through which Casaulx ruled Marseille, led seven of his friends in founding this confraternity. Although Alexandre Jullien, who wrote the definitive history of these penitents did not mention it, Fontanier relates that Mascaron and his seven friends were all members of the Franciscan third order, which had been established at the monastery of the Observant Franciscans in 1535.[39] This information complements what we know about the pénitents Bourras, particularly about Mascaron, one of the most fervent of the Leaguer-Republicans who followed Charles de Casaulx.[40] In 1593 on a trip to Rome, Mascaron's son Guillaume negotiated with the company of disciplinati of Rome under the title of Saint John Beheaded, and gained from this confraternity the right to share in all the indulgences granted to it by various popes for its efforts in burying criminals condemned to death in Rome. As noted earlier, the Bourras shared these indulgences with the penitents of Saint John the Baptist.[41] Late in the eighteenth century the confraternity also saw fit to establish an orphanage for the children of lost sailors.[42]

The pénitents Bourras, like the penitents of Saint John the Baptist, were a hotbed of political activity during the period 1591–96 when Casaulx and the Holy League ruled Marseille. But instead of disbanding the company in 1596 when Marseille returned to his control, Henry IV simply exiled Mascaron and his sons from Marseille.[43] The pénitents Bourras went on to become one of the most popular and successful confraternities of penitents in Provence.

During the first ten years of its existence the confraternity had a chapel in the monastery of the Fathers of Saint Anthony. In 1604 they moved to a chapel they had built in the garden of the Trinitarian monastery. For most of the ancien régime the Trinitarians served as their chaplains.[44]

Many stories exist that try to explain why these penitents were popularly called the Bourras. The most sensible, offered by Jullien, is that the name stems from a type of coarse grey cloth called "bure" that was used to make their habits.[45] The pénitents Bourras limited their membership to seventy-two in honor of the seventy-two disciples of Christ.[46] Because of this limited membership, and because of a set of strict statutes Jullien claims were culled from various sets of statutes from Franciscan tertiaries, the Bourras prospered until the early years of the Revolution.[47]

LES PÉNITENTS ROUGES DE LA SAINTE CROIX (1607)

In 1607 the reverend father Binans (called the "Anglais"), a member of the Minims order, preached a mission in Marseille. As a result of his efforts, a group of Marseillais on May 1 of that year decided to establish themselves as a confraternity of penitents. They went to Father Binans for direction, and he established them under the protection of the Holy Cross. He limited their membership to ninety-six in honor of the years in the lives of Jesus and Mary, and for habits gave them red robes similar to those of the Minims.[48]

Originally the pénitents rouges also had a chapel in the monastery of the Fathers of Saint Anthony, but in 1612 they built their own chapel outside the Carmelite monastery. In 1641 in a great procession, these penitents marched to the Minim monastery where they changed the cord with which they belted their waist for that of the Third Order of Saint Francis of Paoli. For their charitable enterprise they buried the dead of the Hôpital de la Charité.[49] In processions in Marseille they carried the statue of Notre Dame de la Garde, the greatest of all local devotions.[50]

LES PÉNITENTS GRIS DE NOTRE DAME DU MOUNT CARMEL (LES PÉNITENTS CARMÉLINS) (1621)

In 1621 the second of the great scapular confraternities in Marseille also established itself as a confraternity of penitents. With the Sabbatine Bull of 1251, the Carmelites had established one of the more popular of medieval confraternities, that of Our Lady of Mount Carmel. Like the Trinitarian confraternity of Our Lady of Good Help, the Carmelite confraternity offered its members a scapular that brought with it the privilege of sharing in several indulgences. The Carmelite scapular was brown.[51]

Marseille was one of the centers of the Carmelite order, and the confraternity was very strong there. In August 1621 the *marguillers* (trustees) of this confraternity petitioned the diocese for permission to establish themselves also as a confraternity of penitents. Permission was granted, and they were established on September 21 of that year.[52] They built their chapel outside the Carmelite monastery. Although their scapulars were brown, they chose to wear gray habits. They limited their membership to 120 in honor of the number of disciples who had elected Saint Mathias to replace Judas, and only members of the scapular confraternity were allowed to join. The Carmelites also put them under the protection of Saint Joseph and Saint Theresa, the secondary patrons of the order. They chose as their charitable enterprise the burying of the poor of the suburban parishes.[53]

The church of the monastery of the Carmelites was a fairly active one, and the pénitents gris figured in most of their processions, especially in the grand procession the first Sunday of the octave of Our Lady of Mount Carmel, July 16, when they carried the statue of Our Lady of Mount Carmel given to the monastery by the scapulars in 1665.[54] According to Lazare de Cordier, the penitents fell into decadence soon after they were established and were disowned by the Carmelites. Later they reformed and were accepted back by the Carmelites. In honor of their return they brought a gift, a dais in blue silk and gold, for the monks to use in their processions.[55]

LES PÉNITENTS GRIS DE NOTRE DAME DE LA CHARITÉ (DE SAINT MAUR) (1662)

There are conflicting stories about the founding of this confraternity. Fontanier, following Lazare de Cordier, states that in 1662 five individuals, along with several men expelled from the pénitents Bourras, established the penitents of Saint Maur.[56] But L. de Gonzague Jullien argues instead that the confraternity was born in the oratory of the monastery of the reformed Benedictines of Saint Maur.[57] Whatever the truth, this was a small confraternity—its membership was limited to thirty-three in honor of the years of Christ's life. Fontanier claims that for most of its life it was essentially a confraternity of priests. It was affiliated with the Fathers of the Good Pastor, who presumably performed its chaplain services. For its charitable enterprise it chose to bury the poor of both sexes in the parish of Saint Martin.

The confraternity had a difficult time surviving. It spent most of the latter part of the seventeenth century searching for a suitable chapel, a search terminated only when the confraternity itself was disbanded during the final decade of the century. It was reestablished by order of Bishop Belsunce in 1714 because he felt that the confraternity served as a useful example to the other confraternities. In the latter part of the eighteenth century, the confraternity was again forced to look for a new meeting place because their chapel was taken over by the city to make way for the building of a new hospital. In 1768 the confraternity was awarded, by royal letters-patent, the former chapel of the pénitents blancs of the Holy Spirit. They remained there until their dissolution during the Revolution.

LES PÉNITENTS GRIS DE SAINT HENRI (1717)

The final confraternity of penitents established in Marseille is less interesting in itself than for what it reveals about its founder.

Monseigneur Henri de Belsunce de Castelmoron became bishop of Marseille in 1709. He was to reign for forty-six years. Belsunce is best known in French history for his role in the battle over the bull *Unigenitus;* but he was also an outstanding bishop, credited with finally implementing the reforms of the Council of Trent in Marseille.[58] One of his efforts was the reforming of the confraternities of penitents. In this effort he created a confraternity of penitents under the protection of his patron saint in 1717. The pénitents gris of Saint Henri are interesting for what they reveal about the episcopal ideal for confraternities of penitents. They chose for charitable work the burying of the dead and the caring for the sick of the Hospital of Saint Esprit. This was the same task chosen two centuries earlier by the pénitents blancs of the Holy Spirit, and it is worthwhile to speculate on the influence the arrival of the pénitents gris had on the decline of the once-thriving company. The chaplains of the pénitents gris were selected by the bishop from the secular priests at the cathedral.

NOTES

1. Ruffi simply states that it was established, "au milieu du siècle de 1400;" but all other sources—Lazare de Cordier, Guibert, and the *Déliberations* of the penitents of Saint Anthony—narrow the date to March, 1499. See Ruffi, 84; *Lazare de Cordier,* bk. 2, chap. 2; Guibert, 56; DSA, f. 178.

2. Guibert, 56.

3. DSA, f. 178; *Lazare de Cordier,* bk. 2, chap. 2; Dasprès, 7.

4. *Lazare de Cordier,* bk. 2, chap. 1.

5. Dasprès, 7.

6. Doc. 5G-863, Archives départmentales des Bouches-du-Rhone, 430; *Livre du Saint Esprit.*

7. Collection Fontanier, 24F-11; *Livre du Saint Esprit.*

8. Guibert, 56, n. 3.

9. On the pénitents bleus see Fontanier, *Notes sur les pénitents bleus,* n.p., Collection Fontanier, 24F-116; *Lazare de Cordier,* bk. 2, chap. 3; Ruffi, 85; Guibert, 56. Note that Guibert gives May 20

as the date of the confraternity's founding. The March date comes from *Lazare de Cordier,* bk. 2, chap. 3.

10. DSA, f. 179. Note that in his manuscript Fontanier mistakenly claims as a source the *Déliberations* of the penitents of Saint Lazarus, when the actual source is the *Déliberations* of the penitents of Saint Anthony.

11. Fontanier, *Notes sur les pénitents bleus.*

12. Ibid., and *Lazare de Cordier,* bk. 2, chap. 7.

13. Fontanier, *Notes sur les pénitents blancs;* 24F-116; also see Ruffi and Guibert.

14. Fontanier, *Notes sur les pénitents blancs;* 24F-116; also see Ruffi and Guibert.

15. Fontanier, *Notes sur les pénitents blancs.*

16. Ibid.

17. Paul Deslandres, *L'Order des Trinitaires pour le rachat des Captifs* (Paris and Toulouse, 1903), chap. 3, passim.

18. Franz Beringer, *Les Indulgences,* 2 vols. (Paris, 1905), 2: 107–13; for an unsympathetic but still useful account of scapular confraternities see H. Charles Lea, *A History of Auricular Confession and Indulgences in the Latin Church,* 3 vols. (reprint, New York, 1968), 3: 495–500.

19. *Lazare de Cordier,* bk. 2, chap. 5.

20. *Notes sur l'origine des Confréries des Pénitents de Marseilles et de Banlieu* (Marseille, 1853), 17–18.

21. Ibid., 18; *Lazare de Cordier,* bk. 2, chap. 5.

22. *Notes sur l'origine des Confréries,* 20–22; Deslandres, 533–37.

23. Deslandres, 528. Note that Fabre would offer the opposite argument. According to him it was the success of the pénitents blancs that gave a boost to the Trinitarians in the seventeenth and eighteenth centuries. See Fabre, *Histoire des hôpitaux,* 2: 300–306.

24. Fontanier, *Pénitents noirs,* 11.

25. Ibid., chap. 2.

26. Harding, "Mobilization of Confraternities," 93–95. The confraternity paid dearly for the distinction it knew under Casaulx.

27. Fontanier, *Pénitents noirs,* 21.

28. Ruffi, 85; *Lazare de Cordier,* bk. 2, chap. 8; L'abbé C.

Nicolas, *L'ancien Couvent des Dominicains de Marseille, 1223–1790* (Nimes, 1894), 56.

29. Guibert, 107–19.

30. Guibert, 61; Régis de la Colombière, 16–17.

31. Ruffi, 85; *Lazare de Cordier*, bk. 2, chap. 9.

32. Guibert, 58.

33. Available records for the confraternity date from 1566. Ruffi, 85; Guibert, 58; DSA, f. 179; *Lazare de Cordier*, bk. 2, chap. 10. Also see Collection Fontanier, 24F-112.

34. *Lazare de Cordier*, bk. 2, chap. 10.

35. Ruffi, 87.

36. Ibid.

37. Guibert, 62.

38. Ruffi, 87.

39. Jullien, *Chronique Historique de l'Archiconfrérie;* Fontanier, *Le Tiers-Ordre Observantin*, 1.

40. The Mascaron family figured prominently in the Marseille of Casaulx. Along with Mascaron senior's efforts to develop a coinage system for Casaulx, his son Pierre was put in charge of establishing the first publishing house in Marseille. See Jullien, 161–63; Harding, "Mobilizations of Confraternities," 95–96.

41. Jullien, 46–50.

42. Fontanier, *Le Tiers-Ordre Observantin*, passim.

43. Ibid., 55.

44. Ibid., 15; Ruffi, 85; *Lazare de Cordier*, bk. 2, chap. 11.

45. Jullien, 12; see *Régis de la Colombière*, page 10 for an example of other explanations.

46. *Régis de la Colombière*, 10.

47. Jullien, 11.

48. Later in the eighteenth century they changed the color of their robes to gray. See Ruffi, 86; Fontanier, *Pénitents Rouges*, 24F-105.

49. Fontanier, *Notes sur les pénitents rouges*, 24F-105.

50. *Lazare de Cordier*, bk. 2, chap. 12.

51. On the Carmelites and their scapular confraternity see Lea, 253–70; Berenger, 244–60; *Catholic Encyclopedia* (1912), s.v. "scapulars."

52. Ruffi, 87; J. B. Cantal, *Monographie de Notre Dame du Mont Carmel à Marseille* (Marseille, 1874).

53. Lucien Fontanier, *Notes sur les pénitents gris du Mont Carmel,* Collection Fontanier, 24F-105.

54. Régis de la Colombière, 127–29; *Lazare de Cordier,* bk. 2, chap. 13.

55. *Lazare de Cordier,* bk. 2, chap. 13.

56. Ibid., bk. 2, chap. 14; Fontanier, *Notes sur les pénitents de la Charité,* Collection Fontanier, 24F-105. This story is given independent support by the archives of the Bourras which tells how Raphael Brunel, expelled from the confraternity in 1658, went on to found another confraternity. See Registre matricule, 24F-51, note 68.

57. Cited in Fontanier, *Notes sur les pénitents de la Charité.*

58. Berengier, *La vie de Monseigneur Henri de Belsunce.*

BIBLIOGRAPHY OF
SECONDARY SOURCES

Agulhon, Maurice. *Pénitents et Franc-Maçons de l'ancienne Provence* (Paris, 1968).

Antier, Jean-Jacques. *Marins de Provence et du Languedoc; Vingt-cinq siècles d'histoire du littoral français méditerranéen* (Avignon, 1977).

Ardoin, Paul. *La Bulle Unigenitus dans les dioceses d'Aix, Arles, Marseille, Frejus, Toulon, 1713–1789,* 2 vols. (Marseille, 1936).

Baratier, Edouard, ed. *Histoire de Provence* (Toulouse, 1969).

———, ed. *Histoire de Marseille* (Toulouse, 1973).

Barnes, A. E. "From Ritual to Meditative Piety: Devotional Change in French Penitential Confraternities from the 16th to the 18th Century," *Journal of Ritual Studies* 1/2 (1987).

———. "The Wars of Religion and the Origins of Reformed Confraternities of Penitents: A Theoretical Approach," *Archives de Sciences Sociales de Religion* 64/1 (juillet-septembre 1987).

———. "Cliques and Participation in a Pre-Modern French Voluntary Association: The Pénitents Bourras of Marseille in the Eighteenth Century," *Journal of Interdisciplinary History* 19, no. 1 (Summer, 1988).

———. "Religious Anxiety and Devotional Change in Sixteenth Century French Penitential Confraternities," *Sixteenth Century Journal* 11, no. 3 (Fall 1988).

————. "On the Necessity of Shaping Men Before Forming Christians: The Institutionalization of Catholicism in Early Modern Europe and Modern Africa," *Historical Reflections/Réflections Historiques* 16 (1989).

Benoit, Fernand. *La Provence et le Comtat Venaissin; Arts et traditions populaires* (Avignon, 1978).

Bercé, Yves Marie. *Fête et Révolte: Des Mentalités populaires du XVIe au XVIIIe siècle* (Paris, 1976).

Berengier, Thomas. *La vie de Monseigneur Henri de Belsunce, évêque de Marseille* (Paris and Lyon, 1887).

Bertrand, Régis. *Les confréres de pénitents de Marseille à travers quantre siècle d'histoire* (Marseille, 1980).

————. "Les pénitents," *Marseille au XVIIe siècle*, Archives communales de Marseille (Marseille, 1980).

Boileau, Jacques. *Histoire des flagellans, ou l'on fait voir le bon et mauvais usage des flagellations parmi les Chrétiens* (Amsterdam, 1701).

Bossy, John. "The Counter-Reformation and the Catholic People of Europe," *Past and Present* 46 (1970).

————. *Christianity in the West 1400–1700* (Oxford, 1985).

Boucher, Jacqueline, "Henri III, mondain ou dévot? Ses retraites dans les monastères de la région parisienne," *Cahiers d'histoire* (1970).

————. *Societé et Mentalités autour de Henri III,* 4 vols. (Lille/ Paris, 1981).

Boursiquot, Jean-Luc. "Pénitents et societé toulousaine au siècle des Lumières," *Annales du Midi* 88 (1976).

Brookes, R. *The Coming of the Friars* (New York, 1975).

Busquet, Raoul. *Histoire de Marseille* (Paris, 1978).

Caro-Baroja, Julian. "The City and the Country: Reflections on Some Ancient Common Places," in *Mediterranean Countrymen*, ed. Julian Pitt-Rivers (Paris and The Hague, 1963).

Châtellier, Louis. *The Europe of the Devout: The Catholic Reformation and the Formation of a New Society* (Cambridge, 1989).

Chenu, M.D. "Monks, Canons, and Laymen in Search of the Apostolic Life," in his *Man, Nature, and Society in the Twelfth Century* (Chicago, 1968).

Chiffoleau, Jacques. *La Comptabilité de l'au-dela: Les hommes, la mort et la réligion dans la région d'Avignon à la fin du Moyen Age (avers 1320–1420)* (Rome, 1980).

Christian, William A., Jr. *Local Religion in Sixteenth Century Spain* (Princeton, 1989).

Cremieux, A. *Marseille et la royauteé pendant la minorité de Louis XIV,* 2 vols. (Paris, 1917).

Dasprès, Abbé. *Notice Historique sur l'Eglise et la Parvoisse Saint Laurent* (Marseille, 1867).

Davis, Natalie Zemon. *Culture and Society in Early Modern France* (Stanford, 1975).

De Ruffi, Antoine. *Histoire de la ville de Marseille,* 2 vols. (Marseille, 1696).

Delaruelle, E. *L'Eglise au temps du Grande Schisme et de la crise conciliaire (1378–1449),* vol. 14, *Histoire de L'Eglise,* ed. Fliche and Martin (Paris, 1964).

Delumeau, Jean, *Catholicism between Luther and Voltaire* (London, 1977).

Duhr, J. "La confrèrie dans la vie de l'Eglise," *Revue d'histoire ecclesiastique* (1939).

Eire, Carlos M. N. *War Against the Idols: The Reformation of Worship from Erasmus to Calvin* (Cambridge, 1986).

Fabre, Augustin. *Histoire des Hôpitaux et des Institutions de Bienfaisance de Marseille,* (reprint, Geneva, 1973).

————. *Les Rues de Marseille,* 6 vols. (Marseille, 1867–69; reprint, Marseille, 1977).

Felix et Thomas Platter à Montpellier, 1552–1559 et 1593–1599 (Paris, 1892; reprint, Marseille, 1979).

Fontanier, Lucien. *Histoire de la Confrérie des pénitents noirs de la Décollation de Saint Jean Baptiste* (Marseille, 1922).

————. *Le Tiers-Ordre Observantin et son Bureau d'Assistance et l'Oeuvre de la Pénitence du Bon-Jésus en faveur des Enfants des Marins Pauvres* (Aix-en-Provence, 1922).

Froeschlé-Chopard, Marie. *La Religion Populaire en Provence Orientale au XVIIIᵉ siècle* (Paris, 1980).

———— (and Régis Bertrand). "Les pénitents et la rupture révolutionnaire," *Pratiques religieuses dans l'Europe Revolutionnaire (1770–1820),* Actes du Colloque Chantilly, 27–29 novembre 1986 (réunis par Paule Lerou et Raymond Dartevelle, sous la direction de Bernard Plongeron.

Guibert, Louis. *Les Confréries de Pénitents en France et notamment dans la diocèse de Limoges* (Limoges, 1879; reprint, Marseille, 1978).

Harding, Robert R. *Anatomy of a Power Elite: The Provincial Governors of Early Modern France* (New Haven, 1978).

Henin, Beatrice. "L'agrandissement de Marseille (1660–1690): Un compromise entre les aspirations monarchiques et les habitudes locales," *Annales du Midi* 98 (1986).

Hoffman, Philip. *Church and Community in the Diocese of Lyon, 1500–1789* (New Haven, 1984).

Jullien, Alexandre. *Chronique historique de l'Archiconfrérie des Pénitents Disciplinés sous le titre du Saint Nom de Jésus (dits Bourras) de la Ville de Marseille* (Marseille, 1865).

Kaiser, Wolfgang. *Marseille Au Temps Des Troubles 1559–1596: Morphologie sociale et luttes de factions* (Paris, 1991).

Kiesler, Charles. *The Psychology of Commitment: Experiments Linking Behavior to Belief* (New York and London, 1971).

Leff, Gordon. *Heresy in the Later Middle Ages*, 2 vols. (New York, 1967).

L'Etoile, Pierre. *Mémoires-Journaux*, 4 vols. (Paris, 1875).

Little, Lester. "Pride Goes Before Avarice: Social Changes and the Vices in Latin Christendom," *American Historical Review* 76 (1971).

———. *Religious Poverty and the Profit Economy in Medieval Europe* (London, 1978).

Lottin, Alain. *Lille, Citadelle de la Contre-Réforme (1598–1668)* (Dunkerque, France, 1980).

Marchetti, Francois. *La Vie de Jean Baptiste Gault, évêque de Marseille* (Marseille, 1645).

Martin, A. Lynn. *Henri III and the Jesuit Politicians* (Geneva, 1973).

———. *The Jesuit Mind: The Mentality of An Elite in Early Modern France* (Ithaca, N.Y., 1988).

Meeks, Wayne. *The First Urban Christians: The Social World of the Apostle Paul* (New Haven, 1983).

Meerseman, Gilles Gerard. "Etudes sur les anciennes confréries dominicaines," *Archivum Fratum Praedicatorum,* 20–24 (1949–53).

———. *Ordo Fraternitatis: Confraternite e Pieta dei Laici nel Medievo,* 3 vols. (Rome, 1980), in particular vol. 1.

Monti, G. M. *Confraternité medievali dell'Alta e Media Italia,* 2 vols. (Venice, 1927).

Nisbet, Robert. *The Social Bond: An Introduction to the Study of Society* (New York, 1970).

Norberg, Kathyrin. *Rich and Poor in Grenoble* (Berkeley, 1985).

Ousset, P.E. "La confrérie des pénitents bleus de Toulouse," *Revue historique de Toulouse,* no. 11 (1924).

Palanque, J.P. *Le Diocèse de Marseille* (Paris, 1967).

Pecquet, Marguerite. "La compagnie des pénitents blancs de Toulouse," *Annales du Midi* 82 (1972).

Phythian-Adams, Charles. "Ceremony and the Citizen: The Communal Year at Coventry, 1450–1550," in *The Early Modern Town,* ed. Peter Clarke (London, 1976).

Pullan, Brian. *Rich and Poor in Renaissance Venice: The Social Institutions of a Catholic State* (Cambridge, Mass., 1971).

Régis de la Colombière, Marcel. *Fêtes patronales et usages des corporations Marseillaises* (Paris and Marseille, 1863; reprint, Marseille, 1977).

Rosenwein, Barbara. "Feudal War and Monastic Peace: Cluniac Liturgy as Ritual Aggression," *Viator* 2 (1971).

Sauzet, Robert. "Sociabilité et Militantisme: Les Pénitents Blancs de Nîmes au XVIIIe siècle," *Actes du Colloque de Rouen 24/26* (November, 1983).

Taveneaux, René. *La Catholicisme dans la France Classique, 1610–1715,* 2 vols. (Paris, 1980).

Tavernier, Felix. *La vie quotidienne à Marseille de Louis XIV à Louis-Phillipe* (Paris, 1973).

Terrisé, Michel. "La population de Marseille vers 1750: Evidences et problèmes de la démographie des metropoles de type ancien," *Annales du Midi* 98 (1986).

Turner, Victor. *The Ritual Process: Structure and Anti-Structure* (Ithaca, N.Y., 1969).

Venard, Marc. *L'Eglise d'Avignon au XVIe siècle* (Lille, 1980).

Vernet, F. *Les Ordres Méndiants,* (Paris, 1933).

Villard, H. "La Chapelle des Pénitents Bourras de Marseille et le Musée des Pénitents," *Bulletin official de Musée du Vieux Marseille* 10 (1934):22.

Vovelle, Michel. *Piété baroque et déchristianisation en Provence au XVIIIe siècle* (Paris, 1973).

————. *De la Cave au Grenier: Un itineraire en Provence au XVIIIe siècle: De l'histoire sociale à l'histoire des mentalités* (Quebec, 1980).

Weissman, Ronald. *Ritual Brotherhood in Renaissance Florence* (New York, 1982).

Whyte, William Foote. "Corner Boys: A Study in Clique Behavior," *American Journal of Sociology* 46 (1941).

————. "Small Groups and the Larger Organizations," in *Social Psychology at the Crossroads,* ed. John Rohrer and Muzafer Sherif (New York, 1951).

————. *Street Corner Society,* 3rd ed. (Chicago, 1983).

Wright, A.D. *The Counter-Reformation: Catholic Europe and the Non-Christian World* (New York, 1982).

Zarb, Mireille. *Les Privilèges de la ville de Marseille; Du Xe siècle à Revolution* (Paris, 1962).

INDEX

THEOLOGICAL INQUIRIES:

Serious studies on contemporary questions of Scripture, Systematics and Moral Theology. Also in the series: